Prime-Time Society

The Wadsworth Modern Anthropology Library

Prime-Time Society

An Anthropological Analysis of Television and Culture

Conrad Phillip Kottak
The University of Michigan

Wadsworth Publishing Company
Belmont, California
A Division of Wadsworth, Inc.

Anthropology Editor: *Peggy Adams*
Editorial Assistant: *Karen Moore*
Production Editor: *Vicki Friedberg*
Designer: *Donna Davis*
Print Buyer: *Randy Hurst*
Permissions Editor: *Robert M. Kauser*
Copy Editor: *Jennifer Gordon*
Cover Designer: *Donna Davis*
Cover Illustration: *Adriann Dinihanian*
Compositor: *Kachina Typesetting, Inc.*

Printed in the United States of America   19

1 2 3 4 5 6 7 8 9 10—94 93 92 91 90

Library of Congress Cataloging-in-Publication Data

Kottak, Conrad Phillip.
   Prime-time society : an anthropological analysis of television and culture / Conrad Phillip Kottak.
      p.   cm.—(Wadsworth modern anthropology library)
   Includes bibliographical references.
   ISBN 0-534-12498-4
   1. Television broadcasting—Social aspects.   I. Title.   II. Title: Anthropological analysis of television and culture.   III. Title: Television and culture.   IV. Series.
PN1992.6.K67   1990
302 · 23'45—dc20   89-37664
                                                                                        CIP

To my son,
Nicholas Charles Kottak.
Live long and prosper.

 Contents

✿ List of Tables

🐚 Foreword to the Series

Modern cultural anthropology encompasses the full diversity of all humankind with a mix of methods, styles, ideas, and approaches. No longer is the subject matter of this field confined to exotic cultures, the "primitive," or small rural folk communities. Today, students are as likely to find an anthropologist at work in an urban school setting or a corporate boardroom as among a band of African hunters and gatherers. To a large degree, the currents in modern anthropology reflect changes in the world over the past century. Today there are no isolated archaic societies available for study. All the world's peoples have become enveloped in widespread regional social, political, and economic systems. The daughters and sons of yesterday's yam gardeners and reindeer hunters are operating computers, organizing marketing cooperatives, serving as delegates to parliaments, and watching television news. The lesson of cultural anthropology, and this series, is that such peoples, when transformed, are no less interesting and no less culturally different because of such dramatic changes.

Cultural anthropology's scope has grown to encompass more than simply the changes in the primitive or peasant world, its original subject matter. The methods and ideas developed for the study of small-scale societies are now creatively applied to the most complex of social and cultural systems, giving us a new and stronger understanding of the full diversity of human living. Increasingly, cultural anthropologists also work toward solving practical problems of the cultures they study, in addition to pursuing more traditional basic research endeavors.

Yet cultural anthropology's enlarged agenda has not meant abandonment of its own heritage. The ethnographic case study remains the bedrock of the cultural anthropologist's methods for gathering knowledge of the peoples of the world, although today's case study may focus on a British urban neighborhood or a new American cult as often as on efforts of a formerly isolated Pacific island people to cope with bureaucracy. Similarly, systematic comparison of the experiences and adaptations of different societies is an old approach that is increasingly applied to new issues.

The books in the Wadsworth Modern Anthropology Library reflect cultural anthropology's greater breadth of interests. They include introductory texts and supporting anthologies of readings, as well as advanced texts dealing with more specialized fields and methods of cultural anthropology.

However, the hub of the series consists of topical studies that concentrate on either a single community or a number of communities. Each of these topical studies is strongly issue-focused. As anthropology has always done, these topical studies raise far-reaching questions about the problems people confront and the variety of human experience. They do so through close face-to-face study of people in many places and settings. In these studies, the core idiom of cultural anthropology lies exposed. Cultural anthropologists still, as always, go forth among the cultures of the world and return to inform. Only where they go and what they report has changed.

James A. Clifton
Series Editor

🦋 Foreword to the Book

For professional anthropologists it is commonplace to say that anthropological knowledge (or at least conventional anthropological knowledge) begins with the exotic and ends up transforming what was strange, irrational, or simply bizarre into something intelligible and humanly acceptable. This involves a necessary demystification and clarification of the connections between apparent social discontinuities that are often perceived as irreconcilable. It is precisely this gap between the exotic and the familiar that gives rise to what we have traditionally called, perhaps a bit pompously, "anthropological theory."

It could be said that this has been the characteristic pattern of all the classic anthropological adventures or journeys. In those cases, the researcher must leave his or her own society in order to visit strange lands and experience exotic customs, which, after considerable time and effort, he or she finally manages to discern and *understand*. The direction of this journey, however, is outward and downward. One meets the "primitives," seeks out "savages," wants to live with "Indians," wishes to interpret customs of "traditional" societies and "underdeveloped" peoples. Our subject matter has been the systematic study of those who are far away, of those less "rich" and modern than we are. We have been trapped in a chalk circle inscribed by restricted anthropological knowledge and concept, by a formula that dictates a process in which the "other" ends up being like us. Then, after the journey and the essays, the other, whether Trobriander or Balinese, remains there, while we are here.

That, it seems to me, is the process that Conrad Kottak resolutely refuses to follow in his pioneering work *Prime-Time Society*. In fact, what he does here is just the opposite. He has decided to take as his object of study television, and with it our own system of representations, and to examine that system through an anthropological lens. Reversing the usual course, he adds a necessary other side to the conventional mode of anthropological understanding. The most interesting aspect of this book is precisely the transformation of the familiar into the exotic. Kottak leads us to distance ourselves from the ordinary world in which we live and that we take as much for granted, and interpret with as little imagination, as the air we breathe. In studying television in Brazil, Kottak takes a different approach, a risky and original one. He does not adopt the simplistic view that in Brazil the universe of television slavishly mimics a cosmopolitan and universalistic pattern that typifies our system and that television leads, therefore, to the dissolution of cultural differences. Perhaps as a result of knowing from personal experience and academic training that cultural realities are similar on some levels and different on others, Kottak, with intelligent suspicion, reverses the usual course and shows how television itself constitutes, in the case of Brazilian society, a landscape of its own, one that is expressive of the dramas and values of the society in which it functions.

As a result, this book is more than a study based on empirical research. It is also a true epistemological experiment of a sort that few have the courage to attempt. Critically observing the modern anthropological scene, one quickly discovers a kind of fear of the observer's own cultural universe. When "we" enter the picture, the old anthropological taboo immediately rises in confrontation. Thus, the people who have "culture," "rituals," and "values" are the Nuer, the Chinese, and the Brazilians. "We"—that is, North Americans and English—have "customs," "ceremonies," and "social sciences." We should only speak of the other—or of those among and before us who have spoken of the other. We are not supposed to adopt the opposite procedure of speaking of ourselves as others on the basis of observations of parts of our own system in which we can discern something concrete and systematic. If we choose to convert the familiar into the exotic, we adopt an epistemological option that takes us to the circus rather than to the opera, to the movies rather than to the theater—indeed, to our own living rooms, where our TV sets reign, rather than to the writers that history and the critics have consecrated. It's a matter of taking more seriously, as *Prime-Time Society* does, that we, too, have a culture. We also live in a society filled with beliefs, rituals, and preconceptions. By following such a path, this book leads us away from being American, transforming us into "Nacirema" (*American* spelled backward, as in Horace Miner's famous article "Body Ritual Among the Nacirema").

This is not an easy process. As a systematic observer of the social life of the United States, I have noted the instantaneous respectability of discourse that cites the Bible, Shakespeare, or some illustrious German or French philosopher. Authors from other worlds do not exist. It remains true, as Clifford Geertz teaches, that anthropological understanding is a dialog between the most particular of particulars and the most universal of universals. But we also know that the universal is socially constructed. Still, we have paid too much attention to singularities and to the exoticism of particulars. We have taken these to be the exclusive object of anthropology. Whether or not one studies primitives has distinguished anthropologists from other social scientists.

Why have we proceeded in this way? This book helps us answer this question through its subject matter and approach. First, there is a tradition of going outward and not inward as *Prime-Time Society* does. Next, there is a world system marked by specific ideological values, based on a

Puritan–Calvinist individualism that piously affirms the rule of the individual as an axiomatic moral entity. This view, as we learn from the work of Louis Dumont, has consequences. One of them is myopia in viewing value systems in which the whole dominates, in interpreting institutions in which hierarchy and relationships are primary. From this comes a tendency to see everything as dissolving into a cloud lacking form and depth, instead of trying to discover new discontinuities and differences that appear in the world and, in a way, reconstitute the old cultural boundaries. Or, are we really supposed to believe that Arab fundamentalism is simply a matter of interpretation, or that Brazilian nationalism is only a way of writing about Brazil?

But this is not all. Along with the question of the values of a world society, we also have the basic problem of the authority of anthropological knowledge. Studies of our own society help demystify this authority. They do this because in them the ethnologist is not alone. The ethnologist speaks of social phenomena that are part of an experience shared by hundreds, or, in the case of this book, millions of people. This is very different from spending a few months on a Pacific island or studying a lost tribe in the Australian interior (even in a world with jets and computers).

As a student of similar phenomena, I know very well the price one pays for such boldness as Kottak's. The problem we face is that almost everything that arises in any system tends to be seen from a certain angle or perspective. To describe Brazilian soccer to North Americans, to propose a theory of Rio's Carnival for the English, or to analyze Brazilian popular music in Paris is very different from doing the same thing in Brazil for Brazilians. In the first case authority resides in the realism of a narrative that has no apparent bias. In the second case, however, the observation tends to be received as trivial or as mere opinion. When studying phenomena that are familiar, that are ours, the anthropologist can no longer whip out the classic line, "But in my tribe it's different." In this case authority no longer resides in the singular personal experience of the classic field-worker (alone in "his or her tribe") but must be won through discussion and exhaustive demonstration of the arguments.

A book about the familiar will also lack a classic type of charm found in orthodox anthropological descriptions, of the boy who was our informant in Morocco or in discussions of Asiatic rituals that cite English philosophers. The anthropologist who studies his or her own society will be closely questioned by readers. He or she is, after all, describing something that everyone knows, experiences, and has an opinion about. Here the anthropologist lacks the dubious benefit and authority of a descriptive narrative that invokes a first time with a tribe or first encounter with a custom. But in compensation, it is through such endeavors that anthropology is effectively democratized. By studying phenomena that are to us "naciremally" familiar, we may discover where anthropological theory really helps and where it is only a pompous obstacle to intellectual progress.

Because of all this, I think that *Prime-Time Society* has the merit of initiating a sort of demystification of television, showing how our knowledge about ourselves, despite our rationalistic universe, is also bound by preconceptions that serve our interests. Thus, Brazilian television has not followed the impersonal rules of a supposed American imperialism but has invented its own system of domination, availing itself of authoritarian legislation and a hierarchical society in which the public has too little faith in its own opinion. In this sense Brazilian television is simultaneously a copy and an act of great creativity, as well as (in my opinion as a Brazilian) a mirror of Brazil's public irresponsibility.

In *Prime-Time Society* Conrad Kottak also shows that there is no exclusivity of productive methods of research and analysis. Effectively combining statistical and structural arguments, he realizes an analysis dominated by the goal of studying a phenomenon culturally. Kottak confronts issues involving academic disciplines and cultural experience. It seems to me that this book demystifies on several levels. It shows how television has multiple and diverse functions and meanings, depending on particular situations and historical moments. The aim, clearly, is to understand how TV represents and expresses Brazil. However, in this study Brazil is not inanimate but a mirror in which Kottak sees himself as an American and as a citizen of the world.

I think, by the way, that this goal of being radically comparative may be the most important feature of *Prime-Time Society*. We need such comparisons to stave off all ethnocentrisms, including universalistic and individualistic ones. By realizing his comparative agenda, Kottak manages to liberate television from a bundle of preconceptions, thus revealing it as a powerful cultural object. This object—contradictory, or as is said nowadays, polyphonic—can work in Brazil like a chorus, having a dominant rhythm and harmony. Brazilian TV helps also to maintain hierarchy and to reproduce a very traditional system of power. Such relentless comparison culturally situates the researcher's own society, creating a mirror through which it can perceive itself more clearly.

For all of this, I believe, the reader will appreciate *Prime-Time Society*, which is written in a clear style that dispenses with the pompous conventions of traditional academic discourse. This book commands attention because, for the first time, it discusses a series of questions that are fundamental to television and to modern society, in the South and in the North.

Roberto DaMatta
University of Notre Dame

🎋 Preface

Like other books in the Wadsworth Modern Anthropology Library, this one is intended for use in a variety of courses—at many levels. It can serve as a supplemental text in introductory anthropology and cultural anthropology, world ethnography, applied anthropology, development and social change, Latin American societies and cultures, and research methods.

I have written *Prime-Time Society* for college students and nonspecialists, although it will also interest professionals. In order to keep the book clear, readable, and interesting, references and appendices with statistical documentation, which specialists will wish to consult, appear at the end of the book. This information supports statements made in the text, but there is no reason for it to intrude on the ordinary reader.

Prime-Time Society is of multidisciplinary interest. It is a comparison of television's social context and cultural effects in the United States and Brazil, which has the most watched commercial TV network in the world. As such, it may prove useful in courses in sociology, American studies, Latin American studies, English, and communications.

My interest in television developed out of my prior work in anthropology—on the one hand my research on modern American culture, on the other my work on social change and development in the Third World. I am not trained in communications, nor do I purport to be an expert in that discipline. Although I try to read as much of the communications literature as I can, I remain an anthropologist, with my own perspectives, methods, interpretive frameworks, and sense of problem and solution.

Nevertheless, I am very pleased with the encouragement offered me by colleagues in communications, broadcasting, and telecommunications departments. Arthur Asa Berger originally encouraged me to write this book for a series he was planning to edit. Joe Straubhaar has been a generous collaborator in common research efforts and has helped a novice learn some of the tricks of the trade. Reviewers for the *Journal of Communication* and its editorial staff made useful and encouraging comments on an article they are publishing based on this project.

For all these reasons, I hope that *Prime-Time Society* will also prove useful in communications courses. In that field, it may be of special interest to instructors who wish to provide a detailed Third World case study, made relevant to students through constant comparison with their own experience in the United States.

Conrad Phillip Kottak

❧ Acknowledgments

Several organizations have supported the research behind this book. I thank them all. The University of Michigan gave me a sabbatical leave in 1983–84, which permitted me to do research in Rio de Janeiro and to plan the rural fieldwork that followed. The Wenner-Gren Foundation for Anthropological Research also supported that work in Rio with a grant to study the electronic mass media and social change in Brazil (1983–84). I am especially grateful to Dr. Lita Osmundsen, who headed Wenner-Gren at that time, for her encouragement, confidence, and support.

Later, the National Science Foundation awarded me a research grant to study the social impact of television in rural Brazil. This partially supported fieldwork in the states of Bahia, Pará, Santa Catarina, and São Paulo. The National Institute of Mental Health funded the main data collection and quantitative analysis. The NIMH grant, entitled "Television's Behavioral Effects in Brazil," supported field team research and data analysis in six Brazilian communities.

In Rio de Janeiro, the Department of Social Anthropology of the National Museum, a division of the Federal University of Rio de Janeiro, gave me an institutional affiliation. The Museum also introduced me to field researchers Rosane Prado and Alberto Costa. At the Museum I developed my friendship with Brazilian anthropologist Roberto DaMatta, who served as Brazilian liaison for the project. I am also grateful to Professors Giralda Seyfurth and Ione Leite and particularly to Professor Gilberto Velho (all of the National Museum) for help with the project.

To Alberto Costa, Roberto DaMatta, and Rosane Prado I offer my deepest gratitude, which I also extend to researchers Celeste DaMatta, Iraní Escolano, Betty Kottak, Pennie Magee, Richard Pace, and Edward Potter. Without them this book would not be.

Throughout the project, we encountered very few problems. All the researchers had social science training. All were fluent in Brazilian Portuguese. All worked meticulously, conscientiously, and indefatigably. Because other researchers gathered much of the data on which this book is based, I want to emphasize my appreciation to them for their efforts and their friendship.

Alberto Costa worked in Ibirama, Rosane Prado in Cunha, and Richard Pace in Gurupá. A field team of four worked in Arembepe: Iraní Escolano,

Pennie Magee, Betty Kottak, and Conrad Kottak. Iraní Escolano and Celeste DaMatta did the research in Niterói, and Edward Potter worked in Americana–Santa Barbara.

In the summer of 1986, two other colleagues helped us round out the national-level component of our research. Dr. Joseph Straubhaar of Michigan State University's Department of Telecommunication worked with Rio-based project consultant Lucia Ferreira Reis in Rio and São Paulo. They gathered data from the major Brazilian public opinion and media research organizations. Thanks also to Cid Pacheco, Paulo Alberto Monteiro de Barros (Artur da Távola), and Otavio Costa Eduardo for help with the national-level work.

Throughout the project Marian Bulcão de Moraes was of inestimable help to many members of the project, and we are all grateful.

I thank my children, Juliet Maria Kottak and Nicholas Charles Kottak, for giving up their Ann Arbor friends to spend a year in Rio. Fortunately they encountered new friends and family there.

Betty Wagley Kottak, my wife, quit a professional job that she liked in order to travel to Brazil with me in 1983–84. I thank her for her support in doing that and for contributing to this project at all stages, including fieldwork in Arembepe. In particular, drawing on her native knowledge of Brazilian culture, and on what we have learned together, Betty spent many days working with me to develop and test the interview schedules on which much of this field research was based.

In Ann Arbor, during data entry and analysis, Barry Cerf consulted on statistical analysis. Linda Swift solved problems with computer hardware and software and typed my field notes. Abdollah Dashti, Edward Potter, Celeste DaMatta, and Iraní Escolano entered our field data.

Iraní deserves special thanks. Not only did she do fieldwork at three of our sites, she was also my research associate in Ann Arbor, where she organized data coding, entry, and analysis.

I am pleased that so many of the people who worked on this project have used it to progress with their own studies. Costa, Escolano, Pace, and Prado have defended master's theses or doctoral dissertations and written papers based on the project. Roberto DaMatta, Edward Potter, and Joseph Straubhaar have incorporated some of its results in papers. Currently we are preparing an edited volume in which all the researchers describe their work and findings at the community level in much greater detail than I can do in this book.

Since his arrival at the University of Michigan in January 1987, Alberto Costa has read and reread this developing manuscript. He has corrected all kinds of errors. His incisive comments have helped me rethink many key concepts and interpretations. He has been as much my teacher as I have been his.

Special thanks are due Roberto DaMatta, whose ideas have enlivened my own and whose enormous intellectual energy always fuels mine. For the fascinating and continuing lessons he teaches me about Brazil, I am very grateful.

I thank James Clifton, fellow anthropologist, who is series editor for the Wadsworth Modern Anthropology Library. Jim made excellent editorial suggestions and offered practical ideas that have improved the book. I also thank Sheryl Fullerton and Peggy Adams of Wadsworth for support and encouragement, and Vicki Friedberg, Donna Davis, and Jennifer Gordon for seeing the manuscript through production.

In addition to Roberto DaMatta, I would like to thank Robert S. Fortner, George Washington University, and Howard Harris, Western Washington University, who reviewed the manuscript and made useful suggestions, many of which I have followed.

For their long-term or indirect contributions to this book, I also thank Atahydes Alves de Souza, Daniel Gross, Marvin Harris, Maxine Margolis, Tony Robben, the Roxos, the Summs, the Wagleys, and three generations of Kottaks, from Mariana to Nick.

I dedicate *Prime-Time Society* to my son Nicholas, who shares my interest in media content and analysis. Nick has always embarked for Brazil, and particularly for its remote villages, with enthusiasm. He visited all the field sites, and in Arembepe he took part in fieldwork on which this book is based. Nick's interests in film and TV have grown along with mine, and his enthusiasm and insight helped guide me to and through this project.

Conrad Phillip Kottak

PART ONE

Television and Culture

CHAPTER ONE

🌀 Television and Cultural Behavior

Why should a cultural anthropologist, trained to study primitive societies, be interested in television, which is the creation of a complex, industrial society? My interest in television's impact on human social behavior arose mainly through contacts with young Americans. These include my children, their friends, and particularly the college students at the University of Michigan to whom I have been teaching introductory anthropology since 1968.

I teach my introductory course, which enrolls 600 students a semester, in a large auditorium. A microphone is necessary if the perennial instructor wants to avoid cancer of the larynx. One or two semesters a year, I stand on a stage in front of these massed undergraduates. In 13–14 weeks of lecturing I survey the field of anthropology, one of the broadest in the college curriculum. I cover not only cultural anthropology, which is my own specialty, but also the other three subdisciplines—prehistoric archeology, biological anthropology, and anthropological linguistics. Introductory anthropology is among the first courses taken at Michigan. Many students take it to satisfy their social science distribution requirement. Most do not plan to major in anthropology, and many will never take another anthropology course.

For these reasons, the lecturer must work hard to keep students' attention, and my evaluations usually give me good marks for making lectures interesting. However, students in this setting perceive a successful lecturer not simply as a teacher, but as something of an entertainer. My efforts to keep them interested sometimes have the side effect of creating a less formal and more relaxed atmosphere than is usual in a lecture. The combination of large lecture hall, electronic voice amplification, and relative informality sometimes prompts students to relax too much for my taste. Nevertheless, changes in students' behavior over the past decade, particularly their more relaxed classroom comportment, helped turn my attention to television's effects on human behavior.

TELECONDITIONING

Most of the freshmen I have taught during the past decade were born after 1955. They belong to the first generation raised after the almost total diffusion of television into the American home. Most of these young Americans have never known a world without TV. The tube has been as much a fixture in their homes as mom or dad. Considering how common divorce has become, the TV set even outlasts the father in many homes. American kids now devote 22–30 hours to television each week. By the end of high school, they will have spent 22,000 hours in front of the set, versus only 11,000 in the classroom (*Ann Arbor News* 1985b). Such prolonged exposure must modify Americans' behavior in several ways.

I have discussed the behavior modification I see in my classroom with university colleagues, and many say they have observed similar changes in students' conduct. The thesis to be defended in this book is somewhat different from those of other studies about television's effects on behavior. Previous researchers have found links between exposure to media content (for example, violence) and individual behavior (hyperactivity, aggression, "acting out"). I also believe that content affects behavior. However, I make a more basic claim: The very habit of watching television has modified the behavior of Americans who have grown up with the tube.

Anyone who has been to a movie house recently has seen examples of TV-conditioned behavior—**teleconditioning**. People talk, babies cry, members of the audience file in and out getting snacks and going to the bathroom. Students act similarly in college courses. A decade ago, there was always an isolated student who did these kinds of things. What is new is a behavior pattern, characteristic of a group rather than an individual. This cultural pattern is becoming more and more pronounced, and I link it directly to televiewing. Stated simply, the pattern is this: *Televiewing causes people to duplicate inappropriately, in other areas of their lives, behavior styles developed while watching television.*

Some examples are in order. Almost nothing bothers professors more than having someone read a newspaper in class. If lecturers take their message and teaching responsibilities seriously, they are understandably perturbed when a student shows more interest in a sports column or "Doonesbury." I don't often get newspapers in class, but one day I noticed a student sitting in the front row reading a paperback novel. Irritated by her audacity, I stopped lecturing and asked "Why are you reading a book in my class?" Her answer: "Oh, I'm not in your class. I just came in here to read my book."

How is this improbable response explained? Why would someone take the trouble to come into a classroom in order to read? The answer, I think, is this: Because of televiewing, many young Americans have trouble reading unless they have background noise. Research confirms that most Americans do something else while watching television. Often they read. Even I do it. When I get home from work I often turn on the television set, sit down in a comfortable chair, and go through the mail or read the newspaper.[1]

Research on television's impact in other countries confirms that televiewing evolves through certain stages (see Chapter 9). The first stage, when sets are introduced, is rapt attention, gazes glued to the screen. Some of us can remember from the late 1940s and 1950s sitting in front of our first TV, dumbly watching even test patterns. Later, as the novelty diminishes, viewers become progressively less attentive. Televiewers in Brazil, whom I began studying systematically in 1983, had already moved past the first stage, but they were still much more attentive than Americans.

A study done in Brazil's largest city, São Paulo, illustrates the contrast. The study shocked Rede Globo, Brazil's dominant network (and the most watched commercial TV network in the world). It revealed that half the viewers were not paying full attention when commercials were shown. Afraid of losing advertising revenues, Rede Globo attacked the accuracy of the research. American sponsors are so accustomed to inattention and, nowadays, to remote control tune-outs, that it would probably delight them if even half the audience stayed put.

The student who came to my class to read her novel was simply an extreme example of a culture pattern derived from television. Because of her lifelong TV dependency, she had trouble reading without background noise. It didn't matter to her whether the background hum came from a stereo, a TV set, or a live professor. Accustomed to machines that don't talk back, she probably was amazed that I noticed her at all. Perhaps my questioning even prompted her to check her set that night to see if someone real was lurking inside.

Another example of a televiewing effect is students' increasing tendency to enter and leave classrooms at will. Of course, individual students do occasionally get sick or have a dentist's appointment. But here again I'm describing a group pattern rather than individual idiosyncrasies. Only during the past few years have I regularly observed students getting up in mid-lecture, leaving the room for a few minutes, then returning. Sometimes they bring back a canned soft drink.

These students intend no disrespect. They are simply transferring a home-grown pattern of snack-and-bathroom break from family room to classroom. They perceive nothing unusual in acting the same way in front of a live speaker and fellow students as they do when they watch television. (A few students manage to remain seated for only 10–15 minutes. Then they get up and leave the classroom. They are exhibiting a less flattering pattern. Either they have diarrhea, as one student told me he did, or they have decided to shut off the "set" or "change channels.")

Today, almost all Americans talk while watching television. Talking is becoming more common in the classroom, as in the movie house, and this also illustrates television's effects on our collective behavior. Not only do my students bring food and drink to class, some lie down on the floor if they arrive too late to get a seat. I have even seen couples kissing and caressing just a few rows away.

New examples of teleconditioning pop up all the time. In each of the past two semesters I've taught introductory anthropology, at least one student has requested that I say publicly "Happy Birthday" to a friend in the class. These students seem to perceive me as a professorial analog of Willard Scott, NBC's *Today* show weatherman, who offers birthday greetings (to people 100 and over). Long ago I put into my syllabus injunctions against reading newspapers and eating crunchy foods in class. Last semester I felt compelled to announce that I "don't do birthdays."

All these are examples of effects of televiewing on social behavior of young Americans. They are not individual idiosyncrasies (the subject matter of psychology) but new *culture patterns* that have emerged since the 1950s. As such they are appropriate objects for anthropological analysis. **Culture**, as defined by anthropologists, consists of knowledge, beliefs, perceptions, attitudes, expectations, values, and patterns of behavior that people learn by growing up in a given society. Above all else, culture consists of *shared* learning. In contrast to education, it extends well beyond what we learn in school, to encompass everything we learn in life. Much of the information that contemporary Americans share comes from their common exposure to the mass media, particularly television.

TV CONTENT'S CULTURAL IMPACT

TV *content's* impact on American culture enters the story when we consider that contemporary Americans share common information and experiences because of the programs they have seen. Again, I learn from my students. The subject matter of introductory anthropology includes the kinship systems of the United States and other societies. One habit I acquired about five years ago takes advantage of my students' familiarity with television. My practice is to illustrate changes in American family structure and household organization by contrasting television programs of the 1950s with more recent examples.

Three decades ago, the usual TV family was a nuclear family consisting of employed father (who often knew best), homemaker mother, and children. Examples include *Father Knows Best, Ozzie and Harriet*, and *Leave It to Beaver*. These programs, which were appropriate for the 1950s, are out of sync with the social and economic realities of the late 1980s. Only 16 million American women worked outside the home in 1950, compared with three times that number today. By the mid-1980s, fewer than 10 percent of American households had the composition that was once considered normal: breadwinner father, homemaker mother, and two children. Still, today's college students remain knowledgeable about these 1950s shows through syndicated reruns. Afternoon television is a pop culture museum that familiarizes kids with many of the same images, characters, and tales that their parents saw in recent days of yore.

Virtually all my students have seen reruns of the series *The Brady Bunch*. Its family organization provides an interesting contrast with earlier programs. It illustrates what anthropologists call "blended family organization." A new (blended) family forms when a widow with three daughters marries a widower with three sons. Blended families have been increasing in American society because of more frequent divorce and remarriage. However, a first spouse's death may also lead to a blended family, as in *The Brady Bunch*. During *The Brady Bunch*'s first run, divorce remained controversial and thus could not give rise to the Brady household.

The occupation of Mike, the Brady husband-father, a successful architect, illustrates a trend toward upper-middle-class jobs and life-styles that continues on American television today. TV families tend to be more professional, more successful, and richer than the average real-life family (Pearl et al. 1982). More recent examples include the Huxtables (*The Cosby Show*) and the Keatons (*Family Ties*). There are also ultra-rich night-time soap families such as the Carringtons of *Dynasty* and the Ewings of *Dallas*. Mike and Carol Brady were wealthy enough to employ a housekeeper, Alice. Mirroring American culture when the program was made, the career of the wife-mother was part time and subsidiary, if it existed at all. Back then, women like Carol Brady who had been lucky enough to find a wealthy husband didn't compete with other women— even professional housekeepers—in the work force.

I use familiar examples like *The Brady Bunch* to teach students how to draw the genealogies and kinship diagrams that anthropologists use routinely in fieldwork and in making cross-cultural comparisons. TV family relationships may be represented with the same symbols and genealogical charts used for the Bushmen of the Kalahari Desert of southern Africa, or any other society. In particular, I chart changes in American family organization, showing how real-life changes have been reflected in television content, with which students tend to be familiar. *The Brady Bunch*, for example, illustrates a trend toward showing nontraditional families and households. We also see this trend in day-time soaps and in prime time, with the marital breakups, reconciliations, and extended family relationships of *Dallas*, *Dynasty*, *Falcon Crest*, and *Knot's Landing*. The trend toward newer household types is also obvious in *Kate & Allie* and *The Golden Girls*.

Students enjoy learning about anthropological techniques with culturally familiar examples. Each time I begin my kinship lecture, a few people in the class immediately recognize (from reruns) the nuclear families of the 1950s. They know the names of all the Cleavers—Ward, June, Wally, and Beaver. However, when I begin diagramming the Bradys, my students can't contain themselves. They start shouting out "Jan," "Bobby," "Greg," "Cindy," "Marsha," "Peter," "Mike," "Carol," "Alice." The response mounts. By the time we get to Carol and Alice, almost everyone is taking part in my blackboard kinship chart. Whenever I give my Brady Bunch lecture, Anthropology 101 resembles a revival meeting. Hundreds of young natives shout out in unison names made almost as familiar as their parents' through television reruns.

As the natives take up this chant—learned by growing up in post-1950s America—there is an enthusiasm, a warm glow, that my course will not recapture until next semester's rerun of my Brady Bunch lecture. It is as though my students find nirvana, religious ecstasy, through their collective remembrance of the Bradys, in the rituallike incantation of their names.

Given my own classroom experiences, I was hardly surprised to read that in a 1986 survey of 1550 American adults, more people said they got pleasure from TV than from sex, food, liquor, money, or religion. In that survey (*TV Guide* 1986b), people indicated which of the following "give you a great deal of pleasure and satisfaction."[2] The percentages were as follows:

watching TV	68
friends	61
helping others	59
vacations	58
hobbies	56
reading	55
marriage	45
sexual relationships	42
food	41
money	40
sports	32
religion	32

"Furthermore, when people were asked what they liked to do for relaxation, watching TV again topped the list, followed by just relaxing and doing nothing, vacationing, music, reading and going out to eat. Sex and religion were each chosen by a mere one percent" (*TV Guide* 1986b:A1).

THE CULTURAL DIMENSION

I often wonder how my more traditional colleagues in anthropology have managed to avoid becoming interested in television—so striking are the behavioral modifications it has wrought in the natives we see and talk to most frequently: our fellow citizens in modern society. Nationwide and ubiquitous, television cuts across demographic boundaries. It presents to diverse groups a set of common symbols, vocabularies, information, and shared experiences (Hirsch 1979:251). Televiewing encompasses men and women of different ages, colors, classes, ethnic groups, and levels of educational achievement. Television is seen in cities, suburbs, towns, and country—by farmers, factory workers, and philosophers (although the last may be loath to admit it).

Television is stigmatized as trivial by many people (particularly orthodox intellectuals). However, it is hardly trivial that the average American household has more television sets (2.2 per home) than bathrooms (*USA Today* Feb. 14, 1985:B1). Given the level of television's penetration of the modern home, we should hardly ignore its effects on socialization and enculturation. The common information that members of a mass society come to share as a result of watching the same thing is indisputably *culture* as anthropologists use the term. This anthropological definition of culture encompasses a much broader spectrum of human life than the definition that focuses on "high culture" — refinement, cultivation, taste, sophistication, education, and appreciation of the fine arts. From the anthropological perspective, not just university graduates, but all people are cultured.

Anthropology's subject matter must include features of modern culture that some regard as too trivial to be worthy of serious study, such as commercial television. As a cultural product and manifestation, a rock star may be as interesting as a symphony conductor, a comic book as significant as a book-award winner. It is axiomatic in anthropology that the most significant cultural forces are those that affect us every day of our lives. Particularly important are those features influencing children during **enculturation**—the process whereby one grows up in a particular society and absorbs its culture.

Culture is collective, shared, meaningful. It is transmitted by conscious and unconscious learning experiences. People acquire it not through their genes, but as a result of growing up in a particular society. Hundreds of culture-bearers have passed through the Anthropology 101 classroom over the past decade. Many have been unable to recall the full names of their parents' first cousins. Some have forgotten a grandmother's maiden name, and few contemporary students know many Biblical or Shakespearean characters. Most, however, have no trouble identifying names and relationships in mythical families that exist only in televisionland.

As the Bible, Shakespeare, and classical mythology did in the past, television influences the names we bestow on our children and answer to all our lives. For example, "Jaime" rose from 70th to 10th most popular girl's name within two years of the debut of *The Bionic Woman*, whose title character was Jaime Sommers. The first name of the program's star, Lindsay Wagner, also became popular. *Charlie's Angels* boosted "Tiffany" and "Sabrina." Younger kids are named "Blake," "Alexis," "Fallon," and "Krystle" (spellings vary) after *Dynasty*'s Carringtons (Myers 1985). In other cultures children still receive names of gods (Jesus, Mohammed) and heroes (Ulysses). The comparably honored Olympians of contemporary America lead their glamorous, superhuman lives not on a mountaintop, but in a small square box. We don't even have to go to church to worship them, because we can count on them to come to us in weekly visitations.

Psychologists are still debating the precise effects of television on *individual* behavior and psychopathology; TV murders and car chases may indeed influence kids toward aggressive or destructive behavior. However, television's *cultural* effects are indubitable. Examples of the medium's impact on U.S. culture—on the collective behavior and knowledge of contemporary Americans—are everywhere. One task of this book is to uncover and analyze these examples.

My conclusions about television can be summarized as follows: New culture patterns related to television's penetration of the American home have emerged since the 1950s. As *technology,* television affects collective behavior, as people duplicate, in many areas of their lives, habits developed while watching TV. Television *content* also influences mass culture because it provides widely shared common knowledge, beliefs, and expectations.

I became interested in television because I saw that its effects are comparable to those of humanity's most powerful traditional institutions—family, church, state, and education. Television is creating new cultural experiences and meanings. It is capable of producing intense, often irrationally based, feelings of solidarity and *communitas* ("community feeling") shared widely by people who have grown up within the same cultural tradition. Nothing so important to natives could long escape the eye of the anthropologist.

Intrigued by the television-conditioned behavior around me, I started reading about television's effects on human beings. The next chapter summarizes what I discovered from previous research and explains why I decided to extend my interest in television to the Western Hemisphere's second largest nation—Brazil, home of the world's most watched commercial TV network.

CHAPTER TWO

🌸 Studying Television

Many researchers have commented on television's impact on contemporary society. Comstock and colleagues (1978) see television as a major socializing agent competing with family, school, peers, community, and church. Gerbner (1967) likens television to a new religion, cultivating a homogeneous outlook on social reality, uniting the population exposed to it in a common set of images and symbols. Hirsch (1979) underscores television's role in focusing attention on national events. Lazarsfeld and Merton (1971) label television "narcoticizing." They fault it for diverting attention from serious issues and for replacing effective thought and action with passive absorption in portrayals. Some researchers have argued that television reinforces the existing hierarchy and impedes social reform by portraying so many wealthy and powerful people (Gerbner and Gross 1976a, 1976b). Television executives have become "key gatekeepers," regulating public access to information (Saldich 1979:22). Historically, political and religious leaders have played this role. Television also contributes to consumerism. It stimulates participation in a worldwide cash economy (Hujanen 1976). Television sets agendas, directing our attention toward some things and away from others (Gerbner and Gross 1976a; Hood 1987:10–15). Although television may not tell us what to think, it is very successful in telling us what to think about (Comstock et al. 1978).

TV's worldwide spread has raised concerns about cultural imperialism. For example, French Minister of Culture Jack Lang has lamented the extent to which American programs (purportedly) dominate the airwaves in many countries. He has decried an "intellectual imperialism" that "grabs consciousness, ways of thinking, ways of living" (Gutis 1987). Many political and cultural leaders react similarly, although others see television's global role more positively. Ignatieff, for example, calls television "the privileged medium through which moral relations between strangers are mediated in the modern world" (Bernikow 1986). It promotes

> the breakdown of the barriers of citizenship, religion, race, and geography that once divided our moral space. . . . Television has become the instrument of a new kind of politics, one that takes the world rather than the nation as its political space, and that takes the human species itself rather than specific citizenship or racial, religious, or ethnic groups as its object. (Bernikow 1986:6)

THE AMERICAN PERSPECTIVE

Television is one of the most powerful information disseminators, public-opinion molders, and socializing agents in today's world. However, many judgments of television are ethnocentric: They are based solely or primarily on American data, yet American TV is merely one national example. Ethnocentrism in the evaluation of television and its effects can be remedied through cross-cultural research.

The ongoing Cultural Indicators Project of George Gerbner and his associates at the University of Pennsylvania's Annenberg School of Communications has revealed many relationships between TV content and impact. (I discuss their possible applications in other cultures in later chapters.) The Gerbner group has found that the more time people spend watching television, the more apt they are to perceive the real world as being similar to that of television.[1]

> Heavy viewing is part and parcel of a complex syndrome which also includes lower education, lower mobility, lower aspirations, higher anxieties, and other class, age, and sex related characteristics. We assume, indeed, that viewing helps to hold together and cultivate elements of that syndrome. But it does more than that. Television viewing also makes a separate and independent contribution to the "biasing" of conceptions of social reality within most age, sex, educational, and other groupings, including those presumably most "immune" to its effects. (Gerbner and Gross 1976a:191)

Labeling this process the "cultivation effect," Gerbner and associates have assessed relationships between heavy television watching and (distorted) perceptions of reality.

TV RESEARCH AND MODERN ANTHROPOLOGY

The National Institute of Mental Health sponsored one of the most thorough surveys yet done of TV research (Pearl et al. 1982). That study, begun in 1979, resulted in a two-volume report (1982) reviewing more than 2500 titles concerned with television's impact on human behavior. Despite the high quality of many of those studies, almost all had been done in the United States.[2] When research on television's influence in other countries is mentioned in the North American literature, it usually involves English-speaking nations. Whether American or foreign, many of the TV impact studies done so far focus on a limited target group (for example, children) and range of effects (for instance, violence).

Despite television's huge cultural significance (see Carey 1989), anthropologists have not paid much attention to television. To be sure, some anthropologists have applied qualitative techniques (including *structuralism*—an analytic technique developed by the French anthropologist

Claude Lévi-Strauss) to mass media content.[3] However, most of these works have been interpretive essays rather than detailed reports based on in-depth field research either inside or outside the United States.[4] The research project that is the basis of this book helps fill that gap.

Anthropology's late entry into TV research probably reflects the discipline's characteristic suspicion of the modern and its resistance to cultural destruction through homogenization. Television's worldwide dissemination is usually seen as spreading cultural similarity and thereby reducing diversity. For years anthropology has been known for expounding cultural relativism, focusing on diversity, and revealing the "other." However, a growing number of modern anthropologists believe that their discipline must provide "accounts of difference that nonetheless recognize real homogenizing factors in the contemporary world" (Marcus and Fischer 1986:vii, 38–39, 135).

Although it may threaten cultural diversity, television is spreading. Anthropology's traditional role has been to provide a broader perspective on aspects of human behavior through systematic study in other cultures.[5] Local studies in varied settings are necessary because "external systems [such as television] always have their thoroughly local definition and penetration, and are formative of the symbols and shared meanings within the intimate life-worlds of ethnographic subjects" (Marcus and Fischer 1986:39). Many modern anthropologists see compelling reasons for research of the sort described in this book.

THE SPECIAL SIGNIFICANCE OF BRAZIL

In 1982 I became interested in television in Brazil. The world's most watched commercial network—Rede Globo—shows mainly its own productions. The research project I planned and eventually directed included systematic field research in six communities in different areas of Brazil. The project, which began in January 1985, investigated television's role in molding knowledge, attitudes, perceptions, emotions, and images of the world, and in stimulating economic development. The general objective was to increase understanding of television through research in an important setting that was non-English speaking. My co-researchers and I asked many questions similar to those that American researchers have used. We wanted to determine whether television has had comparable effects in the Western Hemisphere's second most populous nation.

Brazil has had television since 1950. By 1979 it had built up the world's fifth largest TV audience size, with more sets than the rest of Latin America combined (Miranda and Pereira 1983:48). Brazilian TV households increased from 7 percent to 51 percent between 1964 and 1979. The figure exceeds 75 percent today. Through communications satellites, reception dishes, and networks of retransmitting ground stations, people in remote villages now receive national programming. Reflecting Brazil's huge population (145 million people) and its degree of economic development (the world's eighth largest economy), its middle class includes 40–50 million people. This is a tantalizing market (second in the Western Hemisphere) for television and consumerism.

Brazil's dominant Globo network moved quickly and efficiently to hook a product-and-information-hungry population. Globo blossomed under the aegis of an authoritarian centralized state and military dictatorship. Today, it blankets Brazil's airwaves as no single network has ever dominated North America. Globo consistently attracts a nightly audience of 60–80 million people. Brazil's most popular TV programs are native productions, and Globo makes most of them.

Several factors led me to research on the cultural context and effects of Brazilian television. First, I had been studying popular culture and mass media in the United States since 1976 (Kottak 1982). Second, my research on television grew out of my previous anthropological fieldwork in Brazil, which began in 1962 in the small village of Arembepe, Bahia. At that time Arembepe was a fairly isolated community with an economy based on Atlantic Ocean fishing in small sailboats (Kottak 1983).

Before the arrival of the electronic mass media (particularly television) Arembepeiros, like many other rural Brazilians, lacked access to national and international information. Contributing to this isolation were poverty, limitations on transportation, educational deficiencies, and massive illiteracy. During the 1960s Arembepeiros were starved for information about the outside world. They quizzed me endlessly about my own distant land and about the Brazilian cities they had heard of but that most had never seen. Because I was a world traveler, my knowledge helped satisfy their appetite for information. The fishermen would gather on the chapel stoop each evening after the fleet had returned and the men had bathed and eaten. I habitually joined them. Villagers were curious about the United States, but their questions were hardly scintillating: Were there camels there? Elephants? Monkeys? They went through a litany of animals they had seen on the lottery tickets that people brought back from Salvador, the state capital.

Having worked in Arembepe several times, I became intrigued with television's impact there in 1980, when I returned after a seven-year absence. By then, national forces were affecting the community much more than previously. After electricity arrived in 1978, villagers had access to television and were much more knowledgeable about international events.

I could only contrast Arembepe's information explosion with the mid-1960s, when villagers endlessly interrogated me about North American fauna. In 1980, as one fisherman remarked, "The whole world is open to Arembepe." Instead of asking "Are there elephants in America?" people told me about a fishermen's strike in France and labor unions in Poland.

They asked me about the chances and merits of President Carter and Senator Kennedy, who were vying for the 1980 Democratic presidential nomination. Other people wanted to talk about Brazilian national politics, during the first free elections since the 1964 military takeover. Arembepe's familiarity with nation and world was well advanced, and television seemed to be the main reason.

Anthropologist Richard Pace, a participant in the research project, reached similar conclusions for the Amazonian town of Gurupá:

> Before the spread of television, conversation often focused on local events, local gossip, soccer, or an occasional diffuse comment on regional or national politics. A foreign anthropologist was often asked vague questions such as—what kind of jungle grows in the United States, are all Americans rich, and what are cowboys like? With the spread of television, however, conversation took on a more cosmopolitan, more diverse nature. Events in North America, Europe, and the Middle East were discussed in detail. National politics were scrutinized (it was the year [1985] that the military regime gave power back to a civilian government). I found myself discussing the goals of the American space program, the ideology of President Reagan, poverty in the United States, international terrorism, and the geophysical causes of earthquakes. (Pace n.d.)

THEORETICAL SIGNIFICANCE

The incorporation of formerly isolated communities and regions into larger information networks exemplifies **cultural evolution**, the development of progressively larger social, cultural, political, and economic systems. Anthropologists have studied the transformation and incorporation of tribes into nations. It is equally appropriate to investigate the contemporary incorporation of communities into national and world systems.[6] Modern anthropology must answer a central question: *How is cultural diversity both influencing and being affected by larger forces?* In this book I focus on the cultural context and effects of mass communication, in the form of television.

Cross-cultural comparison and attention to **cultural variation** are vital to understanding the effects of any technology on human behavior. In the case of television, culture intervenes in determining (1) specific aspects of program content, (2) program preferences, and (3) how people interpret and are affected by televised messages. Cultural variation is obvious in locally produced program content. It is also manifest in the scheduling and shaping of news, advertising, and entertainment, and educational and political messages. There is a reciprocal relationship between television and culture. The pre-existing culture influences indigenous creations and program choice. Long-term exposure to messages then feeds back on social reality, changing old beliefs, attitudes, and behavior. This process contributes to the development of a new (mass) culture.

Purportedly "basic human conflicts" portrayed on television actually vary substantially from culture to culture (Comstock et al. 1978). As Dundes (1975) observes, people perceive nature through the mediation of culture. The cognitive categories that guide perception vary between cultures. Culture intervenes between television's technological form and its effects on people.[7] Through comparative research in nations such as Brazil, where local productions are most popular, we can separate television's impact as technology (relatively constant) from the impact of its content (much more cross-culturally variable).

There is another prime reason for doing television research outside the United States. When television is (virtually) everywhere, researchers can only observe how people behave when it is present, as Comstock and colleagues (1978) have observed. However, in Brazil and other Third World nations, television's diffusion is more recent. Many households still lack sets. In these settings we can still make before–after and absent–present comparisons. We can study effects related to length and degree of exposure at different ages. As in most of the world, the percentage of households with television is rapidly increasing in Brazil. Fortunately, however, our project began in time to locate and interview many people with virtually no TV exposure. This allowed us to isolate television's impact on communities, households, and individuals with different degrees of exposure. I discuss these effects in subsequent chapters.

Before the advent of television, North Americans already lived as mainly literate people in a media-rich environment. However, Brazil's literary traditions are far less developed than those of the United States. There were no printing presses in Brazil until the early 19th century. Although Brazilians composed poetry and addresses before 1850, the best-known Brazilian novels appeared after that date. In the United States, the written word has played a much more substantial role than in Brazil. Television's presence has increased Americans' contact with the mass media by 40 percent (Comstock et al. 1978). The increase has been even greater in Brazil, given its media-poor background.

CULTURAL IMPERIALISM OR CULTURAL DIVERSITY

Despite fears and lamentations about cultural imperialism, a cross-cultural perspective shows that TV is not just a homogenizing force. Instead, television is potentially a means of elaborating on the Great Traditions of different societies and preserving the cultural diversity that such traditions represent. For example, millions of Brazilians who were formerly excluded by isolation and illiteracy have now joined in a single national communication system. They now have better access than ever to distinctively Brazilian themes and representations.

Cross-cultural evidence also contradicts a common ethnocentric belief of Americans about televiewing in other countries. This misconception is that American programs inevitably win out over local products, that *Dallas* and *Dynasty* are as popular abroad as they have been in the United States. Televiewing habits in many nations show that this is not necessarily true. In fact, it is rarely true when there is appealing local competition. In Brazil, for example, the most popular network relies heavily on native productions. *Dallas* and *Dynasty* draw minuscule audiences.

It isn't North American culture but a new pan-Brazilian national culture that Brazilian TV is propagating. Brazil's Globo network plays each night to the world's largest and most devoted audience. The programs that attract this horde are made by Brazilians, for Brazilians. Brazilian productions are also exported to over 100 countries, spanning Latin America, Europe, Asia, and Africa. Even Brazilian intellectuals (who tend to consider TV a low art form) take a certain pride in national achievements in programming and production. They regard television as a means of spreading a positive image of Brazil around the world.

We may generalize that American programming that is culturally alien and inappropriate for local conditions will not do very well anywhere when a quality local choice is available. Confirmation comes from many countries. National productions are highly popular in Japan, Mexico, India, Egypt, and Nigeria.[8] In a survey during the mid-1980s, 75 percent of Nigerian viewers preferred local productions. Only 10 percent favored imports, and the remaining 15 percent liked the two options equally. Local productions are successful in Nigeria because "they are filled with everyday moments that audiences can identify with. These shows are locally produced by Nigerians and not by whites cast in blackface" (Gray 1986). One of the most popular series—*The Village Headmaster*, watched weekly by 30 million people—reminded urbanites of the rural values they had left behind (Gray 1986).

NATIONAL-LEVEL RESEARCH

From 1983 to 1987 I directed the research project described in this book. The field sites, research methods, and findings are described in greater detail in Part 3. The project was a multi-tiered, or multi-level, study. It investigated Brazilian television at both the national and local levels. The national-level work began in August 1983. I had arranged a year's affiliation with the Department of Social Anthropology of the National Museum, a division of the Federal University of Rio de Janeiro. During that year, I interviewed television industry experts and personnel in Rio de Janeiro and São Paulo. I also did archival and statistical research in Brazil's media-research organizations (see Chapters 3 and 4).

CONTENT STUDY

My anthropological training had prepared me to be not an aloof, detached scholar but a participant observer—joining in native life as I learned about that culture. To study Brazilian television I first had to know about it from watching it, as natives do. As I watched TV in 1983–84 I did a *qualitative study* of the social and cultural *content* of the most popular programs (see Chapters 4–6). Specific goals and interests guided my televiewing. I paid particular attention to media portrayal of family, race, ethnicity, occupation, social class, sex-gender roles, and sexism (Chapter 5). I wanted to be able to contrast treatment of these matters in Brazil and the United States. Time and resources did not permit me to do a long-term, quantitative content analysis.[9] Nevertheless, I did gain a general understanding of Brazilian TV content, which I compare with American programming throughout *Prime-Time Society*.

I observed many cross-cultural contrasts in program types, preferences, themes, subjects, plots, and character attributes. These reveal underlying differences in society, culture, and values (see Chapters 5 and 6 particularly). Study of content was intrinsically interesting because of what it revealed about Brazilian culture. Content analysis also provided necessary background information that helped us formulate relevant questions to assess the effects of specific aspects of Brazilian TV content.

IMPACT ON RURAL COMMUNITIES

Besides national-level investigation and content study, the other project component was a coordinated field study of several rural Brazilian communities. The aim was to gather original data permitting comparison of communities and people with different degrees of exposure to television. In January 1985, field research began in four communities in the states of Santa Catarina (south), São Paulo (southcentral), Bahia (northeast), and Pará (Amazon). We added two other sites later. Fieldwork continued into 1987. (See Chapter 8 for map of Brazil with field sites.) Beginning in Chapter 8, I discuss research sites, methods, and findings. First, however, I describe Brazilian television at the national level.

PART TWO

The National Level

CHAPTER THREE

◈ Censors and Gatekeepers

Amerian commercial television is supported by advertising rather than by government subsidies. For this reason it is freer of direct government controls over reporting of public affairs than are broadcasting media in most other countries, including the Soviet Union and many African nations (Hirsch 1979:252). Soviet television, via 80 million sets reaching 90 percent of the citizenry, has become a nationally pervasive propaganda tool. Four channels, all emanating from Moscow, carry the same basic programs. These are the official news, speeches of the Supreme Soviet, lessons in geometry, grammar, and computers, and youth classes about one's obligations in society (Morrison 1986).

The overt propaganda role of television is also obvious in Africa. So concludes a report by the International Development Research Council, a Canadian research group, based on a study of Cameroon, Congo, Gambia, Ivory Coast, Niger, Nigeria, Senegal, Zaire, Zambia, and Zimbabwe (Gray 1986). The report found that (despite a few bright spots such as Nigeria) television in Africa is generally a government mouthpiece (Gray 1986). Typical African TV content includes political speeches, reports on visits of foreign dignitaries, development experts speaking in European languages over the heads of the average viewer, and dramas featuring upper-class characters dealing with Western problems.

In these nations television is characterized by much less competition and variety than in the United States, or even than in Brazil, where, however, a single commercial television network dominates as none has ever done in the United States. Nevertheless, this chapter will illustrate, with primary reference to the world's most watched commercial network, that control by gatekeepers can operate on several levels. Censorship can apply to commercial as well as to government-funded or government-run television.

For instance, even when television is commercial, as in the United States or Brazil, government officials typically allocate access to the airwaves. They also play a role in regulating scheduling and content of news, documentaries, ads, propaganda, information, and entertainment programs. Several forms of censorship have affected Brazilian commercial television:

EXTERNAL	INTERMEDIATE	INTERNAL
government	network executives	self-censorship
public opinion		by creators
sponsors		

GOVERNMENT CENSORSHIP

In 1984, as Brazil prepared for its first presidential election (albeit indirect) in a quarter century, television remained that nation's most censored medium. Brazil's foremost television critic and commentator Artur da Távola contended that this was because the television industry lacked cultural power. (He was referring to elite or "high culture.") Because many intellectuals considered television a low art form, they didn't make the same demands for easing television censorship as they did with theater, film, newspapers, and books. Brazil's high culture power brokers didn't care much if popular entertainment programs were cut. When TV writers protested censorship, they weren't taken seriously because television still had a low value as art.

Although television lacks high culture prestige, as the mass medium *par excellance,* it can have tremendous power. As Hirsch has observed,

> Political leaders and office-holders are generally far more alert and sensitive than social scientists and journalists to the structural characteristics which distinguish television from other news media and provide it with a *different form of power* [emphasis added]. (Hirsch 1979:255)

Brazil's military government (1964–85) never doubted TV's power and was vigilant in supervising its content.

In recent years, the Brazilian government has controlled television by granting access to the airwaves and by supervising program content. A 1962 law granted licenses for 15 years, but under military rule they were revokable at any time (Kehl 1981b:28–29). Brazilian broadcasters therefore held precarious concessions. Government decree could arbitrarily annul these licenses.[2] As a result, Brazilian broadcasters were much more careful than their counterparts in the United States, where licensing is more long term and less arbitrary.

Brazil's electoral freedom ended abruptly on April 1, 1964, when military officers seized the government, ousted elected President João Goulart, and instituted a reign of authoritarianism. Military repression began to abate only in the late 1970s, finally ending in 1985.

In a 1975 speech, Brazil's Minister of Culture explicitly focused on television's huge potential influence as the reason for state control over that medium (Miranda and Pereira 1983:26). Among undesirable TV content features needing government attention, he mentioned violence, distorted presentations of reality, and foreign social and moral values and customs. According to the minister, government authorities should intervene when necessary to preserve authentic Brazilian values, to protect and prepare future leaders (Miranda and Pereira 1983:28).[3]

Government scrutiny of television content was most intense from 6 to 9:30 P.M. During this prime time Brazil's most popular television programs—the Globo network's national news (8 P.M.) and its three nightly soaps or *telenovelas*—are broadcast in three time slots—6 P.M., 7 P.M., and 8:30 P.M. Unlike American soap operas, Brazilian *telenovelas* end. The typical one lasts six or seven months. For each new *novela* Rede Globo (*rede* means "network") had to submit a synopsis and the first 15 chapters to a government censor for approval and modification.

Even after *abertura* ("political opening"), which began in the late 1970s, and as military rule was ending in 1984, censorship continued. Newspapers and TV magazines such as *Amiga* (the number-one fan magazine) routinely published complaints by fans, authors, and actors about government-imposed cuts in *telenovelas*. One actor complained that his character had become incomprehensible because a critical personality transformation took place in two scenes cut by censors. The censor routinely snipped references to politics, political figures, and characters with certain occupations (for instance, numbers racket personnel). Departures from traditional family values were also taboo.

Several cases illustrate the kinds of content that were censored. References to the rallies for direct presidential elections that occurred in 1984 were cut from an 8 o'clock *novela*. A deranged woman's unfounded suspicion that her brother was having an affair with the mayor's wife, known as "the first lady," was excised from a 6 P.M. *novela*. From a 7 o'clock serial the censor cut a dream of light extramarital romance by an oppressed middle-aged married woman infatuated with a man other than her supermacho husband. In one 8 P.M. *novela*, which started off with two high-class professional thieves as its protagonists, censorship eventually forced both to shift to legitimate businesses. In a very popular 7 o'clock serial, there was doubt about whether the censors would allow the heroine, a glamorous woman in her fifties, to end up with a much younger, divorced man, and whether the hero could marry the (reformed) villainess. (In both cases they did.)

Censorship laws stifled political reporting and debate. In 1984 São Paulo's independent TV Cultura was sued over a live broadcast of an interview in which a former president called a governor "a bandit." Other stations cut this part when showing the tape, but TV Cultura transmitted the interview live. It was not the slandered governor, who was no friend of the military, but the federal government that sued. It was illegal to say scandalous things about any government official.

Brazilian censorship concentrated on politics and violence and paid much less attention to nudity and sex. Brazilians (still) try to limit children's exposure to media violence more than Americans do. Announcers proclaim certain TV hours approved for children of certain ages. A government-imposed rating system continues to regulate movie houses, and managers pay more attention to it than American theater owners do to the G, PG, and R system. My then 13-year-old son, although accompanied by consenting parents, had trouble getting into Brazilian theater showings of *The Twilight Zone* and *Indiana Jones and the Temple of Doom*. They were considered too violent for children younger than 14. Managers enforce the code by asking to see a child's identity card.

Nudity and graphic romance fared better under censorship. The careful monitoring by the military government did not ban certain prime-time commercials that would be considered very risqué or would be banned outright on noncable channels in the United States. Brazilians apparently found nothing unusual in ads featuring ample female bodies spilling out of the same scant bikinis that could be seen by the thousands at any Rio beach. Babies' bottoms are permissible (in diaper commercials) on American TV, but the genitals of male and female toddlers, which are shown in Brazilian ads, are not. A men's underwear commercial, shown in 1984 on the 7 o'clock *novela* and seen by millions of children, featured a young man clad in bikini briefs cavorting in bed with a naked woman. A year later, following the end of military rule, I saw in the same time slot a commercial featuring a rooster that erupted, Woody Woodpecker fashion, from the fly of a pair of men's underpants. By 1987, female breasts and male buttocks were in vogue. Yet Brazilians still considered such American imports as *The Fall Guy* and *Hill Street Blues* too violent for hours when children were watching TV. If shown at all, these programs aired after kids' bed time.

In response to the threat of government interference and network controls, reporters, writers, directors, and commentators have consciously and unconsciously censored themselves. This internal censor can be particularly stifling, because it is a constant brake on creativity.

CONSUMERS AND PUBLIC OPINION

Measuring the Audience

The main purpose of commercial television is neither to entertain nor to enlighten, but to sell. American and Brazilian television strive not to train proper citizens, but proper consumers. Brazil has well-developed market research, public opinion sampling, advertising, audience targeting, and other techniques designed to spur consumption. IBOPE (The Brazilian Statistical Public Opinion Research Institute) is the foremost polling organization, with a historic role equivalent to Gallup's or Nielsen's in the United States.[4] Founded in 1942, IBOPE is headquartered in Rio, with a second major agency in São Paulo and offices in several other cities. One indication of its prominence is that "IBOPE" has come to mean rating. A program's success is measured by its "IBOPE"—the estimate of the number of sets tuned to that channel at that time.

In the mid-1980s IBOPE employed about 800 people nationwide to do 80,000 brief household interviews each day. Throughout Brazil, pollsters gathered data on number of sets in use, channel watched, and age and sex of viewers. American networks use sample precincts to predict elections. IBOPE (which also does political polling) maintains its own sample areas—key neighborhoods. These allow assessment of variation in viewer habits and preferences based on socioeconomic characteristics, particularly class and income. Socioeconomic class is all important in sampling, because it provides the information about consumers' buying power necessary for advertising and programming strategies.

In Rio, IBOPE samples almost 200 households each half hour between 7 A.M. and midnight. This amounts to more than 7000 interviews per day, over 200,000 per month. IBOPE polls regularly in major cities and occasionally in more than 100 smaller cities and towns. The organization thereby covers the nation from extreme south, to far west, to northeast, to Amazonian rain forest. A less prominent organization, Audimarket, compiles TV ratings using audience meters in Rio, São Paulo, and the southern city of Porto Alegre. Audimarket findings (in 1985), based on 220 homes in São Paulo and the same number in Rio, confirmed Globo's nightly dominance between 6 P.M. and 9:30 P.M. Audimarket and IBOPE agreed that Globo *telenovelas* routinely get about 70 percent of the sets turned on (50–70 percent of all sets) in that time period. Later in the evening there is more competition.

An indirect measure of Globo's success is utility company monitoring of mass behavior. Each night, when a Globo *novela* begins, phone use drops, minute by minute, then rises during commercials. Piped water levels also drop across the nation during commercials, as hundreds of thousands of toilets are flushed. (The same thing happens annually in the United States during Super Bowl commercials.)

Brazilian survey research is confined to cities. Neither IBOPE nor any other polling organization works in communities with recent and incomplete access to television. This is one reason why research on television's context and effects in rural areas has been needed and was part of our project in six communities and five states. IBOPE's rationale for its sampling strategy is that Brazilian television is an urban phenomenon, which spreads the metropolitan patterns of Rio and São Paulo to other cities and towns in a highly urban nation. TV's target is the consuming classes, who are most numerous, concentrated, and reachable in urban locales.

In the United States, *Variety, TV Guide*, and newspapers routinely publish ratings. Comparable information is much more restricted in Brazil. Despite constant IBOPE polling, data on the most popular programs of the week, month, season, and even year are publicly unavailable. To obtain ratings data, I had to arrange personal interviews at the market research agencies.[5]

The reason for this secrecy is that these agencies make money selling their data and services. IBOPE sells its voluminous monthly statistical reports to firms that have some business use for them. A single issue of a monthly report cost about $300 in 1984. Except for subscribers, no one knows exactly what the fluctuations in program preferences are, unless one of the networks decides to publish them. Broadcasters occasionally do this as a marketing ploy, to plug the popularity, and hence the commercial value, of an offering. Besides daily sampling, IBOPE (and others) do special studies commissioned by networks, stations, and businesses. If results agree with expectations or help the corporate image, they appear in newspapers and magazines. If not, the sponsor suppresses them.

IBOPE gathers data but does not do detailed analyses of its results. Those who commission a study or purchase IBOPE's reports must do their own calculations of matters such as the effect of age or sex on viewing habits and preferences. My own perusal of IBOPE's monthly survey data for Rio revealed a few obvious patterns. Of *novela* viewers, 41 percent were males, but slightly more men than women watched the news. The percentage of male viewers increases during the evening, with men dominating the audience after 10 P.M.

Results from our six field sites show that various factors affect preferences for particular types of programs. *Telenovelas* and news attract somewhat different audiences. Those who said they liked *novelas* tended to be female, younger, less educated, and of lower social class. News fans were more likely to be male, older, and better educated. A preference for humor was more common in men and in younger, better-educated people. Variety, which ranges from the lowbrow programming of the Sílvio Santos network (SBT) to the elite-oriented shows of the Manchête network, attracted a wide spectrum of people.[6]

For many years the American market has been much more competitive than Brazil's, with nothing like single network domination. Competition leads to open ratings comparisons. Nielsen publishes its results for anyone to consult. American ratings become credentials in advertising in *Variety* and other trade journals. Networks and stations use ratings to attract advertisers. Production companies use them to sell their products, including syndicated reruns, to stations. Something comparable happens occasionally in Brazil. In 1984, the newborn Manchête network commissioned an IBOPE study and then gleefully publicized the results when its coverage of Rio's Carnival far surpassed powerful Globo's programming, which was beaten for the first time ever in certain time slots.

IBOPE has established a *useful social-class scale* to evaluate audience buying power. Its categories are A (upper class), B1 (upper middle), B2 (middle middle), B3 (lower middle), C (upper working), and D (lower working and people without significant income). The basis of the scale is the proportion and amount of household income remaining after certain basic expenditures. These necessities encompass food, utilities (including telephone), school expenses, clothing, transportation, personal hygiene items, medical care, and domestic help. Note that IBOPE uses Brazilian cultural standards to define middle-class existence. For instance, most middle-class Brazilians consider domestic help (a maid or cook) a necessity. (The American equivalent might be the washing machine.)

IBOPE adds the amounts expended on all these items and deducts the total from gross income. What remains is divided by total earnings to give a percentage of gross income (that is, disposable income) available for consumer goods. IBOPE uses this percentage to assign people to social classes. The organization also pays attention to actual gross income. IBOPE recognizes that some very poor people manage to reduce their expenses on basics, yet still lack the money to buy the items hawked on television. Proportional distribution of the classes in Rio in 1983–84 is shown in Table 3.1.

Audience Targeting: Massification Versus Segmental Appeal

Television executives and sponsors make decisions based on socioeconomic characteristics of audiences. Brazil has four national networks—Globo, SBT, Manchête, and Bandeirantes. Only Globo has true **mass appeal**, consistently attracting large audiences in all social classes, regions, and types of community. More than Globo, the other networks target their programming at particular segments of the Brazilian population.

Classes A and B comprise at least 40 percent of the viewers in Brazil's southern cities, and the Manchête network aims many of its programs at this upper segment of the IBOPE scale. For example, in October–November 1983, Manchête showed an attractive documentary series, *The Brazilians*, written and narrated by anthropologist Roberto DaMatta. To cap its 1984 Summer Olympic coverage, Manchête produced and broadcast a handsome historical miniseries. That offering, *The Marquesa dos Santos*, told the story of the love affair between 19th century Brazilian emperor Dom Pedro II and the title character. Well-produced musical and interview programs, a weekly magazine, and recent American film hits (dubbed in Portuguese) rounded out Manchête's schedule.

Globo's huge popularity rests on three main program types: national news, *telenovelas*, and comedy–variety shows. Globo's *novelas* (see Chap-

TABLE 3.1 *IBOPE's Social Classes*

CLASS	PERCENTAGE
Upper (A) and upper middle (B1)	6
Middle middle (B2) and lower middle (B3)	34
Working (C)	34
Abject poverty (D)	26
Total	100

ters 4 and 5), whose production standards and acting professionalism put day-time American soaps to shame, offer the clearest quality contrast with other networks. Other Brazilian networks have competent news programs. Globo, however, hooks the mass audience because six nights a week its national news is sandwiched between its two most popular *telenovelas*. The other networks have managed to compete with Globo only in low-brow and middlebrow comedy–variety programming and outside of prime time (that is, outside 6–9:30 P.M., Monday through Saturday).

Globo's weeknight news and *telenovelas* have a loyal national following. Only on Sundays does the pattern of nationwide Globo viewing break down somewhat. On Sunday night Globo offers a two-hour combined variety show and newsmagazine. This program, *Fantástico*, regularly ranks in the week's top ten. Compared to Globo's weeknight programming, however, *Fantástico*'s audience is more *segmental* (as opposed to *massified*—with across-the-board appeal, attracting all social groups in the nation). *Fantástico* is much more popular in small cities, towns, and rural zones than in the major cities. Availing themselves of urban recreational alternatives, middle-class *cariocas* (residents of Rio de Janeiro) and *paulistas* (residents of São Paulo) watch less Sunday night TV than do other Brazilians.

Globo's quality is less obvious in its humor and variety programs, including *Fantástico*, which tend to have more small-town and down-scale audiences. One *Fantástico*, for example, told viewers that extraterrestrials had been visiting Earth for 50,000 years. As proof it showed motifs of birds purportedly unlike any found on earth in Peruvian architectural reliefs. It also featured a supposed jaguar's head (which looked more like a rabbit's head to me) at Lake Titicaca. Presumably, *Titicaca* means "jaguar."

Globo quality also suffered late Saturday afternoons, when the network offered a live variety show hosted by the (now deceased) "Chacrinha." This clownlike older man wandered around amid a supporting cast of scantily dressed disco-dancing women, professional entertainers, amateurs, and panelists who judged their acts. Punctuated by close-ups of outrageously exposed female bottoms, Chacrinha muttered to his screaming audience questions such as "Who's smarter—men or women?" For years this two-hour program was considered a favorite of maids and cooks throughout the nation. Chacrinha also sponsored contests to determine such notables as Brazil's most beautiful maid, student, black woman, best disco dancer, and queen of the samba schools.

Trailing Globo's almost total national penetration is SBT (the Brazilian Television System), owned by *paulista* impresario Sílvio Santos. Established in 1982, it took only two years for "Sílvio Santos," as the network is known, to become the nation's second in scope. SBT aims at a lower segment of the IBOPE scale than does Globo or Manchête. Its most popular programs are game and variety shows, on the same level as Globo's Chacrinha.

Sílvio Santos himself hosts one of them—a several-hour Sunday marathon. In 1984 this program began Sunday at 11 A.M. and ended at 8 P.M. It has since lengthened, to compete face-to-face with *Fantástico.* The Sílvio Santos marathon has several segments, most modeled on old American game shows, such as *Name That Tune.* Most popular is the last segment, a two-hour amateur program. Eight panelists (mostly men) judge singers, dancers, and oddball performers (for example, a man who rubs his face in broken glass without being cut). The live performances and jurors' she-nanigans are interrupted by clips from the American *Gong Show.* Occasionally someone appears mimicking *Gong Show* acts. Often, untalented singers are gonged.

Globo's only significant competition comes on Sunday afternoon and early evening. The viewers of the Sílvio Santos game-show marathon usually equal or surpass Globo's audiences. Sunday, the only day without *novelas,* is also the day when urban middle-class Brazilians flock to clubs, beaches, and restaurants. From a commercial viewpoint, Sunday afternoon is a television disaster. This is the time slot that the usually dominant network can most afford to lose.

Sílvio Santos's audience includes millions of class C and D viewers. These are people with neither automobiles nor club memberships, who can't afford to eat in restaurants. Sunday is also the national "maid's day off." Often the maid, who leaves her employers Saturday afternoon, spends Sunday with her family watching Sílvio Santos. Another SBT variety show, hosted by Augusto Liberato (Gugú), did so well late Saturday night that Globo enticed Gugú to its own roster in 1987.

On weeknights, SBT airs two prime-time *novelas,* scheduled to overlap as little as possible with Globo's. One is usually a Mexican program dubbed in Portuguese. The other is Brazilian. There is a very obvious contrast in quality between SBT *novelas* and those made by Globo. Globo's are lavish productions, with multiple outdoor scenes and location shots. Globo employs some of Brazil's finest actors and writers. The programs shown on SBT, whether Brazilian or Mexican, are inferior. They take place indoors. Locales are less attractive and varied and well-known actors less evident. Their audiences are mainly lower class.

Like all Brazilian networks other than Globo, SBT has segmental rather than mass appeal. Brazilian elites consider SBT's most popular formats—game and variety shows—lowbrow entertainment (comparable to *The Gong Show, Gomer Pyle,* and *The Beverly Hillbillies*). SBT does rival Globo for the lower half of the IBOPE scale in certain time slots. In Arembepe, the coastal town in Bahia I have studied since 1962, virtually everyone is a member of the national lower class (IBOPE segments C and D). Arembepeiros are faithful viewers of SBT shows, but they also like Globo news and *telenovelas.* SBT also attracts some class B2 and B3 viewers. These middle-class viewers are necessary for its survival. Programs that appeal only to classes C and D, who have little extra money to invest in consumer goods, are doomed.

For example, in 1984 SBT canceled one of Rio's most interesting programs, *The People on TV*, because it did not appeal to the consuming classes. This had been a live afternoon program, shown weekdays from 3 (later 4) to 6. *The People on TV* offered the closest thing I saw in Brazil to consumer advocacy. Poor people (maids, cooks, drivers) appeared each day to report about exposed sewers, economic disputes, and victimization. Two attractive young women sat on a stage and answered viewers' phone calls. A panel including a congressman and a spiritualist helped host Wilton Tupinambá Franco suggest solutions. Occasionally Franco engaged in shouting matches by phone or in person with a purported villain. The program always ended with Ave Maria, as the audience filed out of the studio, stopping to pay homage to a garish statue of the Virgin Mary. Concomitantly, Franco delivered an emotional benediction.

The People on TV suffered the same fate as a series of other shows previously hosted by Wilton Franco. Because it appealed mainly to the poor, it left the air. It never found major sponsors, or earned much of a profit. Most of its ads were for snake-oil remedies, products the poor could afford. The fact that *The People on TV* actually had a large audience share, often beating Globo in its time slot, shows that audience quantity is less important than quality. This is particularly true in Brazil, where the consuming class is numerically much smaller than in the United States. Even the poorest Americans have more disposable income and participate more in consumerism than the poorest Brazilians.

NETWORK DOMINANCE

Hirsch (1979) made these observations about American television before the cable age:

> Some of the "effects" commonly attributed to the television medium should be conceived instead as following from its present organizational form, in which nearly 900 separate channels are effectively reduced to being mere conduits for four centralized TV networks. It is for this reason, and the consequent lack of variation or diversity in program content to which the nation is exposed, that television now serves so well as a proxy for all of the mass media whenever questions arise over mass media effects. (Hirsch 1979:249)

His remarks are even truer of commercial television in Brazil, where production involves the concentration of power and capital in the hands of fewer people (Miranda and Pereira 1983:20).

Globo provides a prime example of the growth of large national monopolies in Brazil during the 1970s (Kehl 1981b:5). The network's success rests on the complexity of its strategy for conquering the public and its cooperation with an authoritarian central government.[7] Globo's critics suggest that years of governmental labor repression facilitated

Globo's success (Kehl 1981b:19). With no strong unions or strike possibilities, workers had to accept the conditions the network imposed.[8] Globo was known for taking the government's side, particularly from 1968 to 1974, at the height of authoritarianism and censorship (Carvalho 1981:37). The network broadcast so many government announcements that it sometimes seemed indistinguishable from the government press agency (Carvalho 1981:33).

However, television executives outside of Globo also made programming decisions out of fear of, or to please, government. In 1983, for example, a government critic employed by a São Paulo station was dismissed because the station's dire financial circumstances required that it seek a government loan.

Still, Rede Globo is the prime example of a broadcasting organization that has prospered in Brazil as a result of nonoffensive popular programming and cooperation with government. Globo has amassed significantly more gatekeeping power than is possible in the United States. Control over multiple media, marketing savvy, and federal intervention and support have combined to create the Globo monopoly. In the public domain, only the Brazilian state rivals Globo's power as national gatekeeper. Recognizing Globo chief Roberto Marinho's huge influence, presidential candidates pay him court, with personal visits.

Monopolistic Control over Multiple Media

American antimonopoly laws have limited media control by prohibiting the same individual or corporation from owning a newspaper and TV station in the same city. There are no such laws in Brazil. Rede Globo's success began in Rio, where a massive support industry reinforces its dominance. The empire built by Roberto Marinho includes production facilities and network headquarters. Add to that empire Rio's Globo TV channel, the best-selling newspaper *O Globo*, popular AM and FM radio stations, and a book publishing house. Finally, Globo owns a record company, which produces best-selling albums of the national and international scores of each *telenovela*.[9] Such media dominance cannot help but restrict Brazilians' access to information, including antigovernment views.

Contributing to Globo's popularity in Rio is extensive press support of its programs. Each morning the newspaper *O Globo* summarizes the previous night's Globo *novela* happenings, ignoring the other networks. The weekly magazine *Tevê*, distributed with Sunday's *O Globo*, gives Globo's offerings much more attention than those of other channels. The magazine mentions the latter only to criticize or castigate their low quality and other faults.

Criticisms of Globo programming in Globo publications are very rare, but each issue of *Tevê* manages to take six to ten potshots at the competition. *Tevê*'s inside front page prints letters derogating non-Globo programs. Columnists take up the tone. The day before the debut of one Globo *novela*, for example, a columnist lambasted the *novela* that had recently debuted on another channel: "Not knowing exactly what to do, TVS offered a remake of *The Right to Be Born* [an old, highly successful *novela*], with poor sets and bad acting" (Távola 1983e:15).

Globo insists on the huge gap between its programming style and others. In the issue of *Tevê* just quoted, columnist Artur da Távola condescended that two Rio stations were "directed at popular programming." He labeled "barbarous" a variety show whose hostess sang along with a pair of guest musicians. Távola also criticized Manchête (known as a high-quality network) for too many announcements of coming programs (a failure fully as obvious any day on Globo) and for showing a music program without naming the concert pieces. Távola also made use of the cultural imperialism argument to extol Globo's national programming, which he contrasted with competitors' tendency to show (cheaper) imported programs. He singled out American westerns for "exploiting the Brazilian fascination with the cowboy, which is rooted in infancy," implying that westerns are juvenile. Távola's final insult in a single column: "There's nothing more tiresome than too much slang—as on TV Record's program *Realce* (perhaps the only good program on that channel)" (Távola 1983e:15).

Generally, Brazilian television management makes it clear that not a lot good can be said about competitors. Consider the situation of the critic and commentator Artur da Távola (later to become a federal deputy). Some regarded Távola as one of Brazil's chief intellects, whereas others dismissed him as a Globo stooge. It was clear that employment conditions permitted Távola to make only occasional favorable comments about other stations. For many years, Távola wrote a daily column in *O Globo* and weekly columns for *Manchête* (a *Life* imitator) and *Amiga* (a popular TV fan magazine). The owner of both magazines was Adolpho Bloch, who also owned TV Manchête and the network of that name. The same rules applied in Bloch's magazines as at Globo: Praise our product, saying as little positive and as much negative as possible about the competition. Thus on November 29, 1983, writing in *Amiga*, Távola (1983c) lauded the technical quality of the Manchête network's daily news broadcasts and two other programs. The column asserted that TV Manchête had entered the realm of quality production until then exemplified only by some Globo productions.

In addition to its cavalier and contemptuous treatment of the competition, Globo also plays down popular culture events that do not fit its schedule and plans. In 1984, for example, the network decided to stick rigidly to its normal programming and leave Summer Olympics (see Chapter 6) and Carnival coverage to the competition, chiefly Manchête. Having made the decision to ignore Carnival, Globo's management ordered directors of its musical programs not to include any of that year's samba scores. An *Amiga* columnist (employed by Manchête) lambasted Globo for trying to deny that samba schools and music were the people's main interest at Carnival time (Halfoun 1984:9). (Manchête, of course, was hyping its own Carnival coverage.)

The Role of the Audience

Besides censorship, audience reactions and preferences constitute another force to which networks respond in program development. In both the United States and Brazil, government officials, sponsors, and network staff routinely cite community standards, public opinion, and the audience in justifying their decisions. Globo encourages public opinion feedback by monitoring and evaluating reactions to its *novelas*. Globo is unique in Brazil in the extent to which it investigates audience reactions to characters and plot developments. Besides consulting daily and monthly IBOPE results, Globo has its own research and analysis department, which does in-depth interviewing. Although leaving no doubt about his own ultimate power, Globo chief Roberto Marinho also delegated authority to the executives under him. He allowed the supervisors of production and direction to define the basic ingredients in Globo productions.

In his voluminous writings about Brazilian television, Távola has stressed again and again that the *telenovela* is a *semi-open work* that the audience has a role in guiding.[10] Globo pays attention to public reaction and modifies *novelas* accordingly because it wants to sell products. This is a very important determinant of what happens to characters and plots.[11] Audience response leads to reduction or augmentation of particular roles. Writers have changed endings in response to letters asking that a romantic couple slated to separate be allowed to stay together. Negative reactions to *Sinal do Alerta (Danger Signal)*, which dealt with pollution and strikes, led Globo to avoid these subjects in later *novelas*. Another serial, *Gigantes (Giants)* depicted not only incest, but also euthanasia of a man attached to a life-sustaining machine. After "mothers" wrote in complaining that these were improper themes for children, that *novela* was shortened to 80 chapters, about half the usual length.

To take the public pulse, researchers and writers consult such information brokers as taxi drivers, hairdressers, and barbers, who are sounding boards of popular opinion. Popular telenovelist Janete Clair, who died in 1983, was particularly adept at modifying her works to accommodate public wishes. She elicited opinions in the supermarket and the street. Another successful telenovelist, Gilberto Braga, purportedly relied on his maid for reactions from her friends. In smaller cities and towns, researchers approach people in the central bar or luncheonette, where announcements are posted and opinion leaders congregate.

The director of Globo's research department can mandate certain changes by *novela* directors. Authors respond in various ways when ratings fall, often reverting to proven formulas. As reward for their popularity, successful telenovelists earn substantially more than actors. On the other hand, management may fire uncooperative writers or those with declining audiences. They can also banish the writer to 6 o'clock (the least prestigious *novela* slot), where, however, an aspiring writer is happy to begin a career.

Telenovelas differ from theater and film in their openness to external input. Actors do not need to cling to a completely predetermined character. Relationships and plots respond to external factors. Of course, production considerations also affect the development of a *novela*. Certain conditions—including the constraints of having to make a chapter a day, and the budget—limit possibilities. The first 50 chapters get the most money, then Globo starts investing in its next project.

Nevertheless, Globo's attention to audience reaction (and, just as important, its publicity about this attention) helps give spectators a sense of participating in the story and its development. Of course, if ordinary people are to influence a *novela*'s course, they must know about intended developments in advance. Radio programs and fan magazines provide this vital information. Once segments have been filmed, some three weeks before being aired, Globo provides fan magazines with plot summaries. The TV magazine *Amiga* summarizes events for the week immediately following its issue date. It also reveals plot plans, such as murders and marriages, well into the future. Occasionally, network officials or writers divulge intended plot developments months before filming.

One interesting case of audience participation involved the *novela O Astro*, during whose last chapters people throughout Brazil were asking "Who killed Salomão Hayalla?" A *Globo* newspaper columnist admitted that she and the writer, Janete Clair, had conspired to dupe the public about the outcome. To maintain the suspense, the columnist reported that Clair had written five endings, with different murderers, when she had really written just one. Sometimes, multiple endings actually are filmed, and *Amiga* publishes all of them—well in advance.

A PRESIDENTIAL CAMPAIGN

President Franklin D. Roosevelt began the practice of going directly to the American people, on the radio. In so doing he wrested control from old-boy newspaper journalists, but he also paved the way for the eventual power of TV gatekeepers.

> The organizational structure of [American] television further underlies and makes possible a wide variety of "effects" often proposed by social scientists as unique to this medium, but which also formerly characterized other mass media when they, too, were organized along the lines which television now follows. For example, the prospect of favorable

television news coverage has accelerated (though did not originate) the staging of conferences, political conventions, press releases, campaign stops, and other "pseudo-events." (Hirsch 1979:251, 255)

Hirsch (1979) finds that American political leaders have little control over the news judgments of broadcast journalists. Still, there is a mutually reinforcing feedback between media, politicians, and government.

Parenti (1986) argues convincingly that the American media have helped recreate a view of reality supportive of existing power relationships. The press generally defines the news as what politicians say. Again and again, the American news media comply with government disinformation campaigns, and reporters, eager to please editors, censor themselves. Thus, censorship works on different levels and in many ways in the United States, just as it has done in Brazil.

In 1984 both the United States and Brazil had lengthy but very differently organized and publicized presidential campaigns. The American campaign was the usual media event. In Hirsch's words (1979:252):

> Candidates for political office seeking to reach the public directly must purchase television advertising time—which has become the single largest item in campaign budgets and greatly accounts for the rising cost of seeking office and pressure to raise funds in ever-increasing amounts.

In contrast, a statute known as the Lei Falcão (Falcon law) regulated media exposure during campaigns in Brazil. According to this law, each candidate received a specified amount of air time of dubious value. Although Brazil had ample know-how, practice, and technology to make slick political ads of the sort that have become so common in the United States, the law prohibited such advertising. TV coverage of candidates remained in the dark ages. It was black and white, with nonmoving pictures. Candidates' TV publicity consisted of typewritten lists of family, memberships, and positions—with mug-shot photos staring out from a silent screen. Government-party candidates had to join the Falcão lineup. However, they also had an advantage. Whenever the president or a minister made an official visit someplace, the welcome by incumbent local officials, who were often government-party candidates, was televised.

In 1984, as the end of military rule approached, Brazil prepared for its first presidential election in two decades. The government wanted an indirect election, through an electoral college, but the people wanted to vote directly. The campaign for direct election produced, in backlash, a halt in the process of "opening," as censorship temporarily increased. The Globo organization, in its most daring political act ever, supported direct election and the presidential candidacy of Brazil's vice-president, a popular maverick. Rallies for direct election were broadcast first by Manchête, then by Globo, in its first coverage of antigovernment protests. After TV gave prominent coverage to plans for rallies, and broadcast actual rallies, the government cracked down. It censored all live broadcasts from Brasília as Congress was voting on (and rejecting) the amendment permitting direct elections.

After Congress mandated indirect election, Tancredo Nêves, a venerable member of the opposition (and the eventual winner, who died soon after taking office), became the overwhelming popular favorite. His election was assured when some government-party members, including the vice-president, formed the Liberal Front and backed Nêves. These votes would guarantee his electoral college victory. The main question now became who would win the government-party nomination, a process involving candidates' personal cultivation of old-boy networks, rather than primaries and the media.

By August 1984, when the government-party held its nominating convention, some Brazilians had been following the concurrent presidential campaign in the United States. An article in *O Jornal do Brasil* reported that Brazilians did not understand the American process of electing a president. Furthermore, after a quarter century of exclusion from presidential voting, they barely understood their own system. Nor did the media offer much help. So deficient was Brazilian television in explaining the electoral process that my best informant in Arembepe didn't realize that he wouldn't be voting for president. He had no idea that the electoral college was scheduled to make the decision, on January 15, 1985. Moreover, the low level of interest revealed by a Gallup poll as the government-party nomination approached was surprising. After all, this was to be the first time since 1960 that the Brazilian president would be chosen without military intervention.

At the same time in the United States, it was clear from media accounts that Walter Mondale needed 1917 delegate votes for the Democratic nomination. When he got them, he would run against President Reagan. The American media kept an accurate delegate count through the Democratic convention. On the other hand, if anyone in Brazil other than candidates and their advisors were keeping tabs on delegates, the media didn't report it. The process remained a mystery. The media kept on speculating, and the candidates continued making counterclaims about the outcome, until the day of the convention.

Nor did television seem to care much who got the nomination. Globo offered only spotty coverage of the vote count, which took place on a Saturday afternoon. In the United States, this would have been one of the biggest political stories of the year, but Globo saw fit to broadcast it in occasional flashes during a Jerry Lewis movie and continuing into Chacrinha—a variety show aimed at maids.

CHAPTER FOUR

❧ *Telenovelas,* Mass Culture, and National Identity

Literature would rehearse the masses in the habits of pluralistic thought and feeling, persuading them to acknowledge that more than one viewpoint than theirs existed—namely that of their masters. It would communicate to them moral riches of bourgeois civilization, impress upon them a reverence for middle-class achievements, and, since reading is an essentially solitary, contemplative activity, curb in them any disruptive tendency to collective political action. It would give them a pride in their national language and literature; if scanty education and extensive hours of labour prevented them personally from producing a literary masterpiece, they could take pleasure in the thought that others of their kind—English people—had done so. [Eagleton's conclusions about the role of *literature in late 19th century England*]. (Eagleton 1983:25, footnote 10)

Network television news shows give the overriding impression that the most important events and activities occur at the national rather than local level, involve the federal rather than local government or private corporations, and arise in major population centers. . . . Local TV news programs . . . contribute further to this impression. . . . Most of the time accorded to "local news" by television stations consists of reports on national sports results . . . and the weather throughout the region. . . . People are implicitly told [that what] is important [is] the nation. [Hirsch's conclusions about the role of *television in late 20th century America*]. (Hirsch 1979:253–254)

TELEVISION AND NATIONAL IDENTIFICATION IN BRAZIL

Working hand in hand with the federal government, Brazilian television has helped spread a changing image of the nation—*from rural-regional to urban-national*. This parallels what literature did in Victorian England and what television has done in the United States. Public service announcements have invoked the image of "government and TV creating a single Brazil—forging *national unity through communication"* (Távola 1983d:26). Concerning television's role in unifying Brazil, Artur da Távola points out that two decades of military rule deprived Brazilians of opportunities to unite through politics or voting. The *telenovela,* soccer, and Carnival became Brazil's most reliable cultural unifiers.

Temporary national mobilization by television has been obvious on certain special occasions. One such event was Pope John Paul II's visit to the world's largest Roman Catholic nation. Brazilians have also tuned in en masse to relief telethons occasioned by such perceived national emergencies as severe flooding in southern Brazil or drought and hunger in the northeast. (These special events are comparable to the American bicentennial celebration or Neil Armstrong's moon walk.)

Globo's image of Brazil has been that of a populace moving together toward modernity, glamour, and a comfortable, materially enriched, upwardly mobile life-style. Globo's preoccupation with creating a national (consuming) culture accompanied the rise of the Western Hemisphere's second largest middle class. This commercially inspired vision challenged previous filmed images of Brazilian backwardness and misery. Globo's "pattern of quality" (explained below) solidified with the arrival of color television around 1973. Its visual opulence was "incompatible with the aesthetics of underdevelopment created by [some of Brazil's best-known] leftist producers" (Kehl 1981b:12).

The theme of national integration was a central point of agreement between military government policies and Globo's objectives of undermining regional traditions and stimulating national mass consumption (Kehl 1981b:24). A priority of the government's 1977 National Cultural Plan was the identification of a Brazilian style of life. Globo simultaneously touted a "global universe" to replace regional programming.

In the late 1970s television helped inform the nation about the emerging political "opening" (*abertura*—the Brazilian equivalent of the more recent Russian *glasnost*). Globo fostered an interest in the rediscovery of Brazil as censorship softened. The network hawked optimism and the idea of a large, solidly unified Brazil. The country could escape underdevelopment. Brazil was "rising in life" just like the central characters in Globo's *telenovelas*—as we shall see. Globo owner Roberto Marinho endowed and gave his name to a foundation supporting preservation of national memory. Television promoted the restoration of historic cities, helping build an image of a national past. Globo urged parents to involve their children in healthful activities, such as gymnastics. During the International Year of the Child, it encouraged joint recreation by parents and children. The network launched national campaigns (such as "Drive Without Hate" and "Get Off Your Duff") that dovetailed with those the federal government was promoting (Kehl 1981b:16).

Globo continues to cultivate a national image, popularizing such expressions as "Move Forward, Brazil" and promoting the idea of nation in various ways. For example, its *Jornal Nacional (National News),* as Joseph

Straubhaar (1982) has observed, avoids city-specific features in favor of national themes. Globo downplays the fact that it is consistently a bit more popular in Rio, where it makes most of its programs, than in São Paulo. When polls show a marked disparity between *carioca* and *paulista* audience shares, Globo hires actors with noticeable *paulista* accents or increases São Paulo-based reports in the national news. Another option is to commission its own poll to show something different.

The urban part of the "global image" of a new Brazil reflected a real demographic shift. In 1950 only 40 percent of Brazilians lived in cities of 50,000 or more. By 1977 the figure had risen to 65 percent. By 1975 Globo reached 96 percent of Brazilian municipalities with more than 50,000 people. Today, television transmits national events and urban life down to the village level. No longer do provincials have to visit Rio or São Paulo to experience what goes on there. Television propagates urban consumers' models of behavior throughout Brazil. Globo helped convert "the national" into a commodity, for internal consumption and export. Touting its own national programming, Globo made savvy commercial use of the epithet "cultural imperialism." It wasn't patriotic to watch imported programs on other channels. National pride dictated that sets be tuned to Globo.

In 1963, after years of studying and living in Brazil, the American anthropologist Charles Wagley, in an essay entitled "If I Were a Brazilian," emphasized that Brazilians had long suffered from a national inferiority complex (1963:278). Through the 1930s Brazil's cultural leaders had depended almost entirely on foreign themes and ideas. However, the nationalistic Getúlio Vargas dictatorship (1930–45) strengthened the federal government. It weakened regional political machines and interests. These political changes promoted a new nationalism, which grew with the return of democracy—free elections in 1950. During the 1950s "Made in Brazil" became a slogan encouraging consumption of national products. Brazilians throughout the country tuned in to Radio Nacional, where they heard their first *novelas*. Soccer became a focus and symbol of the nation and its unity.

According to Wagley, Brazilians retain their national inferiority complex. It is the reason they (still) feel an "overdeveloped" pride when any Brazilian does well outside the country, such as winning the World (Soccer) Cup or a film prize at Cannes (Wagley 1963:283). This pride extends to an area in which Brazil now does especially well both nationally and internationally: television production.

THE *TELENOVELA*

We have seen that Brazil's favorite programs are native productions, rather than imports. Most popular are the Globo network's national news and its soaps or *telenovelas*. Known as the *novelas* of·6, 7, and 8, they actually air at 6:10, 6:55, and 8:25. The 7 and 8 o'clock *novelas*, separated by local and national news, get the largest audiences. Globo's national news is broadcast between 7:55 and 8:25 P.M. six nights a week.

Unlike American soaps, Brazilian *telenovelas* appear six (rather than five) times per week and at night. Perhaps the most important difference is that *telenovelas* end, whereas American soap operas continue for years. The typical Globo *novela* has 150 to 180 chapters and lasts six or seven months. *Telenovelas* are similar to the novels of Charles Dickens, most of which were written in monthly installments and originally published as pamphlets to fit a set length.[1] Also like Dickens' works, *telenovelas* use the serial *(folhetim)* form to treat a series of characteristic conflicts and problems, most often about status reversals—especially upward mobility—and usually with urban settings.

Telenovelas have a readily apparent structure. Each *telenovela* chapter begins with a replay of the previous night's last scene. Next comes an invariant for that *novela*: its recorded opening sequence. This is an attractively filmed introduction, with an upbeat or romantic theme song especially recorded by a Brazilian pop artist, serving as background music for detailed cast credits. One sign of an actor's popularity is the placement of his or her name in these credits. The stars' names can appear first, or they can come at the end of the introduction, as "invited actor" or "special appearance by."

The final chapter of a *telenovela* is broadcast Friday night and rebroadcast Saturday night, with a new serial moving into its slot the following Monday. Globo staggers *telenovela* debuts throughout the year, with a new one starting every two months or so in one of the time slots. It takes a few weeks for viewers to become accustomed to new settings and characters and to get interested in the story line. But Globo manages to retain its audience because they are already hooked on *novelas* that have progressed further in other time slots. As a result, *seasonality* is less marked than on American TV. Brazilian television features no spate of reruns or massive prime-time programming changes during the summer.

During my 13 months in Brazil in 1983–84, I followed six to eight *novelas. Louco Amor (Crazy Love),* a reasonably popular serial in the coveted 8 o'clock time slot, had begun a few months before my August 1983 arrival. I started watching too late in its plot development, with too little knowledge of Brazilian programming conventions, to get very interested in that *novela.* The one that replaced it, *Champagne,* also left me cold, and many Brazilians shared my opinion. As *Champagne* drew to a close, when the audience usually mounts, its share, between 50 and 65 percent (a spectacular rating in the United States), remained well below average for this time slot. Aiming for an average nightly share of 60 percent, Globo considered *Champagne* a ratings failure. A third *novela* had moved into the 8 P.M. time slot by the time I left Brazil, but achieved no special popularity.

In contrast, all the serials that occupied the 7 o'clock slot during my stay (*Guerra dos Sexos—The War between the Sexes, Transas e Caretas— Hipsters and Squares*, and *Vereda Tropical—Tropical Path*) attracted large audiences. They were both ratings and critical successes. They illustrated the formula for the 7 P.M. slot, mixing light comedy, romance, and glamour. The all-star cast of *The War Between the Sexes* included some of Brazil's most respected stage and film actors. Its writer and directors had modeled this serial on classic American romantic film comedies, particularly the light, slightly sophisticated Doris Day movies of the 1950s. Commentators considered *Guerra dos Sexos* a particularly innovative *novela* because its characters included several female executives and other working women. It had more of a workplace setting than the average serial, in which domestic scenes predominate.

Each time slot attracts a particular audience, and Globo targets that audience with a particular *novela*. Six o'clock is the hour of adolescents, maids, housewives, small-town and rural folk. Such people often watch television and eat dinner when urban Brazilians are still at work or caught in a traffic jam. Given this audience, 6 o'clock *novelas* usually take place in county seats in the interior. Among *telenovela* settings, these are most similar to our field sites. The characters of the 6 o'clock *novela* sample the reality of small-town and rural life. They include landowners, ranchers, farmers, mayors, priests, physicians, local businesspeople, and at least one romantic teenaged couple.

Occasionally the 6 o'clock *novela* is a Brazilianized adaptation of a classical work, such as Molière's *L'Avar*. Globo chooses literary classics because they have (or are easily transferable to) such rural, small-town settings. Globo assumes that 6 o'clock viewers are younger, less sophisticated, and include more women and children than later audiences. The network aims the *novelas* of 7 and 8 more at urbanites, but these serials are also popular in rural areas.

The 7 o'clock *novela* occupies a transitional and general hour, and its situations and characters recall the sitcoms that dominate American television between 8 and 9. Many urban Brazilian men get home from work between 7 and 8, in time to catch a glimpse of the 7 o'clock *novela* and to watch the national news at 8, often while dining.

Brazilians writing about their contemporary mass culture state that its three defining elements are *soccer, Carnival, and the 8 o'clock novela*. Globo aims the 8 o'clock *novela* at a more mature audience than its earlier programs. The serial in this time slot is a mystery, usually with a few murders. Several times during the past decade, the entire nation has watched as a murderer is revealed in the last chapter.

An anecdote about the arrival of American Secretary of State Henry Kissinger at the Brasília airport illustrates the intensity of Brazilian devotion to the 8 o'clock *novela*. Kissinger's plane arrived early. Finding no welcomers, the secretary and his entourage walked into the terminal and discovered their greeting party watching the final chapter of an especially popular *novela*. The murderer, whose identity people all over the nation had been speculating about for weeks, was about to be revealed.

Brazilian polling organizations agree that on a few occasions like this, Globo's audience share has approached 100 percent. No program in the United States achieves such a share—not *The Cosby Show*, the Super Bowl, a presidential debate, a World Series game, *Roots, The Day After*, or the last episode of *M*A*S*H*.

Most *novelas* focus on aspects of the *urbanization and modernization of Brazil* (Kehl 1981a:56). Each new one attempts to comment on a current issue, trend, or fad. Each must contain illustrations of *climbing between socioeconomic levels, usually with the central character as the ascendant figure*. Each should have several romances and should end with a series of weddings. Because of censorship, breaches of marital fidelity are rare (although failed marriages are common—see Chapter 5). Purely sexual attractions are only occasionally depicted. In contrast, on American day-time soaps, sexual encounters are often between people who are not married to each other (Goodman 1986).

Romance, however, is the rule on Brazilian television. *Telenovelas* often feature cases of wild, crazy love. A loved one is like a sickness. Many *novelas* portray unrequited love, usually a woman's hopeless devotion to a man destined to end up with someone else. Intergenerational and in-terracial romances occur, but rarely between central characters.

Crazy Love, a 1983 8 o'clock *novela* typifies relationships, issues, set-tings, situations, and characters in that time slot. That serial offered con-fused parentage (from a switch of babies), a sixtyish rich man's marriage to a fortyish lower-middle-class woman, and a late fiftyish woman's marriage to a late-thirtyish man. Also included were an interracial marriage (of a woman and her chauffeur), interracial adoption, two murders, and a detective. Add to all that the magazine industry, working women, a philandering husband, an alcoholic artist, several characters relentlessly pursuing money, and a status hungry mother.

More "adult" (that is, violent) *novelas* and Brazilian miniseries (of one to several weeks' duration) are sometimes shown at 10 P.M. (In times of economic crisis, when Globo must cut production costs, imported series fill this slot instead.) The American program *Roots* probably inspired the Brazilian miniseries, born in 1979 as Globo responded to the new politics of national opening. The network produced several series that together offered a panorama of modern Brazil.

One such series was *Malu Mulher (Maria Luisa, the Woman)*, set in São Paulo. Its protagonist was a divorced woman (living with her mother and daughter) with a degree in sociology but no steady job. In the political climate of opening, *Malu Mulher* could deal with such hitherto avoided issues as marital separation, single motherhood, machismo, and even female orgasm.

Another series *Plantão de Policia,* set in Rio, offered a journalist as protagonist. Unlike American programs with comparable content (for example, *Hill Street Blues, Cagney & Lacey*), this show did not offer a detective or police officer as hero, because law enforcement is not a respected profession in Brazil. Still another series, *Carga Pesada (Heavy Load)*, reminiscent of the old American series *Route 66*, followed two truck drivers around the country.

Finally, *O Bem Amado (The Well-Loved)*, written by Dias Gomes, well-known playwright and TV writer, originated as a *novela* in 1973 and eventually returned as a weekly series. Many Brazilians consider this program the best series ever made in their country. It took place in Sucupira, which served as a microcosm of one common Brazilian locale: the interior town. *O Bem Amado* focused on the effects of the state, the media, international culture, and other external forces on local life. It did so through comedy–melodrama about politics, land title disputes, the arrival of an income tax official—even visits by Frank Sinatra and UFOs.

Ten o'clock has always been more restricted, experimental, elite, and intellectual, attracting people who don't have to get up the next day at 5 or 6 A.M. The most controversial programs, including an unsuccessful 1979 *novela* about pollution and working-class problems, are always shown at 10. Another *novela*, which offered three endings for the public to choose among, plus a final scene in which all the characters, alive and dead, reassembled, was a ratings failure. Critics said it experimented too much.

THE PATTERN OF QUALITY AND MASS PARTICIPATION

Having examined the politico-economic context of Globo's rise, we may now consider Globo programming as a *cultural* product. Globo's success in Brazil is unique, and an important component of the explanation for this achievement is cultural appropriateness. Other networks, after all, also cooperated with the forces of oppression, but didn't succeed as Globo did. Rede Globo is Brazil's most watched network because it has true mass appeal. Its *telenovelas* draw their audiences from all social classes, regions, and types of community.

Globo is fully comparable to the greatest successes of contemporary American popular culture, such as the ubiquitous McDonald's fast-food chain. Globo and McDonald's are commercial organizations that have succeeded in their home cultures by skillfully establishing a nationwide pattern of familiar, culturally appropriate reliability and consistency— rather than excellence—in their products. Just as McDonald's is familiar to virtually every American, Globo is familiar to almost all Brazilians. Americans routinely submerge their individual tastes, thoughts, and feelings in a social collectivity when they consume McDonald's products (Kottak 1978). Brazilians do the same thing when they ingest shared information, a daily dose of national mass culture, by watching the same Globo programs (in audience shares only dreamed of by American network executives). Television's influence, however, is more powerful than fast food's. People must go out to fast-food restaurants, but *TV invades the home*. People are constantly and intimately exposed to its themes and products.

To understand Globo's cultural significance we must answer a larger question: *What constitutes mass culture?* Common to all mass culture successes, no matter what the country, the first requirement is that they fit the existing culture. They must be *preadapted* to their culture by virtue of **cultural appropriateness.** If a product is to be a mass culture success, it must be immediately acceptable, understandable, familiar, and conducive to mass participation.

Participation in an intensely experienced pop-culture event—such as a *telenovela*'s conclusion, a rock concert, a Carnival parade, or a traditional team rivalry—can be a powerful molder of social solidarity. Such participation is comparable to a religious ritual, as people (temporarily) submerge their individuality in a single, attentive, emotionally involved community.[2] Anthropologist Roberto DaMatta recalls occasions on which "all Brazil has cried as one" when a *telenovela* mother and son are reconciled (personal communication). Certain emotion-laden images, dramatic formulas, and stylistic tricks enable *novelas* to penetrate on the national level (Kehl 1981b:7). Recalling the example of *The Brady Bunch* discussed in Chapter 1, a television program—and in Brazil a network—can have a special place in the affective life of millions of people.

However, mass culture has cognitive as well as emotional components. One reason for *soccer's* huge success in Brazil is that its rules and internal (technical) characteristics are known by all who play or watch. Such **mass knowledge** contrasts with the privileged expertise and resultant prestige of professionals such as lawyers and economists. An activity's clarity democratizes it. Soccer, television, and Carnival are alike in that each creates a democracy missing in most areas of Brazilian life (DaMatta 1983).

Lack of understanding is detrimental both to mass culture and to democracy. Common knowledge enhances participation—whether recreational, political, or economic. As Távola has emphasized, in *telenovelas* as in soccer the codes that regulate conduct and conflict are well within spectators' intellectual, verbal, and psychological repertoires (Távola 1983d). The ideas that the audience uses to discuss *novela* subject matter and to identify with particular characters come from everyday life.

If a product is to be a mass culture success, it helps if when natives first encounter it they feel (not necessarily think, realize, or be fully aware) that they have already experienced it, or something similar. The popularity of a new song or movie, for example, can be enhanced if it reminds us of many old ones. The most successful mass culture phenomena blend old and new. They draw on familiar themes, *which they arrange in novel ways*, thus winning a place in the imaginations of whatever culture creates or accepts them.

For decades the serial form has been popular in Brazil. The *telenovela* resembles earlier expressions of Brazilian popular culture. These include radio *novelas*, printed pamphlet serials, and folk sagas (*literatura de cordel*) that are read and told in the interior, particularly the northeast.

The cultural reason that Globo is such a powerful force in contemporary Brazil is its appeal across regions, classes and other social boundaries. The self-proclaimed and endlessly repeated "Globo pattern of quality" has characterized its productions since the mid-1970s. Because Globo offers quality programming, its appeal even extends to upper-income people. Like soccer and Carnival, Globo furnishes a common idiom that crosscuts regions and classes in a continental nation and a hierarchical society. Globo exemplifies the generalization that for a product to be a mass culture success it must be immediately acceptable, understandable, and familiar. It must produce mass participation.

The Pattern of Quality

The three major American networks rely on independent production companies for most of their programming. Globo, in contrast, makes much of what it shows, including virtually everything in prime time. Globo can therefore control the content of its shows much more than NBC, CBS, and ABC do. Globo bases its pattern of quality not on an appeal to a high-brow target market. The pattern did not develop out of the elite-oriented productions (theater, classical music, fine arts, educational, and documentary programs) that characterized Brazilian television during the 1950s. At that time only wealthy people, who regarded television as a means of bringing national and international high culture into their homes, could afford sets.

In Globo's strategy, as in McDonald's, *quality* means something else. It refers to a *consistent, reliable, tolerable, culturally appropriate product, rather than an exceptional one.* In producing its shows, Globo's aims have been to capture and hold the mass audience by offering certain constants that Brazilians appreciate and now expect to see on TV. Globo productions, particularly *telenovelas*, offer culturally familiar and appropriate settings, plots, themes, relationships, behavior, and emotions. Globo introduces new ideas clearly, simply, and sparingly. It aims at a certain basic technical and aesthetic quality, while ensuring that its programs do not threaten public standards and beliefs. The network presents material compatible with preferences and aspirations of Brazilian consumers. In Brazil, only Globo has been successful in achieving

> a pattern of its own, which is responsible for a constant and intense relationship between television and the public. The televiewer already knows the type of service he'll receive. He can disagree here and there, like or not like particular programs. He knows, however, what the network will be offering him in terms of certain predictable types of

content. The Globo pattern accustoms the viewer to a predictable and desirable daily dose of emotion, information, pleasure, entertainment, and general services. (Távola 1983a:28)

Compare these statements about the reasons for Globo's enduring success to observations I have made about the cultural significance of the McDonald's chain in contemporary American culture:

Natives, programmed by years of prior experience, feel completely at home. . . . [Their] devotion to McDonald's rests in part on uniformities associated with almost all its outlets . . . food, setting, architecture, ambience, acts, and utterances. For example, the McDonald's symbol, its golden arches, is an almost universal landmark. . . . The surroundings tell us that we are somehow apart from the variability of the world outside. We know what we are going to see, what we are going to say, and what will be said to us. We know what we will eat, how it will taste, and how much it will cost. . . . Throughout the United States, with only minor variation, the menu is located in the same place, contains the same items, and has the same prices. The food, again with only minor regional variation, will also be prepared according to plan, and will vary little in taste. (Kottak 1978:75–77)

According to Távola, Globo's dogged pursuit of its pattern of quality boosted that network (Távola 1983b:30). The other networks were less consistent and reliable. Some maintained a low everyday standard, occasionally elevated by an outstanding program. Globo, however, fulfilled its audience's expectations with virtually everything it produced. Having reached this level, the network could also make higher-quality (that is, elite-targeted) programs, which it has done.

Globo's coupling of technical know-how with product uniformity is the primary reason the network has been so successful nationally. The quality pattern has also enabled Globo to export its programs, particularly *telenovelas*, to more than a hundred foreign countries. The network has received international prizes. The quality pattern is a primary reason that Globo has nightly audience shares rarely obtained in the United States. To summarize, Globo's pattern of quality is a pattern of *acceptable consistency,* rather than excellence. That is why Globo's strategy for mass culture success is comparable to McDonald's.

CONSTANCY

To maintain the consistency essential to its pattern of quality, Globo must overcome the fact that *telenovelas* end. One way is by employing a stable of popular, reliable, and familiar writers, directors, and actors. Globo thus uses something like the studio system that once prevailed in Hollywood. Actors receive salaries even when not working in a *novela*. In the language of the trade, Globo can buy or sell them, just as a Brazilian soccer player can be sold to Italy. Actors, writers, and directors maintain constancy by carrying their distinctive marks and styles with them between *novelas*.

The Role of the Writer

Traditionally, a single writer penned a Brazilian *telenovela*. Janete Clair wrote dozens of successful serials. She gained a national fame unparalleled among American TV writers, who are virtually anonymous to the people who watch their creations. Few Americans know who writes *The Cosby Show*, but Brazilians know the names, styles, formulas, and plans of their regular telenovelists.

It would be difficult for an American prime-time TV writer to match the heroic schedule of the traditional Brazilian telenovelist. The serial writer must churn out 160 chapters, at a rate of almost one a day, in six months. The burden takes its toll. In 1983–84 Globo was threatened with desertion by some of its writers, who preferred the easier schedules of plays and movies. In response, the network allowed two writers to collaborate on the 8 o'clock *novela* that started in mid-1984. One writer created two chapters, then the other writer wrote two, and so forth. For the 7 P.M. *novela* that began in August 1984, something similar was done. A senior author developed the main idea and plot line, while a junior colleague did the actual scripting. This system is common now.

Successful writers customarily sit out one or two *novelas*, then return— usually to their preferred time slot. Until Clair's death in late 1983, she and Lauro Cesar Muniz alternated regularly at 8 o'clock. As Brazil's most productive and popular telenovelist, Clair was a dominant figure in the creation of national mass culture. Millions of Brazilians felt a sense of profound loss when she died of cancer in 1983, just as many Americans did when Walt Disney, one of our preeminent popular culture creators, died in 1966. Born in the Brazilian interior, the daughter of a Lebanese street trader, Clair grew up in a small town in the state of São Paulo. She began as a radio writer, with a 20-chapter adaptation of Tolstoy's *Anna Karenina*. Clair's first *telenovela*, for the (now defunct) Tupi television network, debuted in 1967.

Clair's own life provided inspiration for the characters she helped make modal in Brazilian popular culture. The telenovelist herself rose in life from a humble origin in the interior to national fame and the good life in Rio. Inevitably, Clair's life history influenced her work and, more generally, the form and themes of the Brazilian *telenovela*. Her creations won easy acceptance. She became an "audience champion" (a term used by Globo to herald its programming). She helped develop the Globo pattern of quality by churning out chapter after chapter, serial after serial. She provided reliable, culturally appropriate entertainment for the Brazilian masses.

Fellow telenovelist and disciple Gilberto Braga has attributed Clair's success in South America, Portugal, and Italy to her intuitive knowledge of the "Latin soul." Clair conceived her public not as intellectual, logical, or rational, but as ordinary people who enjoyed immersing themselves in fiction. She dealt with problems of common people. She didn't mind being mushy and drawing on formulas and cliches, because her use of the simple and the maudlin were popular. On her death commentaries about Clair's work agreed that emotion and intuition were key elements in her success.

Her *telenovelas* blended Brazilian reality (urban family settings, problems, and relationships) with Brazilian escapism (rising in life), as viewers "lived" problems other than their own each evening. The saga of middle-class families who achieve riches was a constant. Most of Clair's works also featured a great victim—someone who, through injustice, had fallen into marginality. In the end the victim always found redemption and rose in life.

For Janete Clair, the basic unit of creation was the chapter. "Our audience is the most faithful of all, and in compensation, the most demanding. They want a show each chapter" (Távola 1983c). Her longest *telenovela* had 328 chapters. Her last and shortest (unfinished by her) had 103. Clair's serials hooked many intellectuals as well as the middle-class target audience. By the early 1970s, in large part because of Clair, the Brazilian *telenovela* had become respectable. It was a diversion that "cultured" people could watch without being embarrassed (Kehl 1981a:50). In urban circles, the expression "my marijuana hour" became synonymous with "my nightly *novela*."

Constancy Through the Actor

Like writers, actors return in new *novelas*—as new characters, but often *in similar relationships*. A common pattern is to reconstitute a love triangle, often with a different outcome. For example, one of Clair's major successes, *Selva de Pedra* (1972–73, remade in 1986), featured a love triangle involving actors Francisco Cuoco, Regina Duarte, and Dina Sfat. The climax came when the Cuoco character, thinking his wife (Duarte) was dead, set a marriage date with Sfat. However, government censors proclaimed the plot adulterous and forced Cuoco to abandon Sfat at the altar. In a later Clair *telenovela*, actress Sfat "got her revenge against Cuoco" (as the press phrased it), by leaving *him* waiting at the altar.

When discussing plot developments, Brazilian fan magazines customarily use the actor's own name instead of the character's. This helps the public identify with actors—constants moving among different *novelas*—rather than with characters, who are transitory. Thus, in December 1983, an *Amiga* (fan magazine) cover proclaimed that "Mario Gomes and Maitê Proença [the actors' names, not their characters'] were going to get married." Another issue carried the statement that Irene Ravache (the actress rather than her character—a thief) wants to rob her partner. Actors working in a *telenovela* "live," rather than merely play, their parts. This idiom is consistent with the focus on the actor as a constant presence, despite the variability of the roles he or she plays.

The prestige of acting and actors has risen in Brazil as a result of Globo's *telenovelas*. Clair's talent and renown in particular helped *telenovelas* become the favored workplace for Brazilian actors. *Novelas* were a boon to professionals otherwise dependent on sporadic theatrical successes and a tentative, commercially unsuccessful, national cinema (Kehl 1981a:50). Synergetically, television has stimulated interest in the national theater and films, because actors, directors, and writers constantly move from medium to medium. Brazil makes little distinction among theater, TV, and film actors. Work in television is taken as seriously as in the theater. For instance, most of the actors who won Molière prizes for theater in 1983 were working concurrently in television.

Other Constants

Other constants are apparent in production—resulting in an unmistakable Globo look. Camera crews cart actors all around Rio, shooting scenes outside. They use the natural beauty and manufactured glamour of "the marvelous city" as backdrop to melodrama. Globo's set decoration is fashionable, from careful flower arrangements and elegant furniture to smartly starched uniforms worn by maids and chauffeurs. The network has helped create certain typical Brazilian roles and characters and a Brazilian style of acting.

Brazilian culture and the Globo style are also apparent in certain characteristic ways of framing TV content. When interacting with other people, even strangers, Brazilians maintain less personal distance than do Americans. Brazilians stand closer together, and this affects television images. Because camera people get closer to their subjects, they can't fit as many in. Commenting about what he saw as a universal limitation of television, which is actually a cultural difference, Artur da Távola told me that the TV screen was unsuited to show more than three people simultaneously. He seemed unaware that American cameras routinely englobe many more—shot from farther back. Globo's camera moves right up to the actor. *Telenovelas* are full of extreme close-ups of mouths, noses, and foreheads. The camera doesn't hesitate to explore pores, crevices, and blemishes on actors' faces.

Another constant is music. Each *novela* has its national and international scores, pop songs that serve as background music. These are eventually assembled on two LP albums, the sales of which increase as the public gets hooked on the serial. Recordings of international singers are used astutely, with some attempt to match foreign lyrics with situations being portrayed. Globo has used songs by Peter Gabriel, Miami Sound

Machine, Rod Stewart, Paul Anka, Spandau Ballet, Julio Iglésias, Michael Jackson, and many other foreign entertainers.

There is also a Globo *novela* conversational style. Eight o'clock serials in particular characteristically fill gaps between significant plot developments with sprinklings of the latest slang. This is often enunciated with a Rio-sophisticate accent. There are numerous trivial conversations and pseudointellectual allusions, such as (mis)quotes of Marx or Sartre. Although religious subjects and characters are rare except in the rural-oriented 6 P.M. *novela*, Globo's serials are chock-full of references to God. Characteristic exclamations include "For the love of God," "God willing," "My God in Heaven," and "Our Lady." The stock expression "I want to have a serious talk with you" brings the prattle, blather, and triviality to an end. It focuses the audience's attention on something important about to happen.

THEMES, SETTINGS, AND CHARACTERS

Common *novela* locales and social settings include fashionable villas, apartments, beaches, and mountains of Rio, and Rio's suburbs (home of lower-middle- and working-class characters). We also see mansions of the (decadent) *paulista* aristocracy, and ranches, churches, and central squares of interior towns. Urban problems are much more common than rural ones.

Some typical issues and themes are conflicts between archaic and contemporary Brazil, rural and urban life, tradition and progress, old and young, agrarian aristocracy and ascendant bourgeoisie. One of the most significant *novelas* in terms of portraying clashes between archaic and modern Brazil was 1973's *O Bem Amado*. It examined the transition between an agrarian and an urbanized way of life, as did Lauro Cesar Muniz's saga, *A Casarão*. The latter serial began in 1900 and followed a traditional family's move from large rural properties to the city of Rio de Janeiro (a move that many families have made).

In stark contrast to the world of the Brazilian *telenovela*, there is not much fluidity in the real Brazilian class structure. Although rural people do move to cities, few Brazilians rise much in life. Nevertheless, as in Charles Dickens' novels about 19th century English society, *status reversals—particularly upward mobility*—are common themes. The predominant theme—*subir na vida*, "to rise in life," escaping from inferior socioeconomic status, obtaining money and prestige—is pervasive. This constant theme is powerfully symbolic of Brazilians' wish to raise their nation's status in the world, to ascend from archaic underdevelopment to progressive modernity.

To their Brazilian viewers, *novelas* offer images of escape and dramatize culturally appropriate fantasies. They suggest several (unlikely) ways to rise in life. Boy from interior moves to city and gets rich. A character rediscovers a lost (wealthy) parent or receives an enormous inheritance. Poor girl marries rich boy. Brazilian TV reversals draw on Pygmalion, *Great Expectations*, and switched-baby themes, but the Cinderella theme is by far the favorite. Interclass romances ("love has no money") are central to most *telenovelas*.

The status reversals addressed by *telenovelas* also include falls. Sudden drops in financial fortune have not been uncommon in Brazil's uncertain economy. *Novela* characters representing all class backgrounds routinely discuss their monetary woes. A common (fallen gentry) character is a woman, usually a widow, from a traditional family who can no longer afford to maintain the life-style that she considers her due. Often she pities herself because she has to work for a living or is in debt. She worries that people talk about her finances, and she wishes to regain status by arranging a career advance and a strategic marriage for her children, usually her son.

On Brazilian television, personal connections and strategic marriages are better ways to rise in life than is achievement through hard work, which is rarely depicted. Formal education is not valued much either, especially for women. *Novelas* say that *women in particular should aspire to rise in life through marriage, not through education or achievement.* But how do they manage this?

In a society whose class system has a large hereditary component, there is profound suspicion of women who "try to make themselves into something they aren't" in order to marry a rich man. A recurrent (and suspect) character is a lower-status woman who attempts to attract a rich man by educating herself. She tries to learn to be (the assumption is that she merely pretends to be) something more than her humble background. (This is not the Pygmalion theme, because it is her idea, not his.) Sometimes she gets the man; sometimes not—depending on her intrinsic goodness.)

For example, in one 8 o'clock *novela* a beautiful, honest woman was initially ashamed to tell her fiancé, a rich and famous plastic surgeon, the truth about herself. Her awful secret was that she was trying to improve herself by taking private lessons in "culture" from a university professor.

"I don't care if you come from a poor family," he responded when finally informed.

"You can't imagine how poor I was."

"I know that your father was a family chauffeur."

Here the man reacted realistically, saying he didn't expect a woman attracted to him to ignore his social position. "My money is part of my totality."

Illustrating the value of personal connections in status reversals, a young man from a fallen gentry family in the same *novela* was urged by his mother to seek improved status as a plastic surgeon by working for a famous specialist, "not a lesser man." The interfering, status hungry woman also pushed her son (against his inclinations) to marry his boss's daughter. (He was in love with a lower-middle-class girl.)

Not just fallen gentry, but also families with humble origins wish to rise in life on Brazilian TV. However (and in contrast to American television), *intelligence, education, good looks, and job performance are not sufficient.* One needs manners and connections to succeed in polite society. An ambitious young man from a lower-middle-class background must develop social skills.

Brazilian *telenovelas* recall Charles Dickens in some respects (serial form, rural–urban transitions, and status reversals). However, it is *a Dickens whose social conscience and concern for the poor have yielded to a preoccupation with glamour.* Of course, this is only partly the writers' fault. Under military rule, neither economic nor class conflicts could be portrayed in *telenovelas.* Censors cut almost all political discussion. *Novelas* occasionally mention pollution, dehumanization, and difficulties in maintaining life-style and status. These are issues debated mainly by the middle class, while the poor struggle with more basic worries. Such unglamorous national macroproblems as poverty, hunger, illiteracy, homelessness, and public health are never central issues. In reality, many of these problems are as blatantly apparent in downtown Rio or São Paulo as they were in Dickens' London. Here the contrast between prime-time and real society is particularly jarring.

Until recently, when telenovelists wished to examine arbitrary power and totalitarianism, they could only do so through analogies and symbols. The changing fortunes of old and new power groups were touched only metaphorically. Conflicts, including intergenerational ones, which are depicted frequently and discussed intensely, are presented as interpersonal rather than intergroup affairs. One exception is the theme of family responsibility and revenge. *Novela* characters are held responsible for deeds by members of their family. The entire family must unite against a perceived enemy. In Chapter 5, I turn to some of the specific social issues and relationships that dominate the Brazilian *telenovela* and contrast them with prime-time society in the United States.

CHAPTER FIVE

✿ Cultural Contrasts
in Prime-Time Society

$\mathbf{M}$y goal in this chapter, which examines significant cultural contrasts in the content of Brazilian and American TV programs, is to demonstrate three key points:

1. The popularity of television programs reflects their cultural appropriateness.
2. Popular media content illustrates fundamental values and institutions.
3. Contrasts in media content across cultures can be keys to perceiving and understanding fundamental cultural differences.

For several years, Gerbner and his associates have been systematically studying American television's content and effects. They have compared Americans' answers to certain questions with their televiewing habits. In so doing they have found a **cultivation effect:** The more time people spend watching television, the more they perceive the real world as being similar to that of television. I believe that a cultivation effect also operates in Brazil. However, it is not simply television as a medium, but *specific TV content* (different in Brazil and the United States) *that does the cultivating.* I therefore began my research on Brazilian TV by studying the social and cultural phenomena that dominate the content of the most popular programs.

The social worlds encapsulated in television programs are constructed not just artistically and technically but culturally, within the societies in which they are imagined, written, performed, and produced. Brazil's characteristic problems, issues, and social units differ from those of the United States, and this affects TV content.[1] Prominent recurring themes in Brazilian television content suggested many of the questions we eventually asked in rural areas.

For instance, we gathered data on beliefs and behavior concerning such key news issues as politics, economic crises (national debt, inflation, shortages), and crime (see Chapter 7). We paid particular attention to *telenovelas*, in order to compare Brazilian and American prime-time television. We also compared *novelas*, daily programs with a continuous story line, with American day-time soap operas. Many of the questions we eventually asked in our field sites were designed to assess local impact of dominant *telenovela* themes. These included social mobility and specific ways of rising socially that *telenovelas* suggest. *Novela* characters typically rise in life by manipulating personal network ties—strategic kin connections, friendships, romances, or marriages. We also considered the impact of *telenovelas'* frequent dramatization of conflicts between marriage and the parental family.

FAMILY AFFAIRS

One striking contrast between American and Brazilian cultures, reflected in TV content, is in the meaning and the role of the family. North American adults usually define their families as consisting of spouse and children. However, when Brazilian adults speak of their *família*, they normally mean their parents, siblings, aunts, uncles, grandparents, and cousins. Brazilian adults may include their children as *família*, but they often exclude husband or wife, who has his or her own *família*.

The presence or absence of spouse and young child(ren) is very important in defining one's social identity on American TV, less so in Brazil. That country has less geographical mobility than the United States. Relationships between parents and their *adult* children, and among extended family members, are more significant there in real life. Brazilian TV content reflects that social reality.

Because contemporary Americans tend to lack an extended family support system, marriage assumes tremendous importance. Marriage provides theme, context, stability, conflict, and dramatic tension for many American programs. The culture's overwhelming emphasis on marital and parental responsibilities places severe strains on the American marriage. Many social issues addressed on American television reflect this.

Surprisingly, however, marriages are at least as unstable in Brazilian *novelas* as in American prime-time series, even though divorce is much less common in Brazil. This reflects a Brazilian social reality that accords relatively less value to the family of procreation (spouse and children) and more value to the family of orientation (parents and siblings). I reached this conclusion by talking to natives and as I watched *telenovelas* during 13 months in Brazil in 1983–84. It struck me that nuclear families of procreation did not have much luck on Brazilian TV. Unlike the durable Cleavers, Bradys, Keatons, and Huxtables, and dozens of other American TV families, the young families depicted at the beginning of a Brazilian *telenovela* rarely survived its course.

In the 8 o'clock *novela Crazy Love*, for example, a young married couple with a small son eventually separated. The wife, a deceptive schemer, was a social climber obsessed with money. Another couple with an 8- to 10-year old son broke up because the husband mistreated the wife and resented her career. At *novela*'s end, he was revealed to be the murderer. (Each 8 P.M. *telenovela* has a murderer.) The next *novela* in this time slot split up a happy family consisting of father, mother, son, and daughter by again making dad a killer. There were similar developments in the next *telenovela*. Barely a month into the program, one husband had committed murder and cheated his wife, her father, and her aunt out of a business and a fortune. He had also legally maneuvered for (temporary) undeserved custody of their son.

In Brazilian productions, the constancy of marriage yields to the continuing relationship between adult characters and their parents, siblings, and extended kin. Furthermore, certain kinds of nuclear family disasters common on American TV (incest, child abuse, wife beating) are rare in *telenovelas*. When one Globo *telenovela* did depict nuclear family incest, fan reaction was so negative that the production was cut short. (Euthanasia in the same *novela* also drew severe criticism and was another reason for a hasty conclusion.) Incest and intrafamily violence do not attract much media attention in Brazil, where one also almost never hears about wife or child abuse.

Does Brazil actually have less abuse within the family, or simply less reporting of that problem than the United States? I suspect that intrafamily violence and sexual abuse *really are* rarer there. One reason is the pattern of regular contact among relatives who live in different households. Brazilians are far less isolated from their extended kin than are North Americans. This helps ensure both physical protection and psychological support for wives and young children. Furthermore, in Brazil domestic violence is curtailed by lack of privacy. Brazilians would be ashamed to have the neighborhood know about family affairs—particularly such scandalous behavior as wife- or child-beating. Indeed, middle-class Brazilians are reluctant to use corporal punishment, even with unruly children.

In the Brazilian life-style, doors and windows are usually open because of the heat. Maids, cooks, relatives, and assorted trades- and servicepeople constantly drift in and out of homes. Brazilians are accustomed to much less privacy than Americans. Open windows and doors mean that people would have trouble minding their own business even if they considered it culturally necessary. With less domestic privacy, a sustained pattern of secret violence is virtually impossible. When domestic violence occurs in small towns, it immediately becomes community knowledge. Villagers voice disapproval, and culprits encounter social ostracism that forces them to mend their ways.

STRANGERS, FRIENDS, AND WORKMATES

Brazilian television reflects the real-life fact that the contemporary Brazilian's social world is more exclusively familial than is the American's. Here a characteristically American theme—preparing to leave home and live with strangers—should be contrasted with Brazilian themes. Americans live with strangers more and more, even at home. According to U.S. census data, only 73 percent of American households were made up of family members in 1980, compared with 89 percent in 1950.[2] Simultaneously, many of the central themes of contemporary American television, films and literature revolve around problems that arise in dealing with strangers. This is true of all our genres, including adventure, suspense, fantasy, and science fiction. The preoccupation with the stranger is missing and the popular genres are different in Brazil. There, television shows people almost always interacting with their families and friends, and rarely with such aliens as roommates, police officers, lawyers, extraterrestrials, pets, wild animals, or mass murderers.

Intervention in personal and family matters by hospitals, courts, social workers, physicians, and other experts is one of the most prominent features of the contemporary United States. It supplies fodder for countless television programs and films, offering yet another illustration of the overwhelming importance of the stranger in American society. On Brazilian TV in contrast, such experts are conspicuous only by their absence.

America's cultural traditions constantly prepare and goad us to leave home and family for independence—faraway places and life among strangers. Familiar themes in American history—frequently seized by literature and the mass media—are pioneer spirit, expanding frontier, and wide open spaces. Americans need space. We are much more private people than Brazilians—or Samoans, whom Margaret Mead described as living in a "civilization which suspects privacy"(1961). Such cultural preferences are rooted in experience. It is hard to be alone, ever, on a tropical island, or in a torrid and densely packed city where windows and doors are almost always open.

A more subtle contrast in television content is in the frequency of domestic versus public settings. Brazilian *novelas* usually take place at home. Family settings also are popular on American TV (from Cleavers through Bradys to Huxtables). Furthermore, many American programs (for instance, *M*A*S*H, The Mary Tyler Moore Show, Cheers, L.A. Law*) mold their unrelated characters into a quasifamily. However, it is obvious to anyone who has watched TV regularly in both the United States and Brazil that American TV much more often depicts its characters in public and work settings. This reflects, among other things, both the North American work ethic and the larger real percentage of externally employed Americans.

Another reflection of the contrasts involving domestic versus public settings, and family members versus nonrelatives, is the difference between Brazilian and American TV in the representation of the sexes. American programming is more male-biased than Brazilian productions. In 1975, for example, American prime time had three men for every woman. By 1984 the ratio was equalizing (National Commission on Working Women 1984). Of 143 new characters introduced that year 47 percent were female (Gunter 1986: 6–8). *Telenovelas* (in which domestic settings predominate) have always had a more equal sex ratio than American prime-time shows. Brazilian television, usually set at home, is faithful to the fact that in the home there are as many females as males. American sitcoms and soap operas also have more balanced sex ratios than do other program types, particularly the male-dominated action series (Gunter 1986: 6–8).

American television recently has been balancing its sex ratio to mirror a changing reality. As more and more real-life women enter the work force, more and more television characters are female. They increasingly populate the workplace settings that dominate programming. Long ago, *The Mary Tyler Moore Show* helped usher in the era of unmarried workplace women in American televisionland. By 1984 the never-married woman had become the modal American TV female (55 percent). Divorced (10 percent) and widowed (9 percent) women reduced the percentage of married women to 26 percent. Three-fourths of the adult female characters introduced to American television in 1984 had paid employment (National Commission on Working Women 1984).

Brazilian TV characters, especially women, more often raise their status through marriage than education or a career. This illustrates contrasting cultural values about work, individual achievement, and family connections. Brazilian feminists often criticized telenovelist Janete Clair, alleging that her female characters (particularly her long-suffering heroines) were too dominated by their husbands and lovers (Távola 1983c). However, since the mid-1970s, independent women and working women have become somewhat more common on Brazilian television. Despite the machismo of the larger society, *novelas* have as many women as men. Furthermore, *telenovela* men are just as fallible as women. Brazilian TV portrays lower-class men in particular as emotionally or morally weak.

OCCUPATIONS AND SOCIAL STATUS IN TELEVISIONLAND

Despite the increasing presence of *working* women on Brazilian TV (still far fewer than in American programs), certain stereotypes persist. A bias again lower-status occupations and characters is common to Brazilian and American television. In both countries TV characters tend to have higher-status occupations than do people in real life (Glennon and Butsch 1979, 1982; DeFleur 1964). In the real-life work force in the United States in 1984, 51 percent of women held clerical and service jobs. However, 75 percent of the TV women introduced that year were doctors, lawyers, or other professionals (National Commission on Working Women 1984).

Although prestige occupations, which can best support—and exemplify—consumerism, dominate both American and Brazilian television, actual occupations differ. Prestige occupations in the United States are in medicine, law, science, engineering, and the top ranks of business and industry.[3] Brazilians also respect successful businesspeople, engineers, and architects and accord high status to successful actors and entertainers. However, professors and writers have more prestige in Brazil than in North America. They outrank all but the most famous physicians, who themselves become celebrities. Detectives and police officers have much less prestige in Brazil and are much rarer on Brazilian than American TV.

Certain occupations predominate in particular time slots. The 6 o'clock *telenovela* usually has a doctor. County seats, where this program usually is set, include at least one general practitioner, who is a valued community member. However, physicians are much rarer in Globo's other prime-time shows. When they do appear, they are usually plastic surgeons, cardiac surgeons, or psychiatrists—the most valued medical specialists in Brazil. Significantly, primarily wealthy people use their services.

Brazil's celebrity face-lifters, such as world-renowned Ivo Pitanguy, usually donate some of their time to the poor. Their reputations, however, come not from their being Mother Teresas, but from the work they do on the rich and famous. Beauty is an obsession among the elites, because Brazilian culture still views women mainly as sex objects and reproducers rather than producers. Women who can afford to lift sagging faces and bodies do so.

In both countries, television dotes on people who can afford to live, or aspire to live, glamorous lives. *Telenovelas* always include a rich family to illustrate consumerism. One set of characters must be able to afford all the products that sponsor the show. (Characters demonstrate and discuss products as part of the story line—for instance, as women talk in the kitchen.) In the United States, *Dallas*, *Dynasty*, and other night-time soaps confirm that life-styles of the rich fascinate Americans as much as Brazilians. Consumers everywhere like to see evidence of the rewards that come at the pinnacle of whatever path one takes to the top.

However, television productions illustrate that different cultures lay out different paths and have contrasting values about work. Glamorous Brazilian characters often do not work if they are independently wealthy. Indolent playboys are much rarer American TV characters. Despite their inherited wealth, many of the Ewings of *Dallas* and Carringtons of *Dynasty* are workaholics. The office is a common setting on those programs.

Our research in Brazilian communities confirmed the contrast with American cultural values about work for its own sake. When asked if they would continue working if they won the lottery, most Brazilian respondents said no. This contrasted strongly with one of the first programs I watched when I returned to the United States in 1984. This was a *20/20* story about Gordon Getty, America's richest man. The well-paid hosts, Barbara Walters and Hugh Downs, both proclaimed that they'd want to go right on working even if they were as rich as Getty.

SOCIAL   CLASS   AND   WAYS   TO   RISE   IN   LIFE

Many social and cultural differences between the United States and other countries, including Brazil, flow from socioeconomic stratification, the allocation and distribution of wealth, prestige, and power. Although the distribution of income in the United States is not as even as in Japan or the Netherlands, it is much more so than in Brazil. Latin nations with strongly hierarchical systems of vested wealth and power resist competition and change. Those values of more open societies can only oppose entrenched privileges. Brazilian society, for instance, is self-consciously hierarchical. American society is self-consciously democratic. This does not mean that the United States lacks socioeconomic contrasts and social classes. However, Brazilian poverty is more extreme than anything in the United States. The most affluent 20 percent of American households average 12 times the income of the poorest 20 percent. The analogous multiple is 33 in Brazil (*Ann Arbor News* November 4, 1984).

Thus, comparing the distribution of resources, Brazil has a much wider gap between richest and poorest, and Brazilians are much more class conscious than Americans. Most Americans, regardless of income, consider themselves to be middle class, and most are. Americans have a hard time dealing with—even recognizing—class differences. Americans prefer to make social distinctions in terms of region, ethnicity, religion, race, or occupation. We do not like to use such labels as "lower class," "working class," or "upper class." Americans are reluctant to acknowledge class differences because we believe that ours is an open society in which capable people can rise through their own efforts. Self-sufficiency and individual achievement are such powerful American values that we resent, and often deny, that class *does* affect chances for success. As our culture reconstructs its history, we forget that many of our "self-made men" came from wealthy families.

The United States has a pervasive, although idealized, egalitarian ethos that is notably absent in Brazil. Our Constitution tells us that all men (and, by extension, women) are created equal. Although it is well known that in practice American justice is neither blind nor equal, there is supposed to be equality before the law. In Brazil all is hierarchy. The penal code authorizes privileged treatment for certain classes of citizens, for example, those with university degrees. High-status Brazilians do not stand patiently on line as Americans do. Important people expect others to attend to their business immediately. Social inferiors readily yield to elites. Rules do not apply uniformly, but differentially, according to class. The final resort in any conversation is "Do you know who you're talking to?"[4] The American opposite, reflecting our democratic and egalitarian ethos, is "Who do you think you are?"

The contrast is one of *doing* (United States) versus *being* (Brazil).[5] In the United States identity emerges as a result of what one does. In Brazil, one's social identity arises from what one is, a strand in a web of personal connections, originating in the extended family. In such a consciously hierarchical society, status reflects extent and influence of the personal network. Brazilians' social identities originate in class background and family connections, and Brazilians see nothing wrong with using their connections for all they're worth. Parents, in-laws, and extended kin are all tapped for entries to desired positions. As DaMatta (1981) has discussed at length, when Brazilians ask "Do you know who you're talking to?" they are conjuring up all the well-connected people within their personal networks. These include relatives, in-laws, school chums, business associates, and friends.

Most Americans, on the other hand, would say that what a person does (achieves) is more important than family background or connections. American culture sees reason for pride in excellence in any line of work. "I may be just a plumber, but I'm a good plumber" is a much more likely to be an American statement than a Brazilian statement. The work ethic influences television. Unemployed people, rich or poor, are suspect in American culture and are rare among TV heroes. The lazy rich man, who in the United States is a playboy or ne'er-do-well, in Brazil enjoys gracefully what family status or fortune was generous enough to provide.

Americans believe that personal worth and moral value come through work, but Brazilian culture has had a "gentleman complex" for centuries (Wagley 1963). Brazilians who can afford to hire others should not do manual work. Menial jobs should be done by menials, millions of whom are available. The do-it-yourselfer or home handyman valued by North American culture would only take jobs away from millions of lower-class people in Brazil. Because of this, one rarely sees those home tool ads that are common on American television. Why would a self-respecting middle-class Brazilian want a drill set or chainsaw for Christmas? Male Brazilian consumers don't want to spend their weekends fixing things around the house. Their wives should have repairs done by appropriate workers during the week, so that the weekend can be devoted to leisure at the club or beach.

Reflecting their respective societies, then, class contrasts are much more obvious on Brazilian than American television. Brazilian TV characters discuss class identities openly. We have seen that *subir na vida* ("to rise in life") is one of the most common *telenovela* expressions. Most *novelas* are modern-day Cinderella stories. A girl or boy from a lower-status family falls in love with and eventually marries someone from a richer family. The interclass friendships and romances shown on Brazilian television link members of classes A (upper), B (middle), and sometimes C (upper working). Only occasionally is there a romance between a working-class character and someone from the upper or upper-middle class. Even rarer in entertainment programming are class D Brazilians (lower working, unemployed poor) with their impoverished, untelegenic life-styles. Even the fantasy world of the *telenovela* recognizes that such people have virtually no chance to rise in life by marrying someone from the elite group.

Obvious class contrasts are far less developed in American productions. The films *Breaking Away* and *Working Girl* stand out as two of the few popular American movies of recent years to focus on issues of social class. Both recall Brazilian *telenovela* themes. The central romance in *Breaking Away* is between a lower-middle-class boy and a girl from a wealthier family. The boy's father is a used car salesman and retired stone cutter. The girl is a college student. The hero enchants her by pretending to be an Italian exchange student. He and his friends are ridiculed by college students because of their background and their lack of the talents and skills that come from being raised in privileged families. On Brazilian TV, the couple would have married. The socially adept boy would have found a job with his father-in-law. However, true to American ideology, *Breaking Away* ended the romance and sent the boy to college. Eventually his social status would rise through education and his own achievement.

Similarly, in 1988's *Working Girl* the heroine realizes her dream of rising in life. In the end she gets a higher-status man. However, as must be true for appropriate success in the United States in 1990, her ascent rests on her own abilities and achievements rather than on connections through kinship or marriage.

In a culture in which self-reliance is a dominant value, Americans voice disapproval when people use marriage or kin ties to gain money, position, or status (Hsu 1975). Relatives who work in the same firm, like the children of famous people who follow their parents' profession, must prove themselves and make it on their own. This, of course, is in the ideal culture. Relatives often do help each other professionally, though much more covertly in the United States than in Brazil. If young Americans are to succeed in a family business, we expect them to work as hard as they would in any other firm.

The themes of work and achievement always emerge in interviews with people who have followed in a parent's profession. The interviewer invariably asks if famous parentage was a help or a liability. A stock answer is that the relationship helped at first, but was more of a hindrance later, because the child's achievements were constantly compared with those of the successful parent. The newcomer had to work hard to convince others that he or she could make it without parental influence. Success achieved merely through family connections—without hard work—is taboo in American ideology.

In both Brazil and the United States, the proportion of certain occupations and social classes on television contrasts markedly with reality. Not only are physicians, attorneys, and other professionals much more common among American television characters than in real life, TV characters also include a much higher percentage of cops and robbers than there are in the American population.

Again, a prominent cultural difference leads to a contrast between American and Brazilian TV content. Neither in Brazil nor the United States is police work a prestige occupation. However, Brazilians give law enforcement officers less respect, and much less TV coverage, than Americans do. This cultural difference has to do with regard for law, and the derivative prestige that goes to those who uphold and enforce it.

Brazilian anthropologist DaMatta, who has spent several years in the United States, explained to me why Brazilians have so little confidence in the police. Americans perceive police officers as figures who uphold the law. Brazilians, on the other hand, see the police as similar to politicians. They view these figures as having little actual respect for the law, as using government and legally constituted power for their own advantage. "Whenever you do something wrong in your country," DaMatta told me, "the police seem to be there to stop you. But in Brazil the police usually stop you when you're not doing anything wrong" (to try to extract a bribe).

Attorneys and law enforcement officers are also much more common on American than Brazilian television because laws are rules designed to regulate behavior in public. Public scenes, and relationships between nonrelatives, are common on American television, whereas domestic settings and family relationships dominate Brazilian TV. In family disaster dramas, American television even allows legal agents to invade the home, converting domestic disputes into matters of public concern and control.

Social class is another important reason police officers are so rare on Brazilian television. The matter of class also explains why state intrusion on the family is much less characteristic of (middle-class) Brazilian society, televised or real, than of contemporary U.S. society. The social network of virtually every middle-class Brazilian includes lawyers and other protectors of private rights. Brazilian police officers, who usually have no more than lower-middle-class status, are reluctant to interfere in the private affairs of their social betters or even to regulate their public behavior.

DARK-SKINNED ACTORS AND CHARACTERS

Another striking culturally derived contrast between American and Brazilian television is in the representation of *dark-skinned characters.* Although Brazil is sometimes called a racial democracy, blacks, who are just as obvious in the Brazilian as in the American population, are much rarer on Brazilian than American TV. Only recently have dark-skinned Brazilian actors started making concerted demands for more, better, and different kinds of parts (but without much obvious success).

Traditionally, blacks, when present on Brazilian television at all, played the same kinds of menial roles they played in real life. (This was also true of American blacks' movie and television roles through the 1950s.) Dark-skinned Brazilian actors mostly still play cooks, maids, drivers, and thugs. However, the poverty that affects a disproportionate number of dark-skinned Brazilians means that there are relatively fewer trained black actors there than in the United States. Because of this, whites often play maids and cooks on Brazilian TV.

Another reason for the paucity of blacks on Brazilian television is Brazilian racial classification. Brazilian racial categories are much more numerous and fluid than American ones, for example, "white" and "black." The lack of precise boundaries between races impedes the emergence of their social identities and any push for collective betterment of dark-skinned Brazilians.

In American culture, race is determined at birth. "Racially mixed" children belong to "the black race" regardless of appearance. In some states, anyone known to have any "black" ancestor, no matter how remote, is classified as black.[6] Such a rule, called *hypodescent,* assigns offspring of a union between members of different stratified groups to the one that is lower socioeconomically. Traditionally, hypodescent has been used to split American society into two groups with unequal access to wealth, power, and prestige.

An American's race, determined at birth, does not change. However, a Brazilian's race can change, depending on personal appearance, economic circumstances, or the person doing the classifying. Furthermore, because race in Brazil is not based on a rule of descent, full siblings can belong to different races. That cannot happen in the United States (Harris and Kottak 1963).

The American system recognizes *blacks* and *whites,* but Brazilian culture uses many more terms to describe an equivalent range of physical variation. Traditionally, when Brazilians—particularly rural ones in the towns we studied[7]—identified someone's race, they chose from dozens of terms. More than 500 terms were in use in Brazil in the 1960s (Harris 1970). In just a few weeks in 1962, I collected more than 40 different racial terms in one of our eventual field sites (Arembepe), which had just 800 people (Kottak 1983).

We have found, as a TV effect, that Brazilian racial terms are being reduced in number as rural people become familiar with urban settings, characters, and vocabulary. Urban Brazilians use fewer racial terms, and they employ them more consistently and pejoratively, than do traditional rural Brazilians.

Still, Brazil has no distinct and coherent "black" category. Indeed, Brazil generally lacks ethnic and minority groups with a strong sense of social identity. In the United States, blacks have such a sense, although they comprise a physically, socially, and economically diverse group. American blacks are both dark and light, rich and poor. In contrast to Brazil, the United States has a substantial black middle class. *These millions of black consumers provide a strong economic incentive to have black actors on TV.* Even poverty-level blacks in the United States, because of food stamps and welfare payments (which are absent in Brazil) participate more in the consumer economy than do poor people in Brazil. According to the U.S. Bureau of Labor Statistics, black households spend a higher percentage of their income on living expenses and consumer products than do non-blacks (Morgan 1986).

Reflecting corporate realization of this consumer clout is the representation of black characters—particularly middle-class ones—on American television (Hill 1982). Broadcasters are aware that American blacks tend to have a certain loyalty to shows with black actors and watch them in greater relative numbers than do whites.[8] American black actors have demanded more parts and better roles and have gotten them. This is not because of network executives' enlightened benevolence. It has happened as a result of recognition of habits and preferences of target audiences.

There are other compelling marketing reasons to have more blacks on American television. In 1986, blacks represented 12 percent of the American population and 9 percent of television households, but 14 percent of all household viewing. Black viewers are growing as a commercial force and target audience. Black households currently average ten hours more than the population average in weekly viewing. One recent study predicts that by 1991 black households will account for one-fifth of network televiewing (Morgan 1986).

The representation of successful black characters on American TV will surely increase. Currently, *The Cosby Show* attracts almost half the black audience for its time slot, versus a third of white households. Its doctor–lawyer parents and consuming Yuppie kids proclaim to millions of black (and white) Americans that hardworking blacks can aspire to and achieve the same life-style as white professionals.[9] Sponsors hope that middle-class blacks will identify with their television counterparts. They want them to emulate their life-styles and buy the products they use. Sponsors also know that white viewers are more sympathetic to, and likely to watch, successful than unsuccessful blacks. *The Jeffersons'* theme song, "We're Moving On Up," is a clear statement of a message that commercial television wants to get to blacks. The message is one of upward mobility, escaping poverty, forgoing welfare, joining the middle class, and participating fully in the consumers society.

CHAPTER SIX

❦ Competition, Achievement, and Information

According to the model presented in Chapter 2, cross-cultural variation shows up in program preferences, and, indeed, different program types are popular in the United States and Brazil. The genres recently popular in the United States include situation comedies, action-adventure, mystery, fantasy–science fiction, movies, continuing series,[1] miniseries,[2] docudramas,[3] sports, awards, game shows, talk shows, variety, news, and soaps. The last three are the mainstays of Brazilian television, as is shown in Tables 6.1 through 6.3.

During our field research in six Brazilian communities in 1985–86, we asked several questions designed to elicit viewing preferences. Table 6.1 lists the responses to "What are your favorite TV programs?" Table 6.2 tabulates answers to "What TV programs do you usually watch?" and Table 6.3 shows responses to "What TV programs did you watch yesterday?"

In all three tables, *telenovelas* win. However, the percentage increases substantially as we move from ideal to actual (that is, from an opinion statement about a favorite program to an actual viewing experience: a program watched yesterday). One reason for the increase is that *telenovelas* air six days a week. People are therefore more likely to watch them "usually" and to have watched them "yesterday." For the same reason, there is a parallel, though less dramatic, increase in the news category.

I also interpret these results to mean that some respondents were a bit embarrassed about their addiction to *novelas* and thus less likely to name them as favorites. However, the viewer devotion to serials on which Globo has built its national success did show up when we asked about actual behavior on a specific recent occasion (that is, "yesterday"). The percentage who said they had watched a *novela* yesterday almost doubled the figure for *telenovela* as favorite program—consistently in all our research sites.

Our variety category includes the Sunday night Globo program *Fantástico*, which, according to IBOPE, maintained the highest average audience for its time slot[4] in 1984 (Table 6.4). Globo considers this program to be particularly popular in small towns and rural areas, such as most of our research sites. In our research results, the variety category was second to *telenovelas* among favorite programs, with news a close third (Table 6.1). However, variety fell to a distant third under "programs watched yesterday" (Table 6.3)[5] and to fourth place among programs "usually watched."

Confirming statements in previous chapters about the popularity of native productions versus imports are the low scores of the American series category in all three tables (6.1, 6.2, and 6.3). American series never rank higher than eighth out of ten categories (Straubhaar 1983).

Table 6.4 compares the top ten TV programs[6] in the United States and Brazil in 1984, the last year for which both Nielsen and IBOPE figures are available. One Nielsen rating point equals 1 percent of the (89 million, as of 1988) TV households in the United States. According to Nielsen's year-end survey, 1984's most popular single program in the United States was the Super Bowl, with a 46.4 rating. About 40 million households were watching. Note that this highest rating of the year (46 percent) contrasts with Globo's *average* nightly audience of between 60 and 100 percent of all households with televisions.

In 1984, Americans were especially attracted to sports, a newsmagazine, awards, docudramas about family disasters, and science fiction. Two sports programs ranked first (Super Bowl—its usual placement) and tenth (Summer Olympics Closing Ceremony). *60 Minutes*, the newsmagazine, made the top ten, but the most popular nightly news broadcast did not. In contrast, Globo's national nightly news normally ranks first or second.

Most popular as a genre in the United States in 1984, however, were docudramas about severe family problems. These included incest and wife and child abuse, issues that three of that year's top programs examined. Respectively, these programs were *Something About Amelia* (fifth), *The Burning Bed* (second), and *Fatal Vision* (third and ninth).

Variety shows, once a mainstay of American television, were notably absent from the top ten. Also missing were action series, the only American productions that have attracted significant prime-time audiences in Brazil. The trend away from network variety and action programs[7] continued in 1985–86, with neither type achieving popularity on American network television (see Table 6.5).

In 1984, Brazilians preferred *telenovelas*, news, comedy, variety, and two imported action series. However, the popularity of the imports faded when Globo, late that year, abandoned them to other networks and moved its own productions into its entire 5 to midnight schedule.

Family themes dominate Brazilian *telenovelas*. Family docudramas were prominent on American TV in 1984, and family-based sitcoms remain popular in the United States today. However, *this apparent content similarity masks important differences.* Contrasts in family structure between Brazilian and American prime-time programs are discussed in Chapter 5. Another contrast is obvious when we consider topics of recent American docudramas. Incest, spouse beating, and intrafamily murder attracted considerable American media attention in the 1980s. These issues are signifi-

TABLE 6.1 *Responses to "What Are Your Favorite TV Programs?"*

FAVORITE TV PROGRAM	GURUPÁ	CUNHA	AREMBEPE	IBIRAMA	NITERÓI	AMERICANA	TOTAL CASES BY CATEGORY
			COMMUNITY				
Novelas	31 25.8%	98 26.1%	76 17.8%	116 24.7%	72 22.6%	48 18.2%	441 22.4%
The news	23 19.2%	66 17.6%	58 13.6%	119 25.4%	46 14.5%	35 13.3%	347 17.6%
Humor	10 8.3%	17 4.5%	47 11.0%	10 2.1%	12 3.8%	26 9.8%	122 6.2%
Films	13 10.8%	47 12.5%	35 8.2%	81 17.3%	53 16.7%	26 9.8%	255 12.9%
American series	4 3.3%	3 .8%	20 4.7%	4 .9%	7 2.2%	42 15.9%	80 4.1%
Variety	17 14.2%	84 22.4%	135 31.7%	38 8.1%	50 15.7%	49 18.6%	373 18.9%
Sports	18 15.0%	27 7.2%	32 7.5%	36 7.7%	18 5.7%	10 3.8%	141 7.2%

Documentaries	3	14	9	35	48	22	131
	2.5%	3.7%	2.1%	7.5%	15.1%	8.3%	6.6%
Children's	1	4	13	18	5	1	42
	.8%	1.1%	3.1%	3.8%	1.6%	.4%	2.1%
Other	15	15	1	12	7	5	40
	4.0%	4.0%	.2%	2.6%	2.2%	1.9%	2.0%
Total cases by Community	120	375	426	469	318	264	1972
	100.0%	100.0%	100.0%	100.0%	100.0%	100.0%	100.0%

NOTE: *Multiple responses are tabulated in this table.*

TABLE 6.2 *Responses to "What TV Programs Do You Usually Watch?"*

PROGRAMS USUALLY WATCHED	COMMUNITY						TOTAL CASES BY CATEGORY
	GURUPÁ	CUNHA	AREMBEPE	IBIRAMA	NITERÓI	AMERICANA	
Novelas	36	127	125	165	104	49	606
	27.5%	30.9%	25.0%	32.9%	22.3%	20.1%	26.9%
The news	33	102	82	157	87	56	517
	25.2%	24.8%	16.4%	31.3%	18.7%	23.0%	22.9%
Humor	6	10	39	10	16	7	88
	4.6%	2.4%	7.8%	2.0%	3.4%	2.9%	3.9%
Films	15	64	71	76	86	46	358
	11.5%	15.6%	14.2%	15.1%	18.5%	18.9%	15.9%
American series		1	10	4	8	2	25
		.2%	2.0%	.8%	1.7%	.8%	1.1%
Variety	12	46	107	20	65	18	268
	9.2%	11.2%	21.4%	4.0%	13.9%	7.4%	11.9%
Sports	22	30	37	24	19	16	148
	16.8%	7.3%	7.4%	4.8%	4.1%	6.6%	6.6%

Documentaries	6 4.6%	11 2.7%	10 2.0%	25 5.0%	48 10.3%	33 13.5%	133 5.9%
Children's	1 .8%	9 2.2%	14 2.8%	11 2.2%	25 5.4%	7 2.9%	67 3.0%
Other		11 2.7%	5 1.0%	10 2.0%	8 1.7%	10 4.1%	44 2.0%
Total cases	131	411	500	502	466	244	2254
by Community	100.0%	100.0%	100.0%	100.0%	100.0%	100.0%	100.0%

NOTE: *Multiple responses are tabulated in this table.*

TABLE 6.3 *Responses to "What TV Programs Did You Watch Yesterday?"*

PROGRAMS WATCHED YESTERDAY	COMMUNITY						TOTAL CASES BY CATEGORY
	GURUPÁ	CUNHA	AREMBEPE	IBIRAMA	NITERÓI	AMERICANA	
Novelas	27	107	121	126	61	71	513
	36.0%	42.8%	49.4%	40.6%	39.6%	43.3%	42.8%
The news	14	46	34	88	30	43	255
	18.7%	18.4%	13.9%	28.4%	19.5%	26.2%	21.3%
Humor	9	6	11	14	8	1	49
	12.0%	2.4%	4.5%	4.5%	5.2%	.6%	4.1%
Films	4	23	26	24	18	15	110
	5.3%	9.2%	10.6%	7.7%	11.7%	9.1%	9.2%
American series	3	2	9	6	6	7	33
	4.0%	.8%	3.7%	1.9%	3.9%	4.3%	2.8%
Variety	9	40	19	25	12	10	115
	12.0%	16.0%	7.8%	8.1%	7.8%	6.1%	9.6%
Sports	4	12	7	6	5	2	36
	5.3%	4.8%	2.9%	1.9%	3.2%	1.2%	3.0%

Documentaries	3	8	8	8	6	14	47
	4.0%	3.2%	3.3%	2.6%	3.9%	8.5%	3.9%
Children's		2	6	10	8		26
		.8%	2.4%	3.2%	5.2%		2.2%
Other	2	4	4	3		1	14
	2.7%	1.6%	1.6%	1.0%		.6%	1.2%
Total cases	75	250	245	310	154	164	1198
by Community	100.0%	100.0%	100.0%	100.0%	100.0%	100.0%	100.0%

NOTE: *Multiple responses are tabulated in this table.*

TABLE 6.4 *1984's Top Ten American and Brazilian TV Programs*

AMERICAN[a]	BRAZILIAN[b]
1. Super Bowl (sports)	*Fantástico* (variety)
2. *The Burning Bed* (docudrama)	National nightly news
3. *60 Minutes* (news) tied with	8 o'clock *novela*
4. *Fatal Vision Part 2* (docudrama)	7 o'clock *novela*
5. *Something About Amelia* (docudrama)	*Os Trapalhões* (comedy)
6. *Lace Part 2* (melodrama)	6 o'clock *novela*
7. Grammy Awards	*The Fall Guy* (action series)
8. Academy Awards	*Hart to Hart* (action series)
9. *Fatal Vision Part 1* (docudrama)	*Chico Anísio* (comedy)
10. *V, Final Battle* (Science fiction) tied with Summer Olympics Closing (sports)	*Bem Amado* (comedy)

[a]*A single broadcast.*
[b]*Average number of sets per time slot.*

cantly different from the topics normally examined in Brazilian *telenovelas*. The American docudramas popular in 1984 were about family disasters, rather than about the "normal" American families whose historic TV popularity was resurrected in 1985. That year, *The Cosby Show* and *Family Ties* became the top two *weekly* programs (among six or seven family sitcoms and four night-time soaps in the top 20—See Table 6.5).

NARROW   WORLD   OF   SPORTS

Television can spread and enhance knowledge and appreciation of sports and spur participation. The extent and effectiveness of sports telecasting has national and international ramifications . A significant part of the explanation for variable success of nations in international sports competition is the availability, extent, variety, and sophistication of media sports coverage.

Why do countries excel at particular sports? Why do certain nations habitually pile up dozens of Olympic medals whereas others win only a handful, or none at all? Why, for example, in the 1984 Summer Olympics did the United States win 174 medals, whereas Brazil managed only 8?[8] Cultural values, society, and the media influence international sports success. It isn't simply a matter of rich and poor, developed and underdeveloped, nations. There is more to international sports success than the virtual cradle-to-medal support that government provides to promising athletes in East Germany and the Soviet Union. It isn't even a question of a national will to win. Certain nations, including Brazil, stress winning even more than Americans do. However, a cultural focus on winning doesn't

TABLE 6.5 *Top 20 Weekly Prime-Time Shows, United States, 1985–86*

1. *The Cosby Show*	NBC	34.0/51	family sitcom
2. *Family Ties*	NBC	30.5/45	family sitcom
3. *Murder, She Wrote*	CBS	25.3/37	mystery
4. *60 Minutes*	CBS	23.9/38	news
5. *Cheers*	NBC	23.7/35	sitcom
6. *Dallas*	CBS	21.9/34	night-time soap
7. *The Golden Girls*	NBC	21.8/36	family? sitcom
8. *Dynasty*	ABC	21.8/33	night-time soap
9. *Miami Vice*	NBC	21.3/36	action
10. *Who's the Boss?*	ABC	21.1/32	family sitcom
11. *Night Court*	NBC	20.9/31	sitcom
12. *Highway to Heaven*	NBC	20.3/31	fantasy series
13. *Kate & Allie*	CBS	20.0/29	family sitcom
14. *Monday Night Football*	ABC	19.8/32	sports
15. *Newhart*	CBS	19.6/29	sitcom
16. *Knots Landing*	CBS	19.5/32	night-time soap
17. *Growing Pains*	ABC	19.5/29	family sitcom
18. *227*	NBC	18.8/31	family sitcom
19. *Hotel*	ABC	18.4/31	series
20. *Falcon Crest*	CBS	18.1/30	night-time soap

SUMMARY

Family sitcoms	7
Night-time soaps	4
Nonfamily sitcoms	3
Mystery	1
Newsmagazine	1
Action series	1
Fantasy	1
Sports	1
Dramatic series	1

SOURCE: *TV Guide,* "The Best and the Worst by the Numbers," July 12, 1986, p. 14.

necessarily lead to the desired result. Indeed, an overemphasis on winning may *decrease* its likelihood.

It is worth recalling here that United States and Brazil are the national giants of the Western Hemisphere. Their populations are 245 million and 145 million, respectively. These countries both have continental proportions and large, physically and ethnically diverse populations with roots in Europe, Africa, Asia, and native America. Each is the major economic power of its continent. However, they offer striking and revealing contrasts in media sports coverage and also in Olympic success.

Over the years our growing media establishment has honed Americans' interest in sports. Along with game shows and award shows, sports provide daily examples of individual and team accomplishments, self-definition through activity and achievement, and, presumably, payoffs from hard work. All these represent dominant values in American culture. Each day we witness the tripartite structuring of our local news broadcasts into news, sports, and weather. There is a steady stream of televised events, matches, games, playoffs and championships. By 1985, U.S. commercial television networks were broadcasting 1500 hours of sports annually, double the 1960 figure. Today, cable TV, which reaches more than half of all American homes, provides almost constant sports coverage. The Olympics, particularly if telecast live when viewers are home and awake, also attract extensive coverage and substantial audiences.

In Brazil, no sports program, not even the Summer Olympics, to which that country sends more than 150 athletes, attracted much of a TV audience either in 1984 or 1988. This isn't surprising, considering that Brazilian television generally has much less sports coverage than does American TV.[9] The coverage that it does offer is amateurish. There is no apparent technical reason for this. Brazil has high-quality television networks (Globo and Manchête), which regularly produce expertly made dramatic and documentary shows. However, as media conduits for sports, Brazil has no cable channels, and sports are not a regular part of either local or national news.

Although soccer is a Brazilian national obsession, engendering fierce team loyalty and passionate interest, regularly scheduled soccer matches aren't televised very often. Fans must either attend local games or follow them on the radio. Nor are championships and major hometown games shown on TV. No Rio channel telecasts the traditional rivalry between the Flamengo and Fluminense (Fla-Flu) football clubs, which routinely attracts 200,000 people to Maracaná, the world's largest soccer stadium. There is no regular nationally televised event like the Super Bowl or the World Series. The World (Soccer) Cup, held every four years, is the only sports event that ever draws audiences comparable to those of Globo's *tele-novelas*.

The Olympics are an international event in which much of the world, including Brazil, may participate via television. The Olympic Games also provide excellent case study material for the understanding of cultural contrasts as applied to sports and the values they express. The Games are supposed to unite nations, providing a peaceful context for competition among them. (The interlinked rings of the official logo symbolize this unity.) However, given flags, anthems, Olympic history, and the tally of medals by country, nationalism is unavoidable.

The media fuel the international competitive aspect of the games. Many people criticized ABC for inciting nationalist fervor in 1984 in Los Angeles. Its cameras seemed rooted to the Los Angeles spectators, largely U.S. citizens, and their victory chants of "U.S.A., U.S.A." (*Newsweek* 1984a). ABC's coverage seemed jingoistic.[10] It irritated athletes and coaches from other countries. Many of them didn't realize that their fans back home were seeing different reports. The President of the International Olympic Committee formally protested ABC's seeming overemphasis on American athletes.

Actually, for the 1984 Summer Olympics, ABC produced not only the broadcasts seen by Americans and tailored to them, but also a more neutral record of each event. The network compiled 1300 hours of total coverage—available to be excerpted for broadcast throughout the world, as it was in Brazil. Fascinating cultural contrasts show up when we consider how television and the press[11] in different countries viewed and interpreted the Olympics. Cultural variation is obvious in the ways in which the same film and events were scheduled, edited, cut, excerpted, explained, and evaluated.[12]

In most countries, if no citizens were participating, the media didn't devote much air time to a sports event. This is the obvious reason Brazilian television pays almost no attention to the Winter Olympics. Cold weather sports are of little interest to Brazilians. However, it is much more surprising that Brazilian television offers so little coverage of the Summer Olympics, to which Brazil routinely sends a large delegation.

In neither 1984 nor 1988 did Globo follow ABC's and NBC's example of substituting Summer Games coverage for regular fare. Globo maintained its normal schedule, offering Olympic summaries outside of prime time. Regular programming was interrupted for just a few special events of strong interest to Brazilians. One of these was swimmer Ricardo Prado's (1984) race in the finals of the 400-meter individual medley, which took place during the 8 o'clock *telenovela*. Globo's strategy made sense, given televiewers' preferences. Brazilians opted for Globo's normal programming 7 to 1 over the Manchête network's broadcast of the 1984 Summer Olympic Games Opening Ceremony (*Veja* 1984b). ABC, on the other hand, had much fuller 1984 Summer Olympic coverage, even though the Games cut into its profitable day-time soap opera schedule. The level of interest in the United States in 1984 was sufficiently high for ABC to meet its pledge to sponsors to deliver 25 percent of American households during prime time[13] (even as Globo was holding 60 percent of Brazilian TV households with routine *telenovelas!*).

To this American analyst, the Olympic coverage that did get broadcast in Brazil in summer 1984 can be criticized on several grounds: There was too little live coverage; it focused too exclusively on events in which Brazilians were participating; it neglected some of the most dramatic events, with certain key races never shown. For example, as far as I know, Brazilian TV never showed the tie between two American women swimmers for first place in the 100-meter freestyle.

Nor did Brazilian TV provide expert commentators, so familiar to American televiewers, to explain sports events to novices. In fact, Brazilian sportscasters demonstrated poor knowledge of sports other than soccer.

This was true throughout the media—press and television. One news-magazine, for example, erroneously reported that West German swimmer Michael Gross had won the 200-meter butterfly, beating a previous world record time of 54.27 (plausible for 100 meters but impossible for 200).

Another missing element in Brazilian sports coverage was the human interest angle so typical of American reporting. This was obvious again in Winter 1988 Olympic stories about skaters Debi Thomas and Dan Jansen (whose sister died just before he was to compete), and the rivalry between two skaters named Brian (Boitano and Orser). In Brazil, just the contest (if even that) was shown, with no commentary about the background, quali-ties, and prior challenges that got the competitors there.

Through visual demonstration, commentary, and explanation of rules and training, the media help introduce sports to people, stimulating interest in participation. *Time* magazine reasonably attributed 1984 Amer-ican Olympic success in bicycling, in which American men won six med-als, to the popularity of the film *Breaking Away*. The media play a major role in stimulating interest in all kinds of sports—amateur and pro-fessional, team and individual, spectator and participatory. Until Brazil has more frequent, reliable, and varied sports coverage, it is unlikely that its international sports success, aside from soccer and car racing (which *is* televised), will increase much.

Besides media neglect, another reason for Brazil's poor Olympic show-ing is that Brazilian culture *emphasizes team sports and victories too much*. Furthermore, and related to the focus on team sports, there is too thin a line between professional and amateur. In the Brazilian sports establish-ment, (professional) team sports have overwhelming weight—with soccer as king. A strong personal connection between fan and soccer team begins on the local level. Proclaiming "I *am* Fluminense" or "I *am* Flamengo," fans yearn for their team's victories and perceive them as their own. This habit fosters an intense personal identification of fan with athletes—professional or amateur—that Brazil's Olympic athletes find oppressive.

The load is heavy because Brazilian athletes in international competi-tion *represent* Brazilians, almost in the same way that Congress represents the people of the United States. A win by a Brazilian team or the occasional nationally known individual athlete is felt to bring respect to the entire nation. However, the media are strikingly intolerant of losers. Ricardo Prado, the most successful Brazilian swimmer ever, swam the finals of the 400-meter individual medley during the 8 o'clock *telenovela*. This occa-sioned a rare interruption in Globo's regular programming. One news-magazine observed, "It was as though he was the country with a swimsuit on, jumping in the pool in a collective search for success."[14] Prado's own feelings confirmed the magazine: "When I was on the stands, I thought of just one thing: what they'll think of the result in Brazil." After beating his old world record by 1.33 seconds, in a second place finish, Prado told a fellow team member, "I think I did everything right. I feel like a winner, but will they think I'm a loser in Brazil?" Leaving the pool, Prado rushed to phone home to find out how the national audience had viewed his performance.

Prado realized as he swam that he was performing in prime time and that all Brazil would be watching. Complaining about having the expectations of an entire nation focused on him, he contrasted Brazilian and American athletes. The United States, he asserted, has so many athletes that no single one has to summarize the country's hopes.

Fortunately, Brazil did seem to value Prado's performance, which was responsible for Brazil's best result ever in Olympic swimming. Previously the country had won a total of only three bronze medals (in 1952, 1960, and 1980)—the last in Moscow for a relay. Labeling Prado "the man of silver," the media never tired of calling his top event, the 400 IM, in which he had once held a world record, the most complete, exhausting, and challenging one in swimming.

However, the kind words for Prado did not extend to the rest of the swim team. The press lamented the "succession of failures that Brazilian swimmers . . . accumulated in the first days of competition." "It was a disaster, nothing went right," said one swimmer. "For an underdeveloped country we did very well," rationalized another. Prado consoled the team, "You gave your best, and that's all you could do." When he returned to Brazil he complained that the Brazilian sports establishment gives swimmers, and athletes generally, poor support. "They think all you have to do is to put athletes up for a week at a good hotel." The president of the Brazilian swimming confederation countered that the team had been given considerable support, but had disappointed the country. Such a statement to the press blatantly violated the American canon that you should not speak ill of amateur athletes.

An article in the newsmagazine *Veja* before Joaquim Cruz's unexpected gold medal in track decried Brazil's "pallid performance." Of Brazil's Olympic contenders only Ricardo Prado had excelled. *Veja* wondered whether the soccer team would "avenge" Brazil's loss of the World Cup in Spain in 1982 (*Veja* 1984b). (It did not. Brazil got a silver medal, to France's gold medal.)

Knowing that the press (as the following quotes from major newsmagazines document) is ever-ready to express "the nation's terrible disappointment" (as it did when the basketball team failed to defend the "national sports dignity"), it is no wonder that Brazilian competitors feel burdened. One yachtsman arrived in Los Angeles a month early so that his fears would diminish, but he still didn't win. "We're only going to relax," said a volleyball player "with the medal in hand." The men's volleyball team also had to settle for "the bitter taste of silver." The eventual failure of the women's basketball team was attributed to tension and apathy. Ricardo Prado expressed his feelings as a Brazilian athlete: "Success in swimming has changed me a lot, has left me harder, less confident. I need to relax. I don't intend to kill myself for anybody."[15]

Expectably, during the 1984 Summer Olympics the Brazilian media focused on the team sports—soccer, basketball, volleyball—and on Prado's swimming success (always juxtaposed with the *team*'s failure). There was little coverage of individuals, other than Prado and Cruz—Brazil's only gold medalist. For example, when eventual silver medalist Douglas Viera disputed the gold medal with a Korean judoist, only five Brazilians (one athlete, two coaches, two journalists) bothered to attend. Hundreds of Koreans were there to cheer on his opponent. The judo matches resulted in Brazil's second, third, and fourth medals ever in that sport, and the first since 1972. However, Brazil received no live coverage of the judo competition, even though all three medalists had previously had international success. The media should have anticipated their medals. The gatekeepers had simply decided that the nation lacked interest in their feats. The names of the three medalists (one silver, two bronze) were mentioned on TV, but I never saw film of their matches.

There is more, of course, to the development of sports than constant and favorable media attention. There must also be encouragement of participation on the amateur and local levels. This is available in the United States through myriad clubs and school athletic teams. In Brazil, swimming, gymnastics, and diving teams are affiliated with money-making professional soccer clubs. Because of this association, the Brazilian sports establishment doesn't pay much attention to the professional–amateur distinction. Brazil's most successful athletes on the international scene— *professional* soccer players—have played in the Olympics. Brazil's 1984 Olympic soccer coach admitted to foreign journalists that his team had just two amateurs, with the others "beginning professionals." The media and fans alike apply the same standards and judgments to amateur athletes that they use for salaried professionals.

A measure of a nation's sports maturity, underlying its international success, is the extent to which it provides public access to athletic facilities. Athletes need places and occasions to practice, develop, and compete. Compared with the United States, Brazil offers few sports opportunities (except for soccer, which people play in town squares and streets, fields, and on beaches). Brazil lacks a well-developed public education system, with the teams, facilities, and schedules that foster athletic competition, as in the United States. The United States can afford to maintain the distinction between amateur and professional sports because it has one of the world's largest sports establishments. Our developed economy, voracious media, achievement orientation, competitiveness, and traditions of joining clubs provide fertile ground for all kinds of sports, team and individual.

Because Brazilians expect their athletes not just to represent but almost to *be* the country, and because they emphasize team sports, the media focus too exclusively on winning. How different is it in the United States? Winning, of course, is also an important American cultural value, but particularly in team sports—as in Brazil. American football coaches are famous for comments such as "Winning isn't everything; it's the only thing" and "Show me a good loser and I'll show you a loser." However, American culture admires moral victories and personal bests and commends athletes who run good races without finishing first. We also honor comeback athletes and hold Special Olympics. In amateur sports, American culture tells us that hard work and personal improvement can be as important as winning. This is particularly true of sports that focus on the individual. These include running, swimming, diving, gymnastics, and skating—in all of which American athletes usually do well.

Accustomed to hearing that our culture overemphasizes winning, many Americans find it hard to believe that other cultures value victory even more. Brazil certainly does. Commenting on the massive coverage he got as a world-record holder, Ricardo Prado observed that Brazilians only notice winners—just number ones, never number twos. He blasted the press for neglecting the achievements of athletes who held no world records.

Brazilian sports enthusiasts are preoccupied with world records, probably because only a win (as in soccer) or a best time (as in swimming) can make Brazil indisputably, even if temporarily, the best in the world at something. Before the 1984 Olympics the media constantly recalled Prado's world record. The best-time standard also provides Brazilians with a ready basis to *fault* a swimmer or runner for not going fast enough, when they don't make previous times. Given this tendency, one would predict, correctly, that sports with very subjective standards (for example, gymnastics, diving) are not popular in Brazil. Brazilians like to assign blame to athletes who fail them, and negative comments about gymnasts or divers are more difficult because grace and execution cannot be measured as easily as time can.

I think that Brazilians value winning so much because it is so rare. In the United States, resources are more abundant, social classes less marked, poverty less pervasive, and individual social mobility easier. American society has room for many winners. Brazilian society is more stratified. A smaller middle class and elite group comprise just 30 percent of the population. *Telenovelas* make rising in life seem more feasible than it is in real life. However, Brazilian sports more accurately echo lessons from the larger society: Victories are scarce and reserved for the privileged few.

Cultural Values in Sports: Being Versus Doing

Favorite sports, the athlete's role, and emphasis on winning vary between cultures. Contrasting values also show up in the interpretations the media and ordinary people offer in discussing performances. The explanations that natives give for sports success belong to a larger context of cultural values. Particularly relevant here is the contrast between ascribed and achieved status (a *status* is simply a position in a social structure). People have little control over the ascribed statuses they occupy (for instance, age, sex). Ascribed statuses depend on intrinsic qualities, what one *is* rather than what one *does*. However, people can *do* more about their achieved statuses (such as, student, tennis player). In the eyes of American law, if hardly in reality, people start out the same. Because of this, American culture emphasizes achieved status and tells us to *make* something of our lives. Success comes through achievement. An American's identity emerges as a result of what he or she does.

In Brazil, on the other hand, as Chapter 5 demonstrated with *telenovela* content, social identity rests on *being rather than doing*. Status reflects what one is from the start, a strand in a web of personal relationships that originate in the extended family. Family position and network membership contribute substantially to individual fortune, and all social life is hierarchical.

The contrasting roles that different cultures assign to ascribed and achieved status extend to sports and to sports coverage. The following description of a 1984 judo medalist illustrates the importance of ascribed status and the fact that Brazilians regard victories as scarce and reserved for the privileged few.

> Middle-weight Olympic bronze medalist Walter Carmona began judo at age six and became a São Paulo champion at twelve. With his fourth place in Moscow in 1980, and subsequent prizes, he is Brazil's winningest judoist. Carmona lives in São Paulo with his family (father, mother, siblings); he trains five hours a day and is in his fifth year of engineering at Mackenzie University. He is fully supported by his father, a factory owner. Walter Carmona's life has been comfortable—he has been able to study and dedicate himself to judo without worries. His situation brings great satisfaction to his father, who says that he is "proud to support a champion." (*Veja* 1984c:61)

Although satisfied with the Los Angeles result, the father thought his son "deserved more than a bronze medal." "We are certain he expected the gold," said his mother. She seems to have been right, because Carmona didn't bother to phone home after receiving his medal. His final match over, the athlete "took a vacation from his team." He toured Los Angeles, not bothering to attend the silver-medal winning judo match of a teammate.

Wealth often does contribute to sports success in the United States, albeit less so than in Brazil. However, it is difficult to imagine *Time*, *Newsweek*, or American television running a similar account. Like American culture, the American media prefer underdogs and rags to riches. Even when an athlete comes from a privileged family, reporters do their best to find some aspect of doing, some special personal triumph or achievement, to focus on. Often this involves the athlete's struggle with adversity (illness, injury, pain, the death of a parent, sibling, friend, or coach). This imagery depicts the athlete as not only successful but also noble and self-sacrificing.

However, given the opposite focus on ascribed status in Brazil, *the guiding assumption in sports as in society is that one cannot do more than what one is*. For example, the Brazilian Olympic Committee sent no female swimmers to Los Angeles because none had made Brazil's arbitrarily established cutoff times. This excluded a South American record-holder, whereas swimmers with no better times were attending from other South American countries. The Brazilian attitude was that only swimmers with these arbitrary times had any chance to place in Los Angeles. No one seemed to imagine that Olympic excitement might spur swimmers to extraordinary efforts.

In contrast, achievement-oriented American coverage dotes on unexpected results. The media adhere to a sports credo originally enunciated by Yogi Berra: "It's not over till it's over." American culture, supposedly so practical and realistic, has a remarkable faith in coming from behind—in unexpected and miraculous achievements.

Contrasting portraits of the United States and Brazil emerge from media coverage of the Olympics. One is of an achievement-oriented society where anything is possible. The other presents an ascribed-status society in which it's over before it begins. Athletes from each culture internalize these values. Key ingredients of sports success according to American culture were apparent in *Newsweek*'s 1984 Summer Olympics coverage.

One issue focused on three athletes. Australian swimmer John Siebin had scored an *upset* win. American gold-medal gymnast Mary Lou Retton was a "piston-driven *pixie*." Japan's Koji Gushiken had finally won the all-round male gymnastics title through *tenacity*. These winners were the products of different nations and had followed different paths to Olympic success. However, *Newsweek* used American values (summarized by the words I've italicized) to interpret their achievements. These three were newsworthy because each embodied an American hero type. These were the underdog (Siebin), the giant-killer (Retton), and the tenacious worker (Gushiken).

Most clearly, Retton and Siebin, pixie giant-killer and underdog kid from out of nowhere, appealed to the characteristic American preoccupation with the unexpected. Their achievements were especially interesting to Americans because they were in some sense extraordinary and unforeseen. Given Siebin's 25th-place world ranking before the event, the odds against his winning his race were almost overwhelming. (Brazilians might have discouraged him from entering key races, or even kept him home.)

Newsweek interpreted Gushiken's victory as the end to a "quest" that had spanned three Olympics. At 27, he would ordinarily be all but decrepit by the standards of his sport. According to *Newsweek*, "things like this don't happen in real life, only at the Olympics."[16]

The credo that *anyone can do anything*[17] is rooted in the doing and achievement orientation of American culture. The American press considered unexpected results, virtually ignored by the Brazilian media, to be some of the brightest Olympic moments. Unheralded swimmer Siebin scored "a stunning upset" over Michael Gross in the 200-meter butterfly. Similarly, "against all odds" an American swimmer with a much slower seed time than Gross anchored the U.S. team to victory in a relay that the West Germans "had seemed destined to win."

Brazilian television paid no attention to the upset nature of these wins. Brazilian culture has little interest in the unexpected. Brazilians assume that if you go into an event with a top seed time, as Ricardo Prado did, you've got a chance to win a medal. Prado's second place finish made perfect sense back home, because one man had bettered Prado's former world record before the race began. Brazilian culture also criticizes not doing as well as expected, given what one was at the outset.[18] However, it doesn't anticipate unexpected success through sudden bursts of achievement during final competition. Because of this, the Brazilian media didn't know what to do with runner Joaquim Cruz's unexpected gold medal, and he received less coverage than Ricardo Prado. However, an American newsmagazine ran a cover story using Cruz's humble upbringing on the outskirts of Brasilia to illustrate classic American values.

American culture accords overwhelming value to work. It therefore seems surprising that our media devote so much attention to unforeseen results and so little to the years of training, preparation, and competition that underlie Olympic performance. The media may be assuming that hard work is so obvious and fundamental that it doesn't need mentioning. Perhaps the assumption is that once athletes enter Olympic competition they are all so similar (the American value of equality) that only mysterious and chance factors can explain variable success. The media apply American culture's focus on the unexpected to losses, too. Chance, fate, mystery, and uncertainty are legitimate explanations for defeat. Runners and skaters fall; ligaments tear; a gymnast inexplicably falls off the pommel horse.

Americans thus recognize chance disaster as the companion of unexpected success. Brazilians, however, place more responsibility on the individual, assigning personal fault. Less is attributed to factors beyond human control. Brazilians blame athletes who don't do as well as expected. Accepting their body's failures, it is culturally appropriate for Brazilian athletes to invoke poor health as an excuse for losing. An American track star, Carl Lewis, could assert that "at the Olympics, it's 100 percent mental, because there's nothing you can change physically." Brazilians would disagree: You can always get sick. Brazilian athletes routinely mention colds or diarrhea as a reason for a poor performance.

For example, because of a cold, runner Joaquim Cruz, Brazil's only gold medalist, withdrew from his second event, the 1500-meter race, in which he was favored. The background to his decision was the intense pressure on Brazilian athletes to win, and Cruz was afraid he wouldn't. A Brazilian newsmagazine's report of his explanation for withdrawing illustrates contrasting national values about the role of illness in sports.

> The night I ran in the finals of the 800 meters, I ate badly, almost didn't sleep, and was awakened at six A.M. by a phone call from "Uncle" [Joao] Figueiredo [then President of Brazil]. I was already weak from running four races in four days. Then I saw I had caught a terrible cold. I went to see the doctor supplied by Nike [the sport shoe company], had acupuncture and massages, and spent a night at the Santa Monica Holiday Inn to see if I could rest better, but it was impossible to recover my form.[19]

Cruz withdrew because he "had no interest in running and placing last." He was flying to Europe to compete again the following week and wanted to "save himself" to set world records later in the year. Brazilians accepted Cruz's decision to forgo the 1500-meter race. An informant told me that he was right to withdraw; he probably wouldn't have won anyway because he was sick.

American and Brazilian athletes and, particularly, the media and the public that interpret and evaluate their performances treat poor health differently. Brazilians use illness negatively, as an excuse. Americans use it positively, as a challenge to be met and bested. To illustrate this, contrast Cruz's behavior with that of top-seeded American breaststroker John Moffet. The swimmer had sprained a leg tendon during his qualifying heat, but in the finals he managed to finish fifth on "arm power and guts." The American media called that performance unbelievable.

A similar focus on overcoming physical limitations was apparent in the American coverage of the English runner David Moorcroft. His last place finish in the 5000-meter finals served as the opening human interest story for the American film *Sixteen Days of Glory*. That segment emphasized that Moorcroft had been plagued with illnesses and injuries. In the 1984 Olympics he ran well in qualifying but faltered during the finals because of leg pain. Realizing he would finish last, Moorcroft's personal triumph was completing the race without being lapped by the winner. He accomplished that goal and finished his long painful journey with pride and honor. (Moorcroft's previously set world record also survived the 1984 Olympics.)

Significantly, the focus on doing in American culture doesn't entail the belief that people can fully control outcomes (chance, or luck, is also recognized). As a result, the American press gives little space to athletes' explanations for less than optimal showings. The Brazilian media, in contrast, find it necessary to assign fault for failure. This usually means blaming the athlete(s).

There are several reasons for this contrast in fault-finding. First, there is less pressure on any given American athlete to win for the United States. Second, American culture recognizes the role of chance. Third, the sheer number of American successes renders discussions of failures somewhat ungenerous. Perhaps Americans are also more optimistic than Brazilians, preferring to focus on what ABC has inculcated as "the thrill of victory" rather than "the agony of defeat." The American press dwells much more on injuries and illnesses of victors and finishers than those of losers and quitters. American culture, applied to sports, uses poor health not as an excuse, but as an obstacle for people to overcome, as in the Moffet and Moorcroft cases.[20]

Illustrating the supreme American value of achieving against the odds is a 1984 *Newsweek* article by Pete Axhelm. "On very special occasions, there appears a quality in sport that defies all plans and diagrams."[21] The athlete's "quest" is a "moving celebration of the potential of the human spirit," the article continued. Near Hollywood, the dream capital of an achievement-oriented society, a succession of American athletes climbed the victors' stand in summer 1984, displaying their medals. They may have felt like *Star Wars* heroes, living a dream, fulfilling a quest, hurdling obstacles, winning out on their own. The closing week of the Olympics "was given to surprises of the spirit." After the 1980 boycott it had not been easy for Americans to return to their grinding training schedules. "I wasn't sure if the sacrifices were worth it," said swimmer Nancy Hogshead. Still, proclaimed Axhelm, in the mood kindled in Los Angeles athletes showed that they could not merely endure, but overcome.

While Americans spoke of spirit, dreams, quests, and victories, Brazilian television found humor in failure. This was chronicled in a montage of Olympic mistakes—pratfalls and stumbles by riders, weightlifters, and runners. ABC distributed this film along with its documentary footage. In the United States these lighter moments illustrated that stunts weren't as easy as the Olympians made them seem. Within American culture, they confirmed that no matter how hard an athlete has trained, the unexpected can always happen, sometimes affecting the result.

In Brazil, the pratfalls were hugely popular on the nightly news. First, they showed that people besides Brazilians could make Olympic mistakes. And the film conveyed a second, less explicit, message: It suggested the futility of trying, or even hoping, to win in a cultural universe in which chances for success are severely limited. (Brazilian TV game shows illustrate the same cultural assumption. Of several [Sunday] game shows copied from American models, the favorite is the Brazilian version of *The Gong Show*. A panel of eight minor celebrities delights in criticizing and ultimately gonging amateurs who dare to perform in this auditorium show, which reaches a national audience.)

AWARDS

Extensive sports coverage thus provides Americans with daily examples of rewards that come from doing. Sports illustrate the value of action, competition, individual and team efforts, discipline, endeavor, and persistence. All these are fundamental in an achievement- and work-oriented society, and they are much less characteristic of Brazil. Awards shows and game programs (see below) also illustrate the key North American values of competition and individual achievement.

Award ceremonies are popular not just on American TV but also in real life. Telecasts of the ever-popular Grammy and Academy Awards were American TV's seventh and eighth most watched programs in 1984. That year, Americans in 26 million households stayed up late to participate in the public recognition of achievements in motion pictures. The Oscar show is carried live in Brazil—between midnight and 3 A.M.—but it attracts a minuscule audience. However, there are no such televised ceremonies honoring Brazilians.

INFORMATION PROCESSING AND BRAIN GAMES

In contemporary North America, math, science, and the computer (accessed through a visual display terminal, in actuality a television monitor) have become strategic resources in a competitive, achievement-oriented, high-tech, information-manipulative society. Manifestations of this society are all around us and include broadcast television content. Our electronic, statistical society rests on the most sophisticated means of data collection, storage, retrieval, and analysis ever developed. Increasingly, social and economic rewards go to adept information processors.

American culture encourages its children to pursue careers demanding skills in math, science, and information processing. They must feel at home with numbers and friendly with computers. Americans must be able to find our way through the maze of numbers that define us. To our addresses and phone numbers have been added area codes and (hyphenated) zip codes. Defining us are salary, tax bracket, grade-point average, college board scores, driver's license, social security number, weight, height, cholesterol level, and blood pressure readings. We carry dozens of credit and registration cards, all computer processed, for all the accounts we have opened. No longer do we have just a name, rank, and serial number. We have serial numbers for every appliance we have ever bought. As the service-and-information economy progresses, these trends intensify.

American culture's obsession with numbers[22]—and the fact that I, as a native, shared it—became apparent to me during my year in Brazil. One of the things I missed most there was accurate information—particularly numbers. When I returned to the United States in January 1984 for a brief visit, I immediately bought several newspapers and magazines. Famished for data I looked through *Sports Illustrated* for bowl game scores. (Had it been summer I would have unconsciously started memorizing batting and earned run averages, runs batted in and home runs. Had it been summer

1989, some entirely new statistics—game winning runs batted in, on-base and slugging percentages—would have fascinated me.)

Next I feasted on a copy of *USA Today*, devouring even its most obscure statistics (such as state with fewest Aleuts). I perused quotations of stocks, mutual funds, and interest rates. I took note of Nielsen's findings on the most popular television programs. (I had almost despaired of getting comparable information about Brazilian programs.) I scanned daily high and low temperatures on the colorful national weather map. After five days of exposure to North American information sources, I felt ready to return to a country where published numbers are scarce and often inaccurate.

The national newspaper *USA Today* provides excellent illustration of the statistical aspect of contemporary American culture. *USA Today* has been dubbed "McPaper" because of its nationwide presence, its uniform, packaged look, its short, concise articles, and its focus on superficial, relatively invariant information that offers quick satisfaction of our appetite for news. It has become the printed-information McDonald's of today's America. A national paper can succeed today because of information gathering and processing facilities and means of national publication and distribution that didn't exist a decade ago.

Relatively invariant is the key in interpreting *USA Today* as a news-paper. A newspaper is, after all, supposed to give us the "news"; events that are new, that have just happened, that vary. However, *USA Today* offers many columns based on statistics that don't change much from day to day. In contrast, we read or hear about more changeable events on the air and in our local newspapers. *USA Today* is, more accurately, an "oldspaper"—based in large part on previously collected numbers. As such it is symptomatic and supportive of our statistical society.

Another manifestation of the information processing, statistical society is the increasing popularity of brain games. Shows like *Jeopardy* are alien to Brazilian TV, where game show contestants play, act, sing, dance, or do tricks. They almost never display their intellect. Consider one example of an American brain-game show. On October 16, 1984, soon after my return to the United States from a year in Brazil, I watched *Nova*'s National Science Test on PBS. Art Fleming, former host of the competitive, fact-retrieval, brain-game show *Jeopardy*, posed several questions to four competitive celebrity brains. They were educator Marva Collins, TV journalist Edwin Newman, ABC science editor Jules Bergman, and actress Jane Alexander.

Newman won, but even Ph.D. professors such as this author had trouble with some of the questions—which illustrate our statistical, information processing society. What percentage of the platinum used for the defense needs of the United States do we import? (2 percent, 22 percent, 69 percent, or *99 percent*—the correct answer) How many red blood cells does the body manufacture every day? (2 million, 2 billion, or *200 billion*) How long does a giant tortoise live? (25, 75, *175*, or 300 years)

These questions amazed me because they were so obscure and statistical. Why do we expect people to memorize such facts, instead of understanding principles? Who (except a physician) cares how many red blood cells the human body makes each day? Can't new military priorities and mineral discoveries change our needs to import raw materials from year to year? This doesn't mean that we shouldn't know facts (Brazilians go to extremes in the other direction), but it does mean that we should be more reflective about their significance.[23]

From a more objective and analytic viewpoint, however, such media-borne facts and figures are important in the larger context of contemporary American society. *They help hook us on information processing*, which will dominate our culture's future. How, after all, do we get our kids interested in facts and numbers? How do we get their little minds comfortable with information storage, retrieval, and manipulation? For the answer, look not only to the classroom and the computer, but also to television, sports (baseball statistics, personal times), toys (such as Teddy Ruxpin), and games. Consider one recently popular game: On my return to the United States from Brazil in 1984, I discovered that one cultural innovation during my absence had been the board game "Trivial Pursuit." Many academics and professionals liked it because it demanded general knowledge, not just familiarity with trivia as its name implied. In addition to entertainment and sports and leisure, "Trivial Pursuit" tested knowledge about science and nature, history, arts and literature, and geography. In choosing its name, the makers had cleverly managed to convince Americans who might otherwise have resisted, particularly kids, that processing data learned in school was fun!

A spin-off of "Trivial Pursuit" was the revival of the TV brain-game program *Jeopardy*, whose popularity has increased as American society has turned more and more toward information processing. By 1987 *Jeopardy* was second in syndication only to the unbrainy but still competitive and information-based game show *Wheel of Fortune*. Both "Trivial Pursuit" and *Jeopardy* value general knowledge. In this they contrast strongly with game shows such as *Let's Make a Deal* and *The Price Is Right*, which were popular during the 1970s. They are yet another expression of the search for excellence, that is processing of facts and numbers, being promoted by our contemporary information processing society. Brazilian game shows, which air Sundays, mainly on the Sílvio Santos (SBT) network, derive from and therefore are much more similar to such older, lowbrow American game shows as *Let's Make a Deal, The Gong Show,* and *Name That Tune*.

Illustrating the power of television, specifically, and its fit with contemporary American life-styles is *Jeopardy*'s increasing popularity, alongside the declining popularity of "Trivial Pursuit." The latter requires assembling real people to play, but *Jeopardy* can be watched effortlessly in isolation. Still, both games are significant manifestations of trends in today's United

States. They hone skills increasingly valued by American culture. Both train people to process facts and figures. Videogames and home computers are additional adjuncts in the enculturation of future information processors. They, too, get young eyes riveted to a screen and perfect the hand–eye coordination needed for a high-tech, computer-dominated future.

WHERE'S THE WEATHER?

Brazil, thus, has deficient sports coverage and totally lacks awards and brain games. It has also avoided the familiar American tripartite division of local news into news, sports, and weather. One of the first "information" hunger pangs to develop within an American in Brazil concerns the weather. When I began to watch Brazilian TV in 1983, I was surprised to discover that evening news programs had no regular local, regional, or national weather reports. Weather was reported only when something unusual happened (a flood or drought). Could a nation larger than the contiguous United States, with nationwide, technically sophisticated television coverage, really do without regular weather forecasts and TV weather maps? Apparently so. I immediately noticed the absence of weather reports for the following personal reasons.

I arrived in Rio in early August 1983, expecting endless summer as a contrast to the Michigan winters I had lived with for 15 years. I found meteorological bleakness instead—70 days of gray skies and day-time temperatures in the seventies. Rio is known as "the marvelous city." However, the human-created blights (pollution, crime) that tarnish its natural beauty stood out vividly against the dreariness of that period.

On rare days when the sun did shine, millions of *cariocas* flocked to the beach. Still, an ocean dip was an adventure. TV news and headlines screamed of shoot-outs on fashionable Ipanema and Copacabana beaches. "Beach rats" (teenaged gangs) roamed unrestrained by police—grabbing and fleeing, sometimes stopping to assault. There were even reports of bathing suit robberies, as thieves "invited" more fashionably clad victims into the surf and demanded a suit exchange. Even if unmolested by robbers, it was hardly safe to take a dip. I tried sharing a wave one Sunday with a dozen other people. Rio's surf is strong and treacherous, and I cracked heads and legs with my neighbors. Under a wave I drank in water that the health department the next day declared polluted with feces. My family and I sought weekend escapes from the weather, the crowds, and the crime. However, the media never offered advice about whether good or bad weather in Rio also meant good or bad weather 100 miles away.

How, I wondered, could a vast nation, which experiences droughts, snows, freezes, and floods, take so little interest in the weather? I eventually discovered three reasons for this contrast with the weather-obsessed United States (which now even has a 24-hour cable weather channel). First, Brazil's weather is less variable than ours. Brazil is largely tropical, has fewer marked seasonal contrasts, and lacks the climatic extremes that show up on a U.S. weather map each winter. A second reason, reflecting a cultural rather than an environmental difference, is the (just-discussed) greater preoccupation with figures in the United States. The increasingly sophisticated and detailed weather reporting on American TV is merely one among many manifestations of a more general American preoccupation with information processing and measurement.

A third reason for Brazil's meager weather reporting is microenvironmental variation. Much of Brazilian television originates in Rio, where microenvironmental contrasts are marked. Because of close juxtaposition of mountains and sea, there is considerable weather variation on the coast near Rio. It is often sunny and warm one place and raining 25 miles away. The media have apparently concluded that there is not much point in trying to predict weather that often changes more within a particular state on a given day than from region to region or season to season.

I have examined contrasts between Brazil and the United States in the most popular program types and in the lessons, themes, settings, and social organization of those programs. Many other differences are apparent when one seeks on Brazilian TV such staples of American television as sports, awards, brain games, and the weather, and numeric information processing generally. News reports offer more similarities but still reveal cultural differences, to which I turn in the next chapter.

CHAPTER SEVEN

❧ What's News: Crime, Violence, and the Stranger

As in the United States, Brazilian network news broadcasts are tailored to fit the usual work day. They air at times when people (particularly consumers) are most likely to be at home. Brazilian men usually get home in time for the evening news. Many professional men also come home to eat a substantial midday meal, during which they may watch the early afternoon national news, which airs at 1:10 Monday through Friday. Linkups to satellite transmissions and international news agencies permit all Brazilian networks to offer competent and visually interesting local and national news. However, Globo, which sandwiches its evening news between its most popular *telenovelas*, is the overwhelming favorite. (This is true despite the fact that Globo, more often than the other networks, has been criticized for politically biased reporting.)

Our field research findings confirm the widespread popularity of Brazilian news broadcasts. These ranked first, second, or third (out of ten categories) among "programs usually watched" and second after *novelas* among "programs watched yesterday" in all our research sites (refer to Chapter 6, Tables 6.2 and 6.3). The most popular national news programs are broadcast from Rede Globo's Rio studios and air at 1:10 P.M. and 7:55 P.M., with the latter, *O Jornal Nacional,* drawing the larger audience. Throughout the nation, to millions of Brazilians—literate and illiterate, male and female, old and young, and of every social class—TV news brings in many cases otherwise unavailable information about the nation, the continent, Latin America, the hemisphere, and the world.

Except for the absence of sports and weather segments (in the local news), Brazilian TV news does not differ as obviously from American television standards and norms as do other program types. For several reasons, most Americans who read and understand Portuguese are probably more comfortable with televised than printed news in Brazil. First, because American and Brazilian networks draw on the same international transmissions and agencies, many of the same news images appear in both countries on a given day. Second, Brazil's TV news broadcasts are just as complete as their U.S. analogs (although focusing, of course, on a different nation).

Americans also may expect less or at least different things from TV news than from print news. For this reason they may find Brazilian TV news less different from its American counterpart than are other programs and newspapers. I personally found Brazilian newspaper reporting (particularly in Rio's *O Globo*) superficial, based on heresay and speculation, incomplete and often inaccurate. As a result, I had greater confidence in TV news.

One contrast between the two countries is that Brazil's national news has multiple anchors. Globo's *Jornal Nacional*, for example, has two anchormen. One is the nationally known, silver-haired, Walter Cronkite-like Cid Moreira. The other is an attractive younger man. Globo's midday news has a principal anchorwoman, Leda Nagle, supported by two lieutenant news readers, a woman and a man. Proportionate female representation is somewhat less in the news than in *telenovelas*, although female reporters and anchors are by no means rare. The female to male ratio among Brazilian TV reporters and news anchors seems about the same as in the United States.

Another similarity is evening scheduling. The pre-dinner local news immediately precedes the national news, and there is a final news wrap-up at 11 P.M. On the other hand, consumers in Brazil are more likely to be home at midday than they are in the United States. For this reason, Brazilian TV offers both national and local news at that time, whereas American networks offer no midday national news. However, many Americans supplement midday local news with Cable News Network, which carries national and international news (and sports and weather) 24 hours a day.

In terms of content and image, news and *telenovelas* present different Brazilian realities. The national news strives to portray Brazil as a large and important nation participating in international events. However, the news also reinforces the image of Brazil as a nation with major and virtually insoluble economic, political, and social problems. (Table 7.1 summarizes the national problems mentioned most often by our respondents.)

DaMatta's (1987) book *A Casa e a Rua (The House and the Street)* delineates three domains of social space recognized by Brazilian culture, running from *home,* through *street,* to the wider *public* world. These categories help us understand the place of the news and other TV program types in Brazilian life. The *telenovela* is about home. It deals with personal and domestic topics, such as family life and problems, marriage, and social climbing. *Novelas* are about Brazilian society rather than the Brazilian state. The news, in contrast, is about civics rather than society, about the public rather than the private realm. Local news focuses on the immediate public sphere—street and city. Specifically, local news examines the threats (crime, protests, strikes, pollution, traffic foul-ups) that the streets pose to person, home, family, and society.

The national news has two main objectives: (1) to report events that are significant for Brazil as a nation-state and (2) to show the multiple links

TABLE 7.1 *Responses to "What Are Brazil's Biggest Problems?"*

	NUMBER	PERCENTAGE
Inflation	375	17.2
Foreign debt	339	15.6
Un(der)employment	240	11.0
Economic crisis/*plano cruzado*	221	10.2
Hunger	182	8.4
Politics	134	6.2
Educational deficiencies	91	4.2
Poverty	71	3.3
All others[a]	518	23.8
Total	2174	100.0

[a]*More than 20 other problems, each mentioned by less than 3 percent of respondents.*

that Brazil maintains with the rest of the world. The national news stresses the Brazilian's role as citizen (rather than as a member of a family, or of a society based on personal social networks). Local news depicts the middle domain—the street—as disorderly and dangerous. However, the national news strives to present the nation as reasonably orderly and, despite its problems, as capable of maintaining its sovereignty in an international community. The portrayal of the Brazilian nation in the national news is analogous to the portrayal of the Brazilian family in *telenovelas*. Families have problems and overcome them while maintaining their dignity and integrity. Family members manage to forge external links and to rise in life. So, too, can Brazil survive, prosper, and increase its international prominence.

We can now perceive the significance of another similarity between American and Brazilian news. Both are about civics, the nation-state, and international affairs. Both recognize that nations are increasingly interdependent participants in international economic and political systems. There are even similarities in specific content. Because the United States and Brazil are the world's foremost debtor nations, it is no wonder that balance of payment figures are newsworthy in both.

Globo's *Jornal Nacional* has a characteristic structure. It habitually starts with economic news, then turns to politics. The economic news, usually bad, focuses on one of the problems identified in Table 7.1 (for example, inflation, the foreign debt, shortages, unemployment). However, some representative of the Brazilian state is always shown seeking a solution. Scenes of meetings in Brasilia with officials of the International Monetary Fund are frequent. The news also broadcasts interviews from abroad, such as one with three governors from the northeast who had traveled to Washington seeking World Bank loans for their drought-stricken region.

As the news widens its lens beyond the Brazilian nation, it first mentions other South American nations. Then comes the rest of Latin America, and finally Europe, the United States, and the rest of the world. Usually, another country finds its way into the news because of some link with Brazil, for instance, a new ambassador or a visit by a high official. The news may mention a European country because of some policy that affects Latin America (for instance, the Soviet Union vis-à-vis Nicaragua).

After economy, the national news turns to politics. In the mid- and late 1980s the main issues were (1) how and when the president would be elected and (2) activities and conflicts within the constitutional assembly, which convened in Brasília following the end of military rule to draft a new constitution. Internationally oriented stories follow; these may be political, economic, or human interest.

The final segment is often about the United States and focuses on some technological aspect of American society. In 1987–88, issues of reproductive technology, such as test-tube babies and surrogate motherhood, proved popular. Brazilians found such stories particularly interesting because they confirmed the stereotype of American society as developed but flawed. The United States may be technologically innovative, but it is an Anglo-Saxon nation that lacks a Latin soul. Because of this, American culture sometimes carries its know-how and inventiveness to inhumane extremes. Such stories appeal to Brazilians because they suggest that power, influence, and technology are insufficient to warrant full international respect. By contrast, they suggest that Brazil, despite its troubled economy and polity, has something enduring and valuable that many other nations lack: warmth and humanity.

CRIME IN THE STREETS

One fundamental contrast between American and Brazilian television is that American entertainment programming presents many more violent acts than occur in reality, whereas Brazilian prime-time programs contain fewer such acts. Despite this difference, there seems to be at least as much violence in Brazilian as in American society. This illustrates that there is no simple relationship between violence on TV and in real life. (Accurate comparisons between televised crime and real crime in Brazil are impossible. Brazilian crime statistics are rarely published, and are inaccurate when they are published.)

Telenovelas are generally nonviolent. Violence and other adult themes increase with the hour. The 8 o'clock *novela* has more violence than the two earlier ones, and 10 P.M. programs have even more. At the start of its 10 o'clock show Globo announces that it is approved only for ages 10 and older. On the other hand, in sharp contrast to entertainment programs, the local *news* offers frequent reports of assaults and other acts of violence. In the Brazilian media, reports of violent acts increase from national TV news (fewest), to local TV news, to newspapers (most). (The rural respondents we interviewed relied on radio and television equally—and 50 percent more than they did on newspapers—as sources of information about crime.[1] However, Brazilians with easy access to all three media say they get more of their crime information from television.)[2]

Expectably, local news concentrates on events in the channel's immediate broadcasting area (such as greater Rio). This is true to a greater extent than in the United States. American local news includes a considerable amount of national information (all the day's professional sports scores, a visit by a national politician, activities of local delegates at a national political convention). Like American local news, however, the Brazilian version dotes on crime. It recites a litany of robberies, assaults, shoot-outs, murders, and prison escapes. It also reports on protests, strikes, and quasihumorous local happenings, such as the appearance of a boa constrictor in the kitchen of a local school.

For reasons discussed in Chapter 5, law enforcement officers are rare *novela* characters. However, civil and military police do show up regularly in the news, particularly the local news, as do criminals and prisoners. All these figures belong to the anarchic middle domain of the street, rather than to either the family or the nation. The low social status of law officers reflects the suspicion that Brazilians have of this social domain.

Brazil offers one particularly striking contrast with the United States in crime reporting. Press and officials alike frequently violate due process and criminal rights (which are virtually nonexistent in Brazil). The difference in legal codes between countries (guilty until proven innocent in Brazil) is obvious in the news. Police routinely declare the guilt of a fugitive or prisoner who would be described as a "suspect' or "alleged perpetrator" in the United States. TV reporters invade police stations and push microphones into a prisoner's face. They ask such incriminating questions as "Hey Pedro, tell us why you killed your wife." In one story about a prisoner who had just escaped with two hostages, a reporter broadcast directly from his newly vacated cell. She proceeded to rummage through the convict's personal belongings, finally holding up a book about the criminal mind that he had been reading just before his escape.

Although crime is more common in Brazil's local news than its national news, real-life violence is by no means missing in the latter. One evening the Globo network showed graphic footage of a man shooting one of his neighbor's three (adult) sons at the fence separating their homes. The sons were confronting the assailant because he had accused their mother of allowing prostitution in her home. Globo gave national coverage to the bloody spectacle of the gunman pumping three bullets into his victim.

Although infrequent in entertainment programming, crime was a news obsession during my 1983–84 stay in Brazil. Infractions of the law, particularly in Rio and São Paulo, received daily attention in news broadcasts and particularly in the press. One of the more ironic incidents occurred in

Rio in December 1983. Globo's local news team, on its way to cover a story about lack of security in an outlying neighborhood, was assaulted by a man who leaned in the window of their car, which had stopped for a traffic light. (Brazilians attribute their habit of running red lights, especially after dark, to fear of such assaults.)

Crime reports occur cyclically, pervading the media at certain times. One such cycle occurred in December 1983, just before Christmas. Another began in June 1984, when *O Globo* launched an attack on the governor of Rio de Janeiro state. The newspaper reported that national congressmen were appalled at Rio's lack of safety and had concluded that bandits were running Rio. Concurrently, Brazil's most popular newsmagazine ran a cover story about people learning self-defense and arming themselves with weapons (easily bought at sporting goods stores).

Crime reports seemed to increase whenever new TV advertising campaigns began. Globo usually started showing new commercials not individually, but with a cluster of ads debuting seasonally. Although I did not investigate the matter systematically, I suspected Globo of deliberately increasing crime coverage to make the outside world seem more dangerous. The effect would be for people to stay home and watch the new commercials. A spate of crime reports a few weeks before Christmas certainly fits this interpretation.

I noticed a similar association between bank commercials and TV crime reports. Bank ads urge viewers to open a savings account. These occur during, and just before and after, Globo's national news (and therefore also just after the crime-filled local news). Just before Globo's national news comes a digital announcement of the correct time (for instance, 7:54:35; the news starts at 7:55) "brought to you by" a particular bank. The news usually begins with the latest on Brazil's monetary problems. A bank commercial intervenes between money and politics, the normal next segment. Later, a savings account ad follows a report of a robbery, assault, prison escape, or counterfeiting ring. Someone seems to be using the following reasoning: News reports about economic uncertainty and crime increase worries about the security of one's money and thus promote banking. I rarely saw bank ads on programs other than the news. (However, illustrating Globo's common use of within-program commercials, *novela* characters often visit or converse in front of an identifiable bank.)

Along with monetary and political turmoil, urban violence (*violência*) has raged in Brazil and has dominated the news since the mid-1980s. This violence was manifest in 1983 supermarket sackings, which the media reported extensively and thereby helped perpetuate. More enduring and frightening than the grocery store sackings were various kinds of assault. The media and word of mouth provided constant reports about crime in the streets. Gangs of boys confronted pedestrians and demanded money or jewelry. Adapting to crime, urban Brazilians carried separately their own and "the thief's" money, to turn over when the confrontation finally occurred. Occasionally, even when victims handed over their money or possessions (but usually only when they resisted) assailants would stab or shoot them.

Foreign tourists were especially vulnerable. Often, they were unaware that jewelry, loaded wallets, purses, and expensive-looking cameras should be left in a hotel safe, rather than taken to the beach or carried in the streets. Furthermore, these tourists didn't understand the Portuguese language or Brazilian culture. They did not respond to assaults as the thieves expected Brazilians to respond. Their unpredictable reactions sometimes frightened perpetrators and resulted in unintended physical harm.

Crime was on everyone's mind, and inaccurate and imprecise reporting exacerbated fears. *O Globo* reported one day that the president of the Brazilian Press Association had been robbed, shot, and killed in his car. The following day the (usually more reliable) *Jornal do Brasil* published the real story. It wasn't the president, but his chauffeur—asleep in the car—who had been robbed, but not shot. The president hadn't been approached at all.

According to a poll published in December 1983, Rio's three most serious problems were inadequate policing, thieves, and lack of hospitals. A Gallup poll in the *Jornal do Brasil* (based on personal experiences with crime) showed violent incidents to be as frequent in São Paulo as in Rio. Almost 40 percent of respondents in each city answered yes to the question "Have you ever been assaulted?" (The fact that no time period was attached to the question augmented the perception of crime's pervasiveness.) The same poll reported that 70 percent of metropolitan São Paulo respondents considered security their city's major problem. Ninety-six percent of *paulistas* and 82 percent of *cariocas* believed that assaults and crimes were increasing in their city.

Rio and São Paulo have several reported murders each week. However, the random, impersonal crimes that Americans often hear about are rare in Brazil. Having lived in Brazil in 1983–84, and visiting annually since, I have yet to hear of an impersonal mass murderer. Never, to my knowledge, has a psychopathic Brazilian killer randomly selected victims in a public place. The most notorious murder case I know of involved a young man who shot and stabbed his mother, father, and three brothers. He did this after his mother shouted at him for playing his stereo too loud in the middle of the night.

Brazilian murders are almost always for gain, and they usually involve people who know one another. (This, by the way, is also truer in the United States than the media accounts, which focus on the unusual and sensational, lead us to believe.) Brazil is a more personal society than the United States.[3] Robbers sometimes engage victims in conversation, telling them intimate details of their lives. Often, assailants take the time to explain that poverty or family problems drove them to crime. Many offer sincere apologies for their actions.

VIOLENCE IN CONTENT

Chapter 3 described how, under military rule (through March 1985), Brazil had much more press and television censorship of various sorts than does the United States. The Brazilian censors concentrated, however, on politics and violence rather than on nudity and sex. There is still much less violence on Brazilian than American TV. Such American cartoons as *Roadrunner*, with its never-ending celebration of animal masochism, are shown throughout the day in Brazil, but attract small audiences. Globo shows its own productions from 5 P.M. to midnight. After several months of watching mostly Brazilian programs, the occasional American movie I saw there on the late show did strike me as brutal. My impression is based in fact. By age 16 the typical young American will have seen 18,000 televised murders (Smith 1985).

Tracking American television content for violence, Gerbner found prime time to contain five to six violent acts per hour. This figure changed little in a 17-year study (Smith 1985). However, another study singled out the 1984–85 television season for particularly violent content. There were fewer situation comedies and more action series that year than in either the preceding or following years. Another reason for more violence that year was that 30 percent of homes were receiving a pay cable service. Cable movie channels routinely show uncut feature films containing graphic violence. Another monitor of violence in American productions is the Illinois-based National Coalition on Television Violence. That group counted an average of 28 violent episodes per hour in movies released in the United States during summer 1984 (*Ann Arbor News* 1984:C1). Nowadays, such films are routinely available to American viewers on cable, through VCRs, and in prime time.

Aiding the visual depiction of the mayhem that is so characteristic of American film content are advances in makeup and special effects, permitting graphic portrayals of cruelty and horror. Another trend in the portrayal of violence on American TV (and in films) is a blurring of images of good and evil. The distinction between heroes and villains is becoming less clear-cut. This reflects the current American tendency to attribute bad deeds to psychological problems, rather than to inherent evil (Smith 1985). To explain antisocial behavior, Brazilians, in contrast, are much more likely to mention economic deprivation or poor law enforcement than criminals' psychological attributes.

One genre of violent movie recently popular in the United States has not done very well in Brazil. This is the dead teenager film, exemplified by *Halloween, Friday the Thirteenth*, and their sequels and imitators. These movies, which are widely available through cable and videocassettes, have virtually the same plot. As a psychopath graphically kills off a group of teenagers one by one, these films offer alienating lessons: The world is dangerous. Friends cannot be counted on. Evil may not win, but it sure does come close. The most ubiquitous lesson, however, is about female sexuality. Girls shouldn't have premarital sex. The survivor is almost always the girl who does not give in to sexual temptation. Murders often take place right after a couple has had sexual intercourse. (One spoof of the genre, *Saturday the Fourteenth*, parodied this. It ran an ad featuring a cheerleader with a button proclaiming "Sex Kills.")

It should come as no surprise that Brazilians don't make slasher films. This American violence goes beyond anything I have ever seen in a Brazilian production. Random impersonal violence, which slasher films depict, is out of place in Brazilian culture. Furthermore, because only people 18 and older would be allowed to see such films, they wouldn't find much of an audience in Brazil.

The antifemale violence of the typical slasher film no doubt has provided symbolic expression for male resentment toward feminism. Feminists are correct that such films degrade women. Slasher movies were also a reaction to a sexual revolution that is now in hasty retreat. The dead teenager film vividly reaffirmed the Puritan belief that sex does not pay. I think that the role of AIDS in curbing promiscuity helps explain the declining popularity (in theaters at least) of slasher movies. Sexual caution has increased for millions of Americans, who are concerned about fatal sexually transmitted diseases. Gazing into the cruel face of a real-life threat from promiscuity, contemporary American culture has less need for hockey-masked Jasons to punish sexual transgressions.

What effect does media violence have on human behavior? We can extend advertising's basic assumption that messages influence behavior. It seems reasonable to suppose that when children watch a daily average of more than six hours of American television, they become somewhat inured to mayhem, injury, and physical destruction. Their perceptions of social reality may be influenced. I am not thinking of cartoons, which do contain multiple violent episodes. I think that kids distinguish between cartoons and the real world. Rather, I have in mind the cops-and-robbers programs that have been popular on American television. Such action series contrast very strongly with real-life events and experiences. How many machine guns or exploding cars has the average American ever seen? How many are seen each week on TV?

Gerbner and associates in the annual "Violence Profiles," published in the *Journal of Communication,* have reported consistent and significant relationships between degree of television exposure and perceptions of the frequency of violent acts in American society. Researchers asked Americans, "During any given week, what are your chances of being involved in some kind of violence—about 1 in 10 or about 1 in 100?" Heavy viewers (at least six hours daily) were more likely than light viewers (less than two hours) to give the "television answer" (1 in 10) versus the "real-life answer." The first answer reflects happenings on television. The second response (1 in 100) more closely matches census data. It reflects the real-life conditions of most Americans.

Comparable Brazilian crime-rate, social, and demographic data are scarce and unreliable. Thus, we could not do a parallel assessment of differences between "real-life" and "television answers" there. However, we did ask many questions derived from characteristic Brazilian TV content. We wanted to determine whether dominant *telenovela* themes and news issues, for example, were associated with particular perceptions among heavy viewers. I discuss the results in later chapters.

DOES TV VIOLENCE INCREASE SUBSEQUENT AGGRESSIVENESS?

Research has yet to confirm any simple causal link between mayhem in the media and in the real world. Antisocial behavior has many causes besides TV. The juxtaposition of predominantly nonviolent programming with real-life violence in Brazil surely confirms this. Poverty and inequality probably make much more potent contributions to violence and crime than does television. Statistical associations between unemployment, poverty, and crime rates have been well documented in the United States and other nations. TV's precise effects on social behavior remain uncertain. However, I see no reason to doubt that TV content can mesmerize and motivate certain types of people. Viewers may mimic behaviors, both positive and negative, they see on television.

Several studies (reviewed by Smith 1985) go further, suggesting that media violence can harm normal people. In one study, steady viewing of graphic violence, including sexual assault, was associated with greater tolerance for and less disapproval of rape and wife-beating.[4] In another study, sampling a 30-year period, the Washington-based Center for Media and Public Affairs focused on violent content of 500 American television programs. It concluded that inordinate violence does affect viewers. A monumental review study published by the National Institute of Mental Health in 1982 also linked exposure to media violence with aggressive behavior in American children. In September 1984, the Attorney General's Task Force on Family Violence concluded that

> the evidence is becoming overwhelming that just as witnessing violence in the home may contribute to normal adults and children learning and acting out violent behavior, violence on TV and movies may lead to the same result. (Smith 1985:25)

However, another study strongly challenges such findings. Freedman (1984) did an extensive review of field and laboratory studies and correlational research on the effects of TV violence on aggressiveness. He wanted to determine just how much scientific evidence there is for the hypothesis that viewing television violence increases subsequent aggressiveness. His review examined "every relevant article" in the main scholarly journals "as well as published books and appropriate government publications." Freedman found a small but consistent (positive) correlation between viewing TV violence and agressiveness. However, he failed to find any "convincing evidence" that television violence causes people to be more aggressive in natural settings.

> There is little difficulty in providing an alternative explanation [rather than the hypothesis stated above] of the relation between viewing television violence and aggressiveness: *Those individuals who prefer violent television programs also tend to be aggressive.* More simply, something in their personalities or behavior patterns, some predisposition, trait, combination of environmental pressures, learning history, or whatever, causes people to like aggressive programming and also to be aggressive. [emphasis added] (Freedman 1984: 244)

DOMINANT THEMES: THE QUEST AND THE STRANGER

There are many causes besides television for fears, insecurities, and violence in the contemporary United States. These include poverty, inequality, the impersonality of American society, and the erosion of family ties, particularly the decline of the extended family. Brazilians still spend much of their leisure time with their extended families. Americans, however, are in constant contact, at work and play, with strangers. These nonkin relationships become increasingly important as a growing percentage of the American population works full time. In Brazil, the extended family, swollen by a population explosion, provides an ample homemade social network. In the United States, our social and economic lives depend on converting strangers into friends. Much of what Americans see and talk about, in media and real life, reflects their dealings with strangers. The need to create and maintain so many relationships beyond the family engenders many insecurities.

In their works of fiction, whether literature, cinema, or television, Brazilians are much less concerned with nonfamily settings and relationships. They are also less fanciful than Americans. Suspense, horror, and fantasy are rare in Brazilian productions, but are key elements of American works. A Brazilian reviewer of a rare Brazilian suspense film, *Shock*, found it "surprising that in Brazil someone would be competent to make a film of terror and suspense"(*Veja* March 14, 1984a:12). It isn't that Americans are escapists, whereas Brazilians prefer realism. Rather, Brazilians imagine their own kinds of escapes, which occur through changes in material circumstances. Thus, as we have seen, the most prominent themes in Brazilian *telenovelas* are transformations in wealth, power, and social position.

There is a Brazilian adage that life in that country requires a sense of humor (Wagley 1963:302). However, I found that humor, which is a playful form of escapism, was much less obvious on Brazilian than American television. The main reason for this was probably censorship. Traditionally, much of the best Brazilian humor has been political satire, which the government monitored more carefully on television than in the press. Brazilians are highly critical of politicians and cynical about their motives (Wagley 1963:296). One illustration of Brazilian political humor was a 1983 column in a São Paulo newspaper (*Folha de São Paulo* Dec. 12, 1983). It described the making (then in progress) of *Return of the Jedi.* The column called the character Jabba the Hut "irresistibly comparable to a well-known figure on the Brazilian political scene [then Finance Minister Delphim Neto]."

Because of cultural background, historical experience, economic necessity, and media reinforcement, Americans are mobile, exploratory people. We dote on wide open spaces. Brazilians, however, prefer densely packed cities and constant human contact. The American pursuit of the frontier has given us a history replete with travel and encounters with strangers. Growing up in America still entails separation from those who raised us. Issues of venturing out, breaking with home, and creating ties with strangers have been critically important in American history. It is no wonder then that so many American creations express these themes. The joy of the journey and the thrill of the quest continue. One illustration is that for more than two decades Americans fans have religiously followed a group of fictional characters whose goal is "to boldly go where no one has gone before."

CASE ANALYSIS: *STAR TREK* AS A SUMMATION OF DOMINANT AMERICAN CULTURAL THEMES

For a case analysis drawn from contemporary American culture, I use a TV series familiar to most readers. This will illustrate that popular media content derives from prominent values expressed in many other domains of culture. With an undiminished, perhaps growing, popularity spanning more than two decades, *Star Trek* is an enduring and powerful force in American popular culture. It provides excellent illustration of such dominant content themes as the quest, and the incorporation of strangers and diversity within an expansive American culture.

Americans first encountered the *Starship Enterprise* on NBC in 1966. *Star Trek* occupied prime time for just three seasons. However, the series not only survives but thrives today in reruns, books, cassettes, and theatrical films. In just a year (1987–88) *Star Trek: The Next Generation* became the third most popular syndicated program in the United States (after *Wheel of Fortune* and *Jeopardy*).

Star Trek has generated a multifaceted spin-off industry, which illustrates TV's potential role in spurring creative activity among natives. Fans write their own stories and novels featuring *Star Trek* characters. They use videocassette recorders to compile collections of *Star Trek* episodes—just as American kids a generation ago hoarded comics and serial pulp literature. Not only are there *Star Trek* fan clubs and annual conventions, there are also special interest groups (such as feminists and Vulcan sympathizers) (Schonauer 1988).

What does the enduring mass appeal of *Star Trek* tell us about American culture? *Star Trek is a transformation of a fundamental American origin myth.* The same myth shows up in the image and celebration of Thanksgiving, a distinctively American holiday. Thanksgiving sets the myth in the past and *Star Trek* sets it in the future. (In Chapter 11, I explore similar associations between an important Brazilian holiday—Carnival—media content, and fundamental cultural values and symbols.)

Encountering the word *myth,* most Americans probably think of stories about Greek, Roman, or Norse gods and heroes. However, all societies have their distinctive myths. Their central characters need not be unreal, superhuman, or physically immortal. Such tales may be rooted in actual historical events.

> The popular notion that a "myth" is . . . "untrue"—indeed that its untruth is its defining characteristic—is not only naive but shows misunderstanding of its very nature. Its "scientific truth" or otherwise is irrelevant. A myth is a statement about society and man's place in it and the surrounding universe. (Middleton 1967: x)

Myths are hallowed stories, expressing fundamental cultural values. They are widely and recurrently told among, and have special meaning to, people who grow up in a given culture. Myths may be set in past, present, future or in a fantasy land. Whether set in real time or fictional time, myths are always at least partly fictionalized.

The myths of contemporary America are drawn from a variety of sources including such popular-culture fantasies as *Star Wars, The Wizard of Oz* (Kottak 1982), and *Star Trek*. Our myths also include real people, particularly national ancestors, whose lives have been reinterpreted and endowed with special meaning over the generations. The media, schools, churches, communities, and parents teach the national origin myths to American children. The story of Thanksgiving, for example, continues to be important. It recounts the origin of a national holiday celebrated by Protestants, Catholics, and Jews. All those denominations share a belief in the Old Testament God, and they find it appropriate to thank him or her for their blessings.

Again and again Americans have heard idealized retellings of that epochal early harvest. We have learned how Indians taught Pilgrims to farm in the New World. Grateful Pilgrims then invited the Indians to share their first Thanksgiving. Native American and European labor, techniques, and customs were thereby blended in that initial biethnic celebration.[5] Annually reenacting the origin myth, American public schools commemorate the first Thanksgiving as children dress up as Pilgrims, Indians, and pumpkins.

More rapidly and pervasively as the mass media grow, each generation of Americans writes its own revisionist history. Our culture constantly reinterprets the origin, nature, and meaning of national holidays. The collective consciousness of contemporary Americans includes TV-saturated memories of "The First Thanksgiving" and "The First Christmas." Our mass culture has instilled widely shared images of a "Peanuts"-peopled Pilgrim–Indian "love-in."

We also conjure up a fictionalized Nativity with Mary, Joseph, Jesus, manger animals, shepherds, three oriental kings, a little drummer boy, and, in some versions, Rudolph the Red-Nosed Reindeer. Note that the interpretation of the Nativity that American culture perpetuates is yet another variation on the same dominant myth. We remember the Nativity as a Thanksgiving involving interethnic contacts (for example, the three kings) and gift-giving. It is set in Bethlehem rather than Massachusetts.

We impose our present on the past as we reinterpret quasihistoric and actual events. For the future we do it in our science fiction and fantasy creations. *Star Trek* places in the future what the Thanksgiving story locates in the past: *the myth of the assimilationist, incorporating, melting pot society.* The myth says that America is distinctive not just because it is assimilationist, but because it is *founded on* unity in diversity. (Our *origin* is unity in diversity. After all, we call ourselves "the United States.") Thanksgiving and *Star Trek* illustrate the credo that unity through diversity is essential for survival (whether of a harsh winter or the perils of outer space). Americans survive by sharing the fruits of specialization.

Star Trek proclaims that sacred principles that validate American society, because they lie at its foundation, will endure across the generations and even the centuries. The Starship Enterprise crew is a melting pot. Captain James Tiberius Kirk is symbolic of real history. His clearest historical prototype is Captain James Cook, whose ship the *Endeavor* also sought out new life and civilizations. Kirk's infrequently mentioned middle name, from the Roman general and eventual emperor, links the captain to Earth's imperial history. Kirk is also symbolic of the original Anglo-American. He runs the *Enterprise* (America is founded on free enterprise), just as laws, values, and institutions derived from England continue to run the United States.[6]

McCoy's Irish (or at least Gaelic) name represents the next wave, the by now established immigrant. Sulu is the successfully assimilated Asian-American. The African-American female character Uhura, whose name means "freedom," proclaims that blacks will become full partners with all other Americans. However, Uhura was the only major female character in the original crew. This reflects the fact that female extradomestic employment was less characteristic of American society in 1966 than it is now.

One of *Star Trek's* constant messages is that strangers, even enemies, can become friends. Less obviously, this message is about cultural imperialism, the assumed irresistibility of American culture and institutions. Even communist nationals (Chekhov) can be seduced and captured by an expansive American culture. Spock, although from Vulcan, is half-human, with human qualities. We learn, therefore, that our assimilationist values will eventually not just rule all Earth, but extend to other planets as well. With *The Next Generation,* Klingon culture, yet more alien than Vulcan and personified by Bridge Officer Worf, has joined the melting pot.

Even God is harnessed to serve American culture, in the person of Scotty. His role is that of the ancient Greek *deus ex machina*. He is a stage controller who "beams" people up and down, back and forth, from Earth to the heavens. Scotty, who keeps society going, is also a servant–employee who does his engineering best for management—illustrating loyalty and technical skill.

The Next Generation contains many analogs of the original characters. Several "partial people" are single-character personifications of particular human qualities represented in more complex form by original *Star Trek* crew members. Kirk, Spock, and McCoy have all been split into multiple characters. Captain Jean-Luc Picard has the intellectual and managerial attributes of James T. Kirk. With his English accent and French name, Picard, like Kirk, draws his legitimacy from symbolic association with historic Western European empires. First Officer Riker replaces Kirk as romantic man of action.

Spock—alien (strange ears), science, reason, intellect—has been split in two. One is Worf, a Klingon bridge officer whose cranial protuberances are analogous to Spock's ears. The other is Data, an android whose brain contains the sum of human wisdom. Two female characters, an empath (Troi) and the ship's doctor (Pulaski), have replaced Dr. McCoy as the repository of healing, emotion, and feeling.

Mirroring its creators' 1980's culture, *The Next Generation* contains prominent black, female, and physically handicapped characters. A black actor plays the Klingon Mr. Worf. Another appears as Geordi La Forge. Although blind, Geordi manages, through a vision-enhancing visor, to see things that other people cannot. His mechanical vision expresses the characteristic American faith in technology. So does the android Data.

During its first year, *The Next Generation* had three prominent female characters. One was the ship's Medical Officer, Dr. Crusher, a working professional with a teenaged son (Wes). Another was an empath, the ultimate helping professional. The third was the ship's Security Officer, Lieutenant Yar.

Contemporary America is more specialized, differentiated, and professional than the same nation was in the 1960s. The greater role specificity and diversity of *Next Generation* characters reflects this. Nevertheless, both series convey the central *Star Trek* message, one that dominates the culture that created them: Americans have varied backgrounds. Individual qualities, talents, and specialties divide us. However, we make our livings and survive as members of cohesive, efficient groups. We explore and advance as members of a crew, team, enterprise, or, most generally, a society. Our nation is founded on and endures through assimilation— effective subordination of individual differences within a smoothly functioning multi-ethnic team. The team is American culture. It worked in the past. It works today. It will go on working across the generations. Orderly and progressive democracy based on mutual respect is best. Inevitably, American culture will triumph over all others—by convincing and assimilating, rather than conquering. Unity in diversity guarantees human survival, and for this we should be thankful.

ANTHROPOLOGY AND THE QUEST

The American preoccupation with adventure, exploration, and forging social relationships among strangers shows up not just in television, films, and fiction, but in science—for example, in anthropology. Every introductory course states that anthropology differs from sociology and psychology because of its global and comparative perspective. American anthropology is rooted in respect for the alien, the different, the other. A basic assumption is that statements about human life, society, and behavior should come from study of many cultures rather than just one.

Sociologists, psychologists, political scientists, and economists study primarily their own societies. However, American (and British and French) anthropology requires fieldwork somewhere else. This is why Margaret Mead studied adolescent behavior in Samoa and why I did my anthropological apprenticeship in a Brazilian fishing village. It is also why I went to Brazil to study television.

However, this quest for the other is undeveloped in Brazilian anthropology. Most Brazilian anthropologists do not undertake fieldwork abroad or conduct cross-cultural studies. Instead, they do research on national issues and Brazilian subgroups, such as homosexuals, prostitutes, working-class communities, and domestic employees. Of dozens of presentations I heard at one annual meeting of the Association of Brazilian Anthropologists, not one reported on research outside Brazil.

Although American anthropologists also study their own society, most do so only after having done prior fieldwork elsewhere. Foreign research removes us from our own culture. It furnishes us with intimate knowledge of another society. It eventually makes us skeptical of explanations that fellow natives of our own society offer and accept without question. Anthropologists who study their own culture after working elsewhere can combine the expertise of the native with the detachment of the observer who knows that human nature varies from one society to another. That is what I am trying to do in *Prime-Time Society*.

Both cultural tradition and practical reasons explain why Brazilians do less foreign research. Brazil lacks the plethora of funding agencies available in the United States. A second reason is that Brazil still has isolated, technologically primitive Indian populations, which may be studied without leaving the country. However, the third reason is cultural: The United States has stronger traditions of exploration and of dealing with strangers than does Brazil.

In 1984, I spent weeks interviewing anthropology graduate students in Rio before finding two to participate in my television impact project. Fieldwork for the project required at least nine months of residence in small communities in other states. Anthropologists had previously studied all those towns, and all were perfectly pleasant places. My main problem was not any lack of competent, interesting graduate students, but finding people willing to leave Rio. Eventually I did find two, Rosane Prado and Alberto Costa, but neither was a native of "the marvelous city."

American history prepares us for exploration, strangers, and alienation. The same is true of the British and French, who became world explorers and later anthropologists, in their empires' most distant territories. Nor, apparently, were the early Portuguese explorers, leaders during the age of discovery, reluctant to travel abroad. Sometime between Brazil's settlement and today, that mentality of exploration has disappeared. The images of sand, surf, glamour, and the good life that characterize Globo *telenovelas* seem to have mesmerized Brazilians, just as staged car crashes and space fascinate Americans.

PART THREE

The Local Level

CHAPTER EIGHT

🐚 The Field Sites

The realization of multilocale ethnographic texts, of even regional analysis as it now exists, may entail a novel kind of fieldwork. Rather than being situated in one, or perhaps two communities for the entire period of research, the fieldworker must be mobile, covering a network of sites that encompasses a process, which is in fact the object of study. (Marcus and Fisher 1986: 94)

Recall that the research project on which this book is based was a multi-tiered study of Brazilian television at national and local levels.[1] My national-level work and content study, basic to previous chapters, occurred between August 1983 and August 1984. During that year, I interviewed television experts and did archival and statistical research in Brazil's media research organizations.[2] The next stage in the project was a series of local-level studies by Brazilian and American researchers.[3]

This local-level research began in January 1985. We eventually studied six communities in different parts of Brazil. Our four main sites were in the southern state of Santa Catarina (Ibirama), the southcentral state of São Paulo (Cunha), the northeastern state of Bahia (Arembepe), and the Amazonian state of Pará (Gurupá). Anthropologists had previously studied all these communities at least 20 years earlier, well before TV reached them.[4]

Our project developed a set of uniform quantitative and qualitative procedures to collect data at each site. We used two printed questionnaires (more accurately, interview schedules, because interviewers rather than respondents wrote down the answers). These served as the basis for 1879 structured interviews, ranging over hundreds of variables. We used one such schedule for 847 households and another one for 1032 individuals.

Our strategy was one of controlled comparison. Thus, our research design held constant several factors across the main sites. First, overriding their diversity in region and background, the people we studied were all Brazilians. They spoke the same language: Portuguese. Second, anthropologists had previously studied the four main sites, using comparable techniques. Third, the four communities were traditional small towns with dependent rural zones. All were fairly poor, considering the scale of socioeconomic variation in Brazil as a whole. Fourth, our methods and instruments were the same at all sites. We started by building rapport and

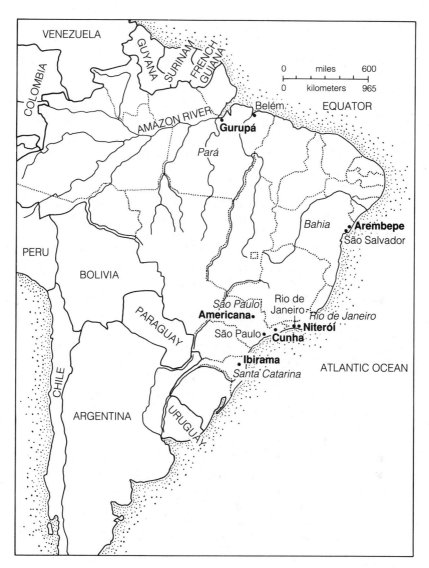

The six field sites.

developing contacts and local networks. We aimed for in-depth understanding of local life before beginning formal interviewing. Fifth, we did these studies simultaneously, so that all our informants (with TV sets) were witnessing the same programs and national events.

As is typical of anthropological research, we used a mixed set of procedures, in this case to assess television's impact in each community. We employed traditional ethnographic procedures: observation of behavior, participant observation, informal interviewing, rapport building, work with well-informed informants, and collection of life histories. Ethnography provided familiarity with each community and, eventually, a basis for representative sampling.

Having developed the ethnographic background, we began formal interviewing, using two detailed interview schedules. Sampling was necessary because our communities were larger than those usually studied by ethnographers. Their populations ranged from 2000 to over 20,000 people. Because we could not interview everyone, we had to choose representative smaller study groups (that is, samples) in each community. Our samples had to represent men and women, people of different ages, rural dwellers and townsfolk, and the gamut of local occupations, income levels, and social classes.

To construct our samples we used a combination of network sampling and random procedures. Procedures developed for village impact studies by Jorgensen (1982) guided our network sampling.[5] These anthropological sampling methods seemed more appropriate for our small-scale locales and in-depth interviewing than did a more impersonal probability sampling design.

What are the steps in constructing a network sample? First, identify local social categories and their demographic characteristics through ethnography and by consulting with experts. These should include locally based government statistical agents, if any. (There were such experts in our larger sites.) Use start-up informants and cross-cutting chains in significant categories to build research networks and for personal introductions to interviewees. Attempt to represent proportionately all significant local social categories.

In our project, we took particular care to represent households and people with and without television, even if this meant oversampling one group or the other. To **oversample** is to include a larger percentage of a particular group in one's sample than there is in the population as a whole. Oversampling is usually done because the group in question is small, but is of special interest to the study. We oversampled (1) the few households with sets in barely exposed communities and (2) the few households without TVs in places where most people had sets.

We used network sampling procedures (informed by locally resident government statisticians) in Cunha and Ibirama. In the Amazon town of Gurupá, more traditional sampling procedures supplemented network sampling. In this low exposure community, researcher Richard Pace mapped the town and randomly chose a representative number of houses in each area. He also interviewed in all TV households, because there were so few of them. In backwater areas, reached by canoe, he interviewed in every other house (all lacked sets).

We also oversampled households without TV and people with no or low exposure in Arembepe—particularly in the rural areas, where there was no electricity. (As in Gurupá, electricity arrived in those areas just as our data collection was ending.)

Why was oversampling necessary? We wanted to maximize cases of households that *lacked television for reasons beyond their own control* (for example, no electricity). We were not looking for Brazilians who had consciously rejected TV or who were too poor to afford a set. Such people would not be typical Brazilians, just as Americans who reject television are statistical oddballs within their mass culture. However, our samples from the more TV-saturated sites inevitably did include a few people who had made conscious choices not to have a television set at home.

Although our sampling was not consistently random, we took care to make our network samples representative. We did this through ethnography and by consulting resident government statisticians with intimate knowledge of each site. We believe that our use of network sampling enhanced our data quality and understanding of local life. However, our sampling procedures do have certain implications for analysis of our data. In particular, we must be cautious in our use of inferential probability-based statistics.[6]

We developed our interview schedules in Rio de Janeiro in early 1984. We pretested them in a pilot study in Arembepe (the northeastern community in which I could draw on long-established rapport) in July 1984. After we had refined, formatted, and printed the schedules, intensive interviewing (using the printed schedules) began in May 1985.

Before this, from late 1984 to early 1985, field researchers Alberto Costa, Richard Pace, and Rosane Prado had been working to build rapport and networks while living in Ibirama, Gurupá, and Cunha, respectively. The final fieldwork in the fourth main site (Arembepe) occurred from June through October 1985. This research was done by a four-person team, two members of which (Conrad and Betty Kottak) had several years of prior field experience there. The other two Arembepe researchers were Iraní Escolano and Pennie Magee.[7]

In each community general ethnography, network construction, sample selection, and structured interviewing took place in that order. Each step was basic to the next. Our interview schedules included a core set of media-related questions. These permitted us to relate television use and exposure to the many other variables queried during the interviews. We cross-checked responses about viewing patterns with viewing logs and random drop-ins.

We completed fieldwork at the four main sites by March 1986. We eventually added two more sites (Niterói and Americana–Santa Barbara) to broaden understanding of television's effects.

An essential part of our research design was comparison of people with varying degrees of TV exposure. As noted, we were able to locate and interview (particularly in Arembepe and Gurupá) many people and households with virtually no exposure. In fact, we chose Gurupá mainly because it was a low exposure community, with no satellite dish and only a dozen sets. All those sets were in the town proper (as contrasted with the rural areas, located along Amazon tributaries). When fieldwork began, all the sets in Gurupá relied on expensive antennas to receive, very badly, signals from the state capital. Our study had begun just in time. A satellite dish arrived, followed by a rapid increase in set ownership, at the end of the fieldwork period.

We did in-depth fieldwork in the four main communities. Each fit the project design of having been studied previously. However, all were rural and poor. As we tried to compare these settings with national-level information from urban sources, we realized that a link was missing. We needed to extend our field procedures, including ethnography and structured interviewing, to the more urban, socioeconomically contrasting settings in which most Brazilians now live.

Another reason for adding such sites is that Brazil has become an urban nation. No project investigating Brazilian mass culture should focus solely on rural areas. Thus we added (in Niterói, Rio de Janeiro state) a suburban upper-income residential compound and a neighboring, dependent, shanty community.

In Americana–Santa Barbara (São Paulo state), we studied a group of textile factory workers and another group that had retained strong ethnic identity (unusual for Brazil). Americana takes its name from this latter group, Americans from the Confederacy who fled the South following the Civil War and established colonies in this part of Brazil. Many still speak English (and Portuguese). We considered this group potentially interesting as a test of an intervening role of surviving North American values on TV impact in Brazil.

Iraní Escolano and Celeste DaMatta did the research in Niterói. Edward Potter worked in Santa Barbara–Americana. Research at these sites was less in depth, with smaller interview schedule samples. Unlike the four main sites, neither Niterói nor Santa Barbara had been studied previously. However, this research does help us connect national statistics, based almost exclusively on urban and suburban survey research, with our local-level strategies and results from the rural areas.[8]

Despite their many similarities, which permitted controlled comparison, our four main sites—Cunha, Ibirama, Gurupá, and Arembepe—did contrast in two important respects. First was ethnic background. Cunha is Luso-Brazilian (that is, deriving mainly from Brazil's Portuguese colonists).

Ibirama had German, Polish, and Italian settlers. Arembepe is Afro-Brazilian, and Gurupá Amerindian-Brazilian.

The second contrast is most important for a TV impact study. Television had reached our research sites at different times. This permitted us to assess relationships between length of TV exposure and other (dependent) variables (while also controlling for such intervening variables as income, class, and ethnic background).

GURUPÁ

Gurupá, a sleepy Amazon town of some 2300 people[9] in Pará state, lies far (60 hours round trip by boat) from the nearest large city (Belém, the state capital). Physically obvious in Gurupá's population is a blend of Portuguese settlers, their African slaves, and native Amerindian inhabitants of Amazonia. The Transamazonian highway is far away, and the river remains Gurupá's only thoroughfare.

Wagley did the original anthropological study of Gurupá during the late 1940s (Wagley 1953). University of Florida graduate student Richard Pace did our television study there, as part of his dissertation research on social change in Gurupá (Pace 1987). Gurupá's lack of a signal-receiving tower had delayed television's diffusion. Townsfolk had to travel (with fair difficulty) to Belém to buy sets and large, expensive antennas, which were never very effective. Because sets and antennas were so inaccessible and expensive, there had been virtually no penetration of Gurupá's rural zones when Pace began his fieldwork in December 1984. Even in town there were only 19 sets. The fact that the town generator provided just six hours of electricity each night was another limit on viewing. Pace did 157 interviews in Gurupá proper and 91 in the rural zone (a total of 248 interviews).

The Dutch founded Gurupá, the oldest of our research sites, in 1609, as an Indian trading post. The Portuguese fought and defeated the Dutch for possession of Gurupá because of its strategic placement overlooking the Amazon. They constructed Gurupá's fort in 1623 to deter the British and Dutch from ascending the Amazon.

Much later, Gurupá, along with the entire region, prospered during the Amazonian rubber boom (1880–1912—especially the years just after 1904). Global interest in rubber arose with the invention of vulcanization around 1880. The process prepared rubber for tires—initially for bicycles, by 1905, for automobiles. Amazonian rubber production rested on small-scale tapping of scattered trees by individual collectors. However, the Brazilian rubber boom and Gurupá's florescence soon ended as a result of Indonesia's more cost-efficient plantation system of rubber production.

Since the Amazonian rubber bust of 1912, Gurupá has followed a downhill path. This decline was halted briefly during World War II, when the Japanese war effort cut off the world supply of Indonesian rubber. This led to an Amazonian mini-boom and a brief (1942–49) resurgence in Gurupá's prosperity.

Perched atop the Amazon's northern bank, Gurupá has a commanding view of a channel that sailboats and steamers still traverse. Visible from the river are architectural reminders of the past. These include a church and city hall, an imposing structure whose construction began in 1910 and halted soon after. Completion of city hall awaited the World War II mini-boom. City hall and a small hospital stand in the central square, from which a long ramp runs down to the river's edge, where boats are moored at the municipal wharf.

The Catholic church, downriver from the square, takes its name from Gurupá's patron saint, Saint Anthony, to whom no one pays much attention. The town's favored saint is Benedict, a dark-skinned miracle worker (who is also honored annually at the Cunha research site). Saint Benedict is the focus of Gurupá's main local celebration, which occurs around Christmas time. Past the church stands the old fort. Farthest downriver is an abandoned saw mill with another wharf, where small boats may be docked.

The main events in Gurupá's history have been in response to world system developments, of which the rubber boom was most important. During Gurupá's heyday (1900–1912) as a thriving collection and deposit site for rubber, the local upper class consisted of rubber buyers and other commercial people. Traders shipped rubber from the rural zone on to Belém.

Wagley's informants still told stories of the town's glorious past. They mentioned the Baron of Gurupá, appointed by Brazil's Emperor Pedro II. They recalled a party given for the governor of Pará, with French wines and champagne, music played on imported grand pianos, and local women in fashionable dresses.

With the rubber bust, however, Gurupá lost its economic base. Its population dwindled. The ghost town became a forlorn reminder of a brighter Amazonian past. Boats no longer stopped in Gurupá. The town remained off the mainstream until World War II, when, during the mini-boom, many rubber trails were reopened, and the town enjoyed new prosperity and growth.

Wagley, who first visited Gurupá during World War II, returned to do ethnographic research in 1949. The town plan was simple, and it remained so through Pace's fieldwork there 35 years later. The main streets ran parallel to the river. Each had an official name, as did each cross street, but no one knew these names. First Street, the one with greatest prestige, today still, is nearest the river. It has the best tile-roofed brick houses. In Wagley's day Second Street, the next one in, had mixed house types—tile-roofed brick and thatched wattle and daub. Third Street had very poor houses with thatched roofs and palm fiber sidings. By the time of Pace's 1984–85 restudy, First, Second, and Third Streets, which in Wagley's days had been unpaved and sandy, had all been paved in concrete. Fourth and Fifth Streets had been added, and Sixth Street was taking form. However, the relationship among prestige, house quality, and proximity to the river persisted.

Wagley studied Gurupá's rural areas along with the town, and we also included them in our TV project. The rural zone is oriented toward small streams, which run into the Amazon. Each stream has a name and forms a neighborhood of people, with houses along the banks. In 1949 the stream people relied on trading posts (most now abandoned) built at the stream's confluence with the Amazon. These posts served as social, religious, and economic centers for that stream's rubber gatherers. They offered a place where people could purchase goods and attend dances and festivals.

Long before Pace's restudy, most of the trading posts were abandoned. Nowadays, Gurupá's rural people live mainly in small villages located further upstream. These sites, which also existed in Wagley's time, consist of a few houses grouped around a chapel. Each village has a name and a patron saint. The saint's "day" is not the one specified by the Catholic ritual calendar. Instead, people honor him or her during the dry season, when they can more easily assemble. Saint Apolonius, for example, is traditionally commemorated in January. Rural Gurupáenses honor him in June, because transportation is easier.

At the time of Wagley's study, a series of rural festivals filled the dry season (May to October). Upstream villages celebrated their saint's day at their chapel, whereas the scattered neighborhoods did so at the trading post. Festivities lasted a week, as people came from several neighborhoods to drink rum, dance all night, and sleep all day. Celebrants didn't invite priests to these ostensibly Catholic events because most padres disapproved of drinking and dancing. (Gurupá lacked a resident priest in 1949, but has one now.)

Wagley noticed several changes between 1949 and his next visit to Gurupá in 1962. There was no longer any emphasis on rubber. Some people had started selling hardwoods, whereas others harvested palm-heart trees. In 1949 Gurupá had neither bicycles nor motor transportation. By 1962, there was a municipal truck, but still no bikes or cars. Miller, at that time Wagley's student at the University of Florida, did a brief restudy of Gurupá in 1974 (Wagley 1976). He described further changes, including small Protestant sects and night clubs with prostitutes. Gurupá also had bikes and automobiles, despite a lack of roads. One could drive only a few miles inland. Today, roads go further inland, but there is still no highway connection. Bicyle riding remains a popular mode of transportation.

Most of the locally available hardwoods, still commercially viable in 1974, had been cut by the mid-1980s, and the saw mill, opened in 1970, had closed. The latest process of extraction, exhaustion, and retraction had worked its way through Gurupá and moved on to other, more distant Amazon communities.

A rural–urban migratory pattern that Wagley observed in 1949 continues today as part of Gurupá's economy. In Wagley's time, when people from the rural zones couldn't find employment either locally or in the town of Gurupá, many went on to the state capital. In the 1970s and 1980s, many people migrated seasonally to millionaire Daniel Keith Ludwig's ill-fated Jarí tree farm north of Gurupá, where they worked for six months at a time.[10]

Gurupá's traditional foods are locally grown manioc, rice, and corn. The poor subsist on manioc and fish. Richer families eat potatoes, squash, and black beans—both locally cultivated and grown outside. In 1949 local fishermen caught in large traps ample supplies of fish, and Wagley remembers three varieties for lunch. Returns from fishing are diminishing now, but, in compensation, Gurupá has more beef.

In evaluating the effects of television on fears (Chapter 10), we have to consider traditional fears. Like other rural Brazilians, Gurupáenses fear real and mythical animals. They are afraid of stepping on poisonous snakes attracted to the warmth retained by the street surface at night. Townsfolk worry about getting sick from eating certain kinds of (taboo) prey. They fear werewolves and the *cobra grande*, a 100-foot serpent believed to travel up the Amazon and endanger river travel at night. Gurupáenses also fear catching bad luck, to which they believe people, animals, and even inanimate objects—such as a fishing line or a rifle—are susceptible.

Of the communities we studied, Gurupá has had the least media, particularly print, exposure. Briefly around 1908 Gurupá had a weekly newspaper. In 1949 Wagley noted that salesmen occasionally brought in newspapers and magazines from the state capital. At that time Gurupá's sole primary school had only 40 students. There were no schools at all in the rural areas. Local teachers were at most primary school graduates. Just one Gurupáense had finished high school. The most literate man in town was an immigrant from Portugal who ran the local hotel. Although many Gurupáenses knew more or less where Rio de Janeiro was, no one had ever been there—or even wanted to go.

In 1949, Gurupá had a diesel-powered electric generator, but no fuel to run it. Wagley brought in a short-wave radio, and people visited him in the evening to listen to it. Gurupá had just one other (nonfunctioning) short-wave radio. By 1962 the town had limited electric light. Transistor radios—which picked up the Amazonian cities of Belém and Manaus, plus Venezuelan stations—had become highly prized possessions. People would lean through the window to listen to a neighbor's radio, as they were to do later when the first TV sets arrived on First Street.

In February 1986, Gurupá's own satellite dish arrived and began receiving Globo *directly* from Rio (with no local programming or advertising). Before that, when Pace's fieldwork began (in December 1984), Gurupá's exposure to Globo had come through Jarí, a small city to the north. Jarí also picked up the network directly from Rio via satellite, with no local programming, advertising, or news. Thus there were open time slots between national programming, when commercials and local news were airing in Rio. These went black in Jarí, or in their place aired a test pattern, music, or an occasional local announcement typed on a solid background. (Earlier, before getting a satellite dish, Jarí had broadcast TV tapes flown in from Rio.)

Before 1986 Gurupá had also received the Bandeirantes network. That channel did offer some local broadcasting, including ten minutes of daily news about the state. However, no one in Gurupá watched Bandeirantes. Reasons for this inattention included poor reception and unpopular programming. Receiving Bandeirantes required a bothersome rotation of the tall antennas to point northeast (toward Macapá—the originating city), rather than northwest toward Jarí, the source of Globo. Once Gurupá got its own satellite dish, townsfolk sold their tall antennas, and no one received Bandeirantes any more.

AREMBEPE

Along with my wife, Isabel (Betty) Wagley Kottak, I have been studying Arembepe, Bahia state—a coastal town whose population (mostly people of Afro-American descent) now numbers 2000 people—since 1962. Youngest of our research sites, Arembepe was settled late in the 19th century by freed slaves from sugar plantations in Bahia's Recôncavo region. In 1985, for the TV project, two other researchers joined Betty and me. Iraní Escolano, a Brazilian, was at that time a graduate student in survey methods at Hunter College of the City University of New York. Pennie Magee, an anthropology graduate student at the University of Florida, had previously spent many years in Brazil.

In 1962 most Arembepeiros had made their living directly or indirectly from ocean fishing in small sailboats. The local economy diversified during the 1970s and 1980s because of the expansion of Salvador, the nearby state capital. That city, which now has well over 1 million people, is less than an hour from Arembepe by car.

Arembepe has changed from a relatively isolated and egalitarian Atlantic fishing village into an economically diverse and socially heterogeneous suburb. I tell the full story of Arembepe's transformation, based on my fieldwork there between 1962 and 1980, in my book *Assault on Paradise: Social Change in a Brazilian Village* (1983).

When we first studied Arembepe during the 1962 rainy season, it took three hours of travel on dirt and sand roads in a four-wheel drive vehicle to reach the village. In 1964, when we did our first census of Arembepe, the population was 750 people living in 160 houses. Fishing was the mainstay of the economy. Men fished for subsistence and cash, and Arembepe's most regular visitors were fish buyers from Salvador.

Over 70 percent of the men fished as a primary occupation, and about 80 percent supported themselves through some role in the fishing industry. The fleet included no motor boats. Fishermen sailed to the continental slope, where they specialized in migratory species.

For decades Arembepe has had a small chapel in its central square, but never a church or a resident priest. Its main local festival, honoring Saint Francis, occurred at the height of the annual fishing cycle, when cash was most abundant. Arembepeiros also celebrated June saints' days (John, Peter, and Anthony), but these were less important than the February festival.

Arembepe's homogeneous traditional economy supported little social differentiation. Aside from fishing, villagers grew and sold coconuts, ran small stores, and sold low-value items from their homes. There was a handful of carpenters and bricklayers. Most houses were simple structures of wattle and daub or palm fronds that required little expertise to build.

Other than in store-keeping, women had few opportunities to make money. Signs of machismo and the social devaluation of females pervaded local life. Arembepe's demographic profile included more males than females in the younger age categories. In part this imbalance reflected neglect of female children and girls' lower survival chances. There was also substantial male emigration, usually for temporary commercial fishing.

With so many men fishing outside, Arembepe had a surplus of marriageable women—too many for all to find husbands. The result was informal polygyny. Some women became secondary spouses, residing separately, of successful fishermen and businessmen. Stigmatized as *raparigas* or "village prostitutes," these women composed Arembepe's only distinct socially deviant category during the 1960s.

Certain leveling mechanisms kept Arembepe's economy and social life egalitarian. For example, social obligations and consequent sharing increased with wealth. Without birth control, family size increased with income. More money meant a better diet, greater resistance to disease, and lower infant mortality. Obligations to in-laws, *compadres*, godchildren, secondary wives, and neighbors also increased with economic success. Arembepeiros received no social security benefits from outside. They had to rely on personal networks to see them through retirement and misfortune. To guarantee their own social security in times of need, the more successful had to share with the less fortunate.

An ideology of equality prevailed, reflecting the reality that everyone in Arembepe was a member of the national lower class. "We are all equal here," said villagers. "No one in Arembepe is really rich." Sailboats and fishing equipment, although manufactured outside, were inexpensive and available to any industrious fishermen. A fully equipped boat cost the equivalent of 400 kilograms of marketed fish. Because boats rarely lasted a decade, few were inherited. Land holdings were meager, produced little cash, and were fragmented through inheritance. Any industrious villager could find land to plant coconut trees, which supplied Arembepe's second export.

When I revisited Arembepe in 1973, after an eight-year absence, these characteristics were in flux. By 1980, when I next did research there, major and dramatic transformations were obvious. The most significant changes were:

Changes in the fishing industry, from windpower to mechanization.

Opening of a paved highway and the rise of tourism; this included an early 1970s invasion by hippies from all over the world.

Construction of a nearby factory and ensuing chemical pollution of Arembepe's water.

The appearance of new categories of social deviance.

The end of the old egalitarian social structure and the rise of social classes.

During the 1970s, during a national era of expansion, Arembepe's economy had grown more diverse. By 1980 fishing—as Aremlepe's primary occupation—had declined to 40 percent of the adult male labor force, down from 74 percent in 1964. Forty young men, 17 percent of male workers, worked at the nearby titanium dioxide factory (Tibrás). Fourteen percent of male and 31 percent of female cash earners now worked in business. Many of them catered to the weekend and summertime tourist trade that had developed because of the asphalted highway that now links Salvador to beaches in and beyond Arembepe.

City people had begun to buy vacation property in Arembepe. Villagers enlarged their houses to rent to outsiders. Reflecting a decade-long flurry of building activity, 16 percent of Arembepe's men now worked in construction. There were over 600 houses in Arembepe and its two new satellite communities, a quadrupling since 1964.

Arembepeiros began motorizing their boats during the early 1970s. They did this with loans from the government agency encharged with developing small-scale fishing. The agency loaned money to successful captains, owners, and land-based entrepreneurs. However, young industrious fishermen, who in the old days would eventually have been able to buy their own boats, lacked sufficient collateral to obtain loans. Nor could they accumulate the money for a motor boat through their own fishing efforts, as they had in the past.

Because of the higher cost of the new technology, boat owners started demanding a larger share of crew members' catches. The owner's net earnings from a normal fishing expedition rose to 1000 percent of the ordinary fisherman's, versus just 140 percent in the mid-1960s. Using their profits, owners bought larger and larger boats.

The fishing pattern changed dramatically. Boats no longer left and returned as a fleet, but individually. No more a day-long affair, fishing became an arduous four-day journey to the north. Fishermen sought waters less affected by the chemical factory, whose pollution of Arembepe's lagoon became a national scandal in 1973.

Villagers no longer assembled on the beach in the afternoon to help unload catches and greet returning mariners. Men no longer congregated on the chapel stoop for an evening chat. Fishermen gave up their nightly communal bath in the chemically polluted freshwater lagoon for indoor showers.

The old leveling mechanisms were ineffective against the wealth contrasts embodied in the new technology. Yet Arembepe's traditional culture, including the old ideology of equality, continued to affect people's actions. Old-time fishermen found the new fishing pattern more like paid employment than a profession. They began to retire, taking advantage of pension benefits that accompanied Arembepe's penetration by the nation-state. Other men turned to the tourist industry, construction, and the factory to avoid working for colleagues who had begun to act like bosses.

The combination of pollution and exploitative relations of production could have doomed local fishing. However, this did not happen because of a steady infusion of immigrant fishermen. These men were attracted by greater cash opportunities in Arembepe, compared with their own more isolated villages, and by the excitement *(movimento)* of the newly electrified honky-tonk town that Arembepe had become.

The rumor of jobs in Arembepe's booming economy attracted not just fishermen but men with other skills. One result was to increase the number of marriageable males. Men between the ages of 20 and 49 now outnumbered women. There were enough husbands to go around.

The new economy also offered women chances to make money in sales, services, and rents. Like fishermen, female cash earners acquired pension rights from the government. Female status rose as access to resources by women and men became more equal. Women became less dependent on men for support.

By 1980, the formerly homogeneous and egalitarian fishing village of Arembepe had become economically and socially diverse. The arrival of outsiders contributed to social heterogeneity. However, differentials arising from the new technology contributed powerfully to the development of stratification among *native* Arembepeiros. A multitude of new social identities appeared. Fully described in *Assault on Paradise,* I can only list them here. A village whose only deviant category had been that of village prostitute during the 1960s now hosts a plethora of socially distinguished groups. They include multiple occupations, residents of satellite communities, immigrants, tourists, the rich, alcoholics, the mentally ill, *candomblézeiros* (participants in an urban-derived Afro-Brazilian cult), and even Assembly of God Protestants.

My observation of television's impact in Arembepe soon after electricity's 1977 arrival led me to the project described in this book. Many Arembepeiros had watched television for the first time on a battery-operated set purchased in 1973 by a local woman named Luminata, appropriately "the illuminated one." During a three-month stay in 1973, I noticed villagers gathering each evening at Luminata's window in the central square to watch TV.[11]

However, television only affected Arembepe significantly after electrification, when many villagers purchased sets and installed them in their homes. Like Gurupá at the time of our study, Arembepe of 1985–86 had retained a few rural areas where electricity and television had not yet arrived. We did 294 interviews in Arembepe proper (and its two satellite villages) and 29 in rural houses that still lacked electricity (a total of 323 interviews).

Arembepe was unique among our field sites in that in many households Globo's signal (Channel 4) was the weakest of the available channels. The best reception I got in Arembepe using my set's own antenna was on Bandeirantes (Channel 7), with Silvio Santos (SBT, Channel 5) second best. One man told me that when he bought a color television to replace his black-and-white one, his Globo reception deteriorated markedly. As a result he shifted from Globo's 7 o'clock *novela* to a dubbed Mexican serial shown on the Silvio Santos network at 7:30 P.M. He said that Globo only came in well when it rained. He planned to buy a new antenna to try to get Globo better.

One woman who had acquired her decrepit black-and-white set as a hand-me-down from a tourist neighbor also had trouble with Globo. She said that her reception varied mysteriously from hour to hour. It sometimes depended on whether her doors and windows were open or closed. Despite the poor reception, Globo was still the people's choice in Arembepe as throughout Brazil.

CUNHA

"The history of Cunha goes back almost as far as the very earliest Portuguese settlement in Southern Brazil" (Shirley 1971:10). Larger than Gurupá or Arembepe, Cunha was founded during the second half of the 17th century. It is a historic town with two colonial churches, the older one built in 1731. Today, about 6000 people live in the town proper, with 15,000 others dispersed in the rural area. The county of Cunha is very large and sparsely populated, reflecting a rugged, mountainous, forested terrain. We did 227 interviews in Cunha proper and 220 in the rural area (a total of 447 interviews).

Cunha is located in Brazil's more developed and prosperous south (São Paulo state). Almost equidistant from Rio (300 kilometers) and São Paulo (227 kilometers), Cunha lies about 50 kilometers off the main highway between those cities. Brazilian anthropology graduate student Rosane Prado did the fieldwork for our TV project there in 1985–86.

Cunha itself, which remains a food-producing community, is far from developed or modern. Situated in one of the more isolated parts of São

Paulo state, the town has a recent history of poor transportation and communication. Anthropologist Shirley reports on his 1965–66 study of Cunha in his book *The End of a Tradition* (1971). Shirley begins by noting Cunha's similarity to the first of the "two Brazils" (rural–traditional versus urban-modern) routinely mentioned by Brazilianists at that time (Lambert 1967). I previously pointed out that television has played a significant role in bridging the opposition between the two Brazils. However, Cunha, which received a substantial number of TV sets at about the same time as Arembepe (1977–78), retains much of its rural and small-town character.

Cunha lies on a road, which is paved but often impassable during the rainy season, linking the coastal town of Paratí, a popular resort 50 kilometers away, to the main Rio-São Paulo highway. This was one of the first roads that the Portuguese built into the Brazilian interior, from one of the largest and best natural ports in Brazil (Paratí). It was a main route between the coast and São Paulo city until late in the 19th century. During this period Cunha was a center of food production and of commerce—catering to travelers. In 1877 the railroad between Rio and São Paulo opened, and this old route became obsolete. The railroad and, much later, the Rio-São Paulo highway left Cunha cut off from the mainstream.

However, none of our research sites has ever been totally isolated, and Cunha is no exception. Gurupá has been linked to cities through boat traffic and seasonal migration. Arembepe has always sold its fish to buyers from outside. During Shirley's mid-1960s fieldwork period, regular bus service linked Cunha (indirectly) to Rio, São Paulo, and towns along the highway. Today, Cunhenses regularly visit Guaratinguetá, the nearest city on the Rio–São Paulo highway, which has services and amusements missing in Cunha itself.

Rosane Prado was a social anthropology graduate student at the Federal University of Rio de Janeiro when she did the Cunha research for our TV project and her own master's thesis (Prado 1986). She was the third anthropologist to study Cunha, after Shirley and an earlier researcher, Willems (1947). Willems chose Cunha for the first community study ever done in Brazil (in 1945) because it was isolated and conservative. It was one of the last remaining centers of the old rural folk culture of São Paulo, known as the *caipira paulista*.[12] (*Caipira* is now a somewhat pejorative term used in São Paulo to refer to the hick peasant farmers of that state.) Although *caipira* culture was in substantial decline when Shirley did his fieldwork, many Cunhenses maintained distinctive speech patterns and accents that set them apart from more urban and modern *paulistas*. Even in 1965–66, Shirley described this region as "one of the most isolated and conservative of the state" (1971:4).

Physically and ethnically, the *caipira paulista*, including Cunhenses, are predominantly Luso-Brazilians. Thus they are light-skinned, dark-haired descendants of Portuguese settlers and their Brazilian offspring. Unlike Cunha, many communities in São Paulo state, including our research site

Americana, were settled by recent immigrants. These late 19th and 20th century colonists included Germans, Italians, Japanese, Middle Easterners, and North Americans.

Situated on a rugged forested escarpment at an altitude (950 meters) conducive to annual frosts, Cunha remained on the periphery of São Paulo's coffee boom, which peaked in 1860[13]. Cunha was a food-producing center in an area that fed the warmer coffee zone in the nearby Paraíba river valley, from which subsistence farming was driven by the cash crop. Agriculture and livestock (pork, beef, leather, and dairy products) are still the basis of Cunha's economy. Its main crops are potatoes, corn, beans, and fruits.

From its *caipira* background Cunha retains a traditional, dispersed rural settlement pattern. Willems and Shirley saw it as having a distinctive culture rich in its own values, organization, and lore:

> The peasantry of southern Brazil, unlike their counterparts in Spanish America, were never wholly subjugated by Church and Crown and hence were not concentrated into villages. Indeed, the agricultural hamlet or village, taken to mean a concentrated settlement of subsistence cultivators, hardly exists at all in Brazil. Towns are very common, but these have specialized urban functions, and the majority of the rural population does not live in them. (Shirley 1971:35)

Shirley classified Cunha's traditional rural residents as peasants because they grew varied crops, had enduring ties to the land, and had commercial links with the town. In Cunha's rural zone the nuclear family was and remains the main productive unit. Despite their dispersed settlement pattern, these rural families are interlinked through marriage, fictive kinship (the godparenthood and *compadre* system), and mutual aid. They also participate in festivities at their neighborhood (*bairro*) chapel, the traditional religious center for between 30 and 50 dispersed rural families. The chapel, a small store, and a primary school often stand near to each other, forming a neighborhood's focus. Traditionally the neighborhood's saint's day was the most important annual festival (also true in Gurupá's rural neighborhoods).

Rural Cunhenses also come to town for major celebrations. During the dry, cool winter, a late July–early August festival honors *Divino Espirito Santo* ("the Holy Spirit"). Next comes the late September–early October commemoration of the dark-skinned Saint Benedict, also a focus of festive activity (in December) in Gurupá. The main festivity held during summer—the warm, wet season (early December)—is for Cunha's patron saint, Our Lady of the Conception. Like Gurupá and Ibirama, but unlike Arembepe, Cunha has a resident priest and regular church services.

Many rural folk have moved to town but have kept their farms. Some family members may live on the farm for most of the year, whereas others visit seasonally, in accordance with agricultural demands. The distinction between rural (*roça*) and town (Cunha) remains important when

Cunhenses speak of social divisions in their community. The focus of rural land use has shifted somewhat from agriculture toward livestock—for meat, milk, and leather. However, farms still produce for their own subsistence and for sale in Cunha, the highway towns, even São Paulo city.

Cunha's rural folk are diverse. They include small farm owners, sharecroppers, squatters, and landless migrant day workers. A few large-scale landowners *(fazendeiros)*—descendants of recipients of land grants from the Portuguese crown—endure from the old slave-holding days when large properties dominated the rural area. Cattle now graze some of the larger properties once used for crops. Absentee owners rely on local cowboys and caretakers.

Average household income and social class were higher in our rural sample than in our urban sample of Cunha.[14] However, strong inequalities in the distribution of land, income, wealth, and prestige were more characteristic of the rural area than of town.

Living in town offers certain advantages. Our Cunha urbanites had better educations, averaging 5.5 years versus 2.7 in the rural sample. Townspeople have better media access. They read more, own many more books, have had TV longer, and watch TV more now. Cunha townspeople watched 1.6 hours daily, versus 1.0 in the rural zone.

Townspeople have more time to watch television and for leisure activities generally. They also visit more. Rural people work harder. Much of the farm land surrounding Cunha is too rugged for efficient use of agricultural machinery. Farmers rely on manual tools, such as the hoe.

The rural people have had sets in their homes four years on the average, compared with six in town. For reasons reflecting stage of TV penetration (see Chapter 9), Cunha's rural folk have a higher opinion of TV, like *telenovelas* more and consider them more realistic than do Cunha's more TV-jaded townspeople.

According to several measures Cunha is more traditional than our other sites, except Gurupá (see Appendix 1—Statistical Comparison of Sites). Cunhenses are more religious, wean their infants later, have more conservative views on sex–gender issues, and more actively maintain the godparent–*compadre* system. Rural Cunha is more conservative than is the town.

IBIRAMA

Ibirama, Santa Catarina, a town of 5800 people in a county of 23,500, was first studied by the Brazilian anthropologist Alberscheim in 1958.* Ibirama lies in the Itajaí river valley, which European farmers settled late in the 19th century. Its founders, mostly German Protestants and Catholics, included many literate people. In establishing a regime of small-scale farm-

*This section on Ibirama was written by Alberto Coelho Gomes Costa.

ing, they vied for land with an aboriginal group, the Xoglens. (There is still a Xoglens Indian reservation nearby.)

Following World War I and especially after World War II, Ibirama's population became ethnically diverse, as Italians and Luso-Brazilians moved in. This immigration was promoted by an assimilationist Brazilian government policy of sending strangers to colonize ethnically homogeneous communities.

Because of its German colonization and its more recent multi-ethnic character, Ibirama attracted Alberscheim's attention. She published the results of her ethnography in a 1962 book. Costa, another Brazilian anthropologist, arrived 27 years later to do our TV-project research and a larger study of ethnicity in Ibirama. He began his study, which lasted more than two years, in February 1985.

The county (municipality) of Ibirama has four districts. Today, two, including Ibirama proper (the county seat), are predominantly German-Brazilian. In the other two, more rural, Italo-Brazilians predominate. Each district has several named settlements, totaling about 60 in the county. The largest town is Ibirama proper, which has stores, factories, government and bank offices, schools, social clubs, and churches. Each district seat also has stores, government offices, schools, ballrooms, soccer fields, boccie (Italian bowling) courts, and churches. Even the interior settlements have a primary school, chapel, soccer field, ballroom, patron saint, and an annual religious festival. Although most of the county's population is Catholic, there are also many Protestants—Lutherans, Presbyterians, and Assembly of God.

In constructing his network sample, Costa received help from local leaders, including the Catholic priest, the Lutheran and Presbyterian ministers, the local agronomist, government statisticians, and political leaders. His sample spanned all four districts, the range of locally significant occupations, and people of different ethnic origin, religion, age, and sex. Costa did 140 interviews in Ibirama proper, 86 in other urban areas (district seats), and 211 in the rural zone (a total of 437).

Historically, Ibirama has been less isolated from region and nation than our other main sites. Even in 1958 daily buses linked Ibirama to Blumenau, Brazil's largest city of German colonization, less than 50 miles away. A paved highway now covers this route. Ibirama has a long history of literacy, and radio and newspapers have been available since before World War II. Ibirama has had television since 1970, longer than Gurupá, Cunha, and Arembepe.

Ibirama's 1958 economy was already linked to region and nation through external commercial and industrial relationships. A wood extraction industry, which has grown substantially, was emerging when Alberscheim did her study. However, local agriculture still had a subsistence orientation, with the family the basic unit of production in agrarian and commercial activities.

The two most important economic changes between 1958 and 1985 were (1) growth of the lumber industry, based on wood from nearby forests, and (2) cultivation of tobacco, which replaced subsistence cultivation and dairying. Despite this commercialization, Ibirama did not become markedly urban or industrialized. It remains a farming area, with more than 70 percent of county inhabitants living in the rural zone.

However, the rural economic structure did change significantly in that monocrop tobacco cultivation for cash replaced subsistence agriculture. Several tobacco companies settled in the region. By 1970 95 percent of the county's arable land was devoted to tobacco, now the main source of local income (averaging about $10,000 per farm per year). Farmers use cash to meet basic living costs, to buy consumer goods and agricultural technology, and for savings.

Although tobacco production links the local economy more strongly to the national one, the structure of rural properties has not changed. Farms are still small, seldom exceeding 25 hectares. Nor has the rural labor force (supplied by the landowner's nuclear family) changed much. The nuclear family remains the basic unit in agriculture and store-keeping. Economic life is still a crucial aspect of family life, and kinship continues to provide the basis of economic relationships.

Asymmetry characterizes Ibirama's traditional marital and family relationships. Although the entire family participates in economic production, the male head controls decision making. Women and children have an excess of work and responsibilities, but they lack authority in agriculture and commerce. However, with increased job opportunities outside family properties, some of Ibirama's women and children are rebelling against this traditional authority structure.

Still, Ibiramenses conceive of the family as the basic social (as well as economic) unit. The social identity of every Ibiramense emerges from his or her family. Every action relates to one's family and affects its name and honor. All Ibiramenses hold this view and idealize their families.

What about politics, especially in the context of Ibirama's German background? Alberscheim saw Ibirama (and German-Brazilians generally) as being somewhat marginal to Brazilian society. She noted a conflict of loyalty between nation (Brazil) and blood (German ancestry). Although political structure, formal legislation, and administrative life were part of the Brazilian national system, the Ibiramenses of 1958 cared primarily about local politics, rather than affairs of state and nation. In their choices of local leaders, an ethnic criterion prevailed. Despite the increasing wealth and prestige of several people of Italian and Luso-Brazilian descent, only German-Brazilians (the majority group) had ever been mayor.

Alberscheim emphasized several expressions of ethnicity in local social life. First, most Ibiramenses were bilingual, speaking German at home and Portuguese in public settings. Second, voluntary associations did not unite people of different ethnic origins. Local clubs were ethnically homogeneous. Alberscheim also noted that strong ethnic stereotypes were held by German-Brazilians. Examples included the lazy Luso-Brazilian, the indolent native (Indian), and the thieving Italian. Today, the stereotypes remain, although clubs have become ethnically heterogeneous and bilingualism is rare. Most younger people do not know German, use of which is confined to meetings of older people.

Today, local political groups still reflect the Protestant–Catholic distinction (with the latter dominant). However, each faction includes people of diverse ethnic origins. When Costa arrived in Ibirama, an Italian descendant who had amassed a fortune from wood extraction and lumber had become not only mayor, but the county's dominant political figure. The new mayor had reoriented Ibirama's old political coalitions and solidarities to align with national parties. Under the military dictatorship (1964–85), the local arrangement of political forces came to mirror the national opposition between supporters and opponents of the military regime.

Between the 1950s and the 1980s the conflict of loyalty between Brazil and Germany disappeared. Today, Ibiramenses criticize Brazil's economic, social, and political problems and compare Brazil with more developed countries. However, their criticisms also demonstrate national pride. They usually mention either Brazil's natural wealth or its lack of ethnic and racial prejudice—its (idealized) racial democracy.

What about TV and its effects (actual and perceived) in Ibirama? As is true of all our research sites, news and *telenovelas* are the most-watched TV programs in Ibirama. *Telenovela* characters are subjects of local conversations, as are economic and political matters reported in the news.

During Costa's stay Ibiramenses were unhappy with the latest national economic plan. They were concerned about agrarian reform and possible land redistribution (locally criticized as communistic). They also discussed economic concerns of mainly local importance, such as the price of the next tobacco crop.

Men conversed about the constitutional convention, the timing of the next presidential election, and other issues at the national, state, and local levels. They discussed sports (mainly soccer) and gossiped about other townspeople (usually about their sexual affairs). *Telenovelas* and food prices were favorite female discussion topics. Women also gossiped about local matters.[15]

What is the relationship between television and change? Changes in economy (subsistence to cash), politics (local to national), and mass communication have all worked together to increase Ibirama's links with outside. However, Ibiramenses see TV as the main culprit in a process of negative social change.

Ibiramenses blame television *almost exclusively* for certain changes in local social life that they view with uneasiness, sorrow, and resignation. Television, they say, closed down the movie house, cut into bar activity, and reduced visiting. Townsfolk regret the decline of social and community life. They complain that TV keeps people at home and isolated from each other and that it inculcates an individualist mentality.

Younger Ibiramenses affirm that "nothing happens in Ibirama," and older people say that Ibirama is a "has-been" place. Townspeople buttress these beliefs with reference to television, which offers daily illustration of an alternative world that invites comparison with Ibirama. In the process of viewing Ibirama in relation to this world, comparisons are sometimes advantageous for the community, sometimes not. The comparison justifies the migratory motives of many local young people. It also supports the local belief in a past golden age, during which community spirit—once pervasive, now lost—allowed a better way of life.

Despite the belief that TV keeps people at home and thereby promotes family and private interests over community ones, townspeople also think that *telenovelas* threaten family life and values by encouraging promiscuous sexual behavior, adultery, and divorce. They think that local sexual and marital behavior has changed, and they attribute this change to *telenovela* content. For example, they complain that a romantic ideal of marriage based on individual choice is destroying traditional principles of mate selection, in which family and community played a larger role.

Historically in Ibirama, premarital sex may have been common (as Alberscheim contended), but it was never completely acceptable. Indeed, it only became acceptable in retrospect after a marriage had taken place. Costa's research in local police archives revealed that defloration and seduction used to be among the most frequent crimes reported to police. Older people blame progress and television for a perceived increase in premarital sexual relationships (even as police reports of defloration and seduction have become rare).

The dominant viewpoint in Ibirama contends that changes in local life are attributable *solely* to external forces. Townsfolk cite those changes, which they view negatively, as examples of TV's cultural impact. Complementing this view, they also idealize a past golden age. In Chapter 9, I begin to examine other local views on relationships between television and social change.

NITERÓI

As mentioned earlier, after our in-depth research at the four sites just discussed, we realized that a link was missing. We needed to extend our field procedures to the more urban, socioeconomically contrasting settings in which most Brazilians now live. We chose two sites for this briefer period of research in 1986.

The first was Niterói, a large city (400,000) just across Guanabara Bay from Rio de Janeiro, which may be reached by ferry or toll bridge. We studied three socioeconomically contrasting neighborhoods in a Niterói suburb located 30 minutes by bus and 20 minutes by car from downtown Niterói.

Reflecting the urban crime threat, the upper-middle-class (B1) Jardim Uba neighborhood is a walled, carefully guarded, suburban residential compound. Most of its 50 male homeowners, including anthropologist DaMatta, are daily commuters to professional jobs in the city of Rio. Its adult women are housewives with maids, cooks, and laundresses. They spend much of their time on child care, shopping, and leisure activities.

We also interviewed in two adjacent communities. Jacaré, just outside Jardim Uba's walls, is a poor shanty community. Most of its inhabitants belong to class D. Socioeconomically intermediate is Piratininga, located on the other side of the road that links Niterói to even its more distant suburbs and Atlantic beaches. Iraní Escolano and Celeste DaMatta did 63 interviews in Jardim Uba, 147 in Piratininga, and 53 in Jacaré (a total of 263 interviews).

The residents of Jacaré work mainly as servants for Jardim Uba. We classified 70 percent of Jacaré's population as class D (poor) and 26 percent as class C (working class). Most people live in wooden shanties, some with dirt floors. Unlike the leisured housewives of Jardim Uba (and the urban elite generally), most Jacaré women work, typically as servants. The most common male occupation was janitor, followed by gardener and caretaker. Other men were fishermen, bricklayers, drivers, salesmen, and doormen.

Across the highway, Piratininga has mixed house types. Some homes are as well constructed as those of Jardim Uba; some even have pools. Others are shanties. The shanty dwellers are squatters who will probably be evicted as the middle class grows and acquires legal title to the land. Piratininga is intermediate between Jacaré and Jardim Uba in all its socioeconomic characteristics. Its men work in a range of occupations. We interviewed fishermen, doormen, drivers, gardeners, artisans, mechanics, businessmen, and engineers. Many women work as maids, but there was also a substantial percentage of housewives. In terms of social class, 90 percent of the population of Piratininga belonged to classes B2 through C, middle-middle to working class.

This suburb is not an area of substantial immigration, either recent or historic. Most people in all three neighborhoods were born in and have family ties with the Niterói area. In general they are descendants of Luso-Brazilians and Afro-Brazilians.

However, there is an obvious economic contrast between this suburb and our four main research sites. Gurupá, Cunha, Arembepe, and Ibirama are all separate, easily identifiable communities. Each has its own traditional economy, even if all are increasingly dependent on external links. Our three suburban neighborhoods in Niterói, in contrast, are fully dependent on external income sources. The elite residents of Jardim Uba make their living in Rio, and the people of Jacaré work mainly in Jardim Uba. Piratininga's residents work in Rio, Niterói, and its suburbs. Rather than self-contained communities, we are dealing here with diverse socioeconomic segments of a complex population, all trying to eke an existence out of urban Brazil.

Every socioeconomic measure significant in Brazilian society increases in linear fashion when we compare Jacaré with Jardim Uba, with Piratininga always intermediate. Jacaré residents have less education, less media exposure, lower incomes, and darker skin color. Thus Jacaré households survived on less than 4 standard income units per month, compared with 14 in Piratininga and 30 in Jardim Uba. The average Jacaré adult had completed less than 3 years of school, compared with 8 in Piratininga and 14 in Jardim Uba. Of significance to our study, the elites of Jardim Uba had much longer home television exposure: They had watched for an average of 28 years, versus 15 in Piratininga and 7 in Jacaré.

AMERICANA–SANTA BARBARA

The second site added in 1986 to enlarge our picture of TV impact, from rural–agrarian areas to urban–industrial Brazil, was Americana–Santa Barbara d'Oeste in São Paulo state. Americana stands less than two hours west of São Paulo city, on excellent highways. Its name derives from Confederate loyalists (*confederados*) who left the southern United States for Brazil at the end of the Civil War. Brazilian Emperor Pedro II, who coveted their technical skills, welcomed them. They established several colonies, of which most, including one in the Amazon, failed. The *confederados* reached Americana in 1866. This turned out to be their only successful colony.

By 1875 a railroad linked Americana to the city of Campinas to the east, an intermediate stop on the way to São Paulo. At first Americana was mainly a farming community. Besides farmers, the *confederados* included doctors, dentists, and store owners, Methodists, Presbyterians, and Catholics. Through the 1890s the main agricultural export (shipped by train to São Paulo) was the rattlesnake watermelon, whose seeds had been brought from the southern United States. By 1900 Italian immigrants were arriving in the area and competing with the Americans in agriculture.

Americans introduced the plow and horse-and-carriage to the region. Companies sprouted up in the area because it was well placed for distributing agricultural machines, including planters and seeders. Many Americans and Italians got rich selling agricultural machines to Luso-Brazilian landowners. Many *confederados* still make and market industrial machines today.

During the early 20th century, the population of the region grew ethnically diverse. The policies of Brazilian President Getúlio Vargas, a staunch nationalist and assimilationist, affected both Ibirama and Americana. Vargas' policy was that Portuguese be the only school language. Previously, basic education of American descendants had been in English. Today, all *confederados* speak fluent Portuguese. Older people are bilingual in English, spoken with a Southern accent.

Eventually the *confederados* spilled over into Santa Barbara, and now they are widely dispersed. Many live in São Paulo city, to which they were attracted because of professional talents and capacities they developed. The largest concentrations of *confederados* today are in São Paulo, Santa Barbara, Campinas, and Americana, in that order. (All those cities are in São Paulo state.)

Researcher Edward Potter spent July through December 1986 in the two adjacent cities of Americana and Santa Barbara. He had previously lived in the western São Paulo city of Andrandina as a high school Rotary Club exchange student. This experience gave him fluent Portuguese. It also opened doors, through connections between Rotary Club members in different cities. From a base in Santa Barbara, Potter studied two groups: (1) textile factory workers and (2) descendants of the American Confederate families.

Potter did preliminary ethnography and network construction with both groups. With less time to spend than our other researchers, Potter focused on intensive study of particular groups within much larger populations. His aim was to learn about those two groups specifically, rather than to study a representative sample of the cities in which they lived. Potter eventually did 59 interviews with factory workers and 102 interviews with American descendants (a total of 161 interviews). He worked mostly in Santa Barbara, where most descendants who remain in the Americana area now live.

Americana and Santa Barbara have similar economies, with urban manufacturing and rural farming. However, Americana is larger (165,000 versus 110,000), richer, more industrial, and more urban. Descendants of many nations (Portugal, Lebanon, Syria, Italy, Germany, Japan, and the United States) now populate the region.

We chose this area because it contained Brazilians unlike those we had studied at the other sites. For example, we wanted to add more factory workers, particularly urban ones, to our inventory of respondents. Americana is a center of Brazil's thriving textile industry. Textiles, Americana's leading product, are a close second in Santa Barbara, where agricultural machine manufacture is the main industry.

Potter lived in Santa Barbara, which had 73 textile factories in 1986—22 in the center of town, the rest in outlying areas. He chose three factories— small, medium, and large—for intensive study.

Small factories lack their own retail outlets, which larger firms have. Castellani, the small factory he studied, produced textiles for sale in a single Americana store. The factory owner gave Potter free rein to visit, observe, converse, and question his employees. In this small, intimate, noisy setting there was less distance between boss and workers than in larger factories. Potter managed to interview almost everyone in that factory. Potter's mid-sized factory manufactured directly for dealers, after receiving orders for a certain amount of textiles.

His large factory site was Wiezel, founded by German immigrants and still family-owned. It made clothing, towels, and sheets from start to finish. Wiezel manufactured its own fabrics and dyes (with a separate factory just for dying). It also spun its own thread and sold its finished products in its own stores. Potter interviewed almost everyone who worked inside the Wiezel factory, located in the center of Santa Barbara. He studied many kinds of factory workers, including thread spinners, loom pattern designers, workers in the cut-and-measure room, and mechanics. When people preferred that he not go to their homes, he interviewed at the factory, during the lunch break and before and after shifts.

Besides factory workers, the inclusion of Brazilians with an American cultural heritage in our project was intriguing. How tenacious, we wondered, were American (and Southern) ethnicity and values? How did American-Brazilians compare with Brazilians of different backgrounds? How did they compare with televiewers in the United States?

Potter actually began his research when he met a young *confederada* studying at the University of Michigan's English Language Institute. With her help he started building the network of contacts and informants he would eventually use for fieldwork in Brazil. She phoned her cousin, Dona Rosa, an older woman in Santa Barbara, who became Potter's sponsor, networking coordinator, and valuable informant. Dona Rosa helped him meet *confederados* and gain entrance to the textile factories.

Santa Barbara is a focal point for *confederado* culture and its enduring ethnicity. In Santa Barbara's rural zone lies the cemetery where descendants are still buried. The main reason that the cemetery was built was that Protestant Americans, who had not been baptized properly, were banned from burial in the existing Catholic cemeteries. In the past, whenever an appropriate minister visited, he conducted a service in the chapel located next to the cemetery. Descendants brought lunches and had potluck—in a haven away from Brazilian society.

Today, the main tasks of the Fraternal Order of American Descendants, officially founded in 1952, are to maintain this cemetery and organize the quarterly reunions there. The fraternity keeps a computerized list of members, with current addresses. It charges dues and employs a cemetery caretaker.

Besides these ethnic reunions, *confederados* also participate in community holidays with nondescendants. *Feira de naçoẽs*, for example, is a popular multiethnic fair in which different ethnic groups (for example, Syrian, Italian, Dutch) are represented, but not necessarily by members of the ethnic group. For instance, Potter observed that the American booth included no descendants. Some real (Protestant) descendants expressed disapproval of its sale of beer.

Americana–Santa Barbara was our research site with the longest TV exposure. The region has had electricity since the 1920s. Because of its relative wealth and proximity to São Paulo and Campinas, it has had television since 1955. Currently, six TV channels—Globo, Sílvio Santos (SBT), Bandeirantes (with poor reception), Manchête, Record, and TV Cultura—are locally available.

Local news originates in Campinas, from which Americana and Santa Barbara are 30 and 45 minutes, respectively, by car. TV has not done in movie theaters in Americana and Santa Barbara, which have larger populations than do Ibirama and Cunha. Santa Barbara has one movie house, and Americana two. Many people (33 percent of Potter's sample) also had VCRs, and both cities had video rental stores. A handful of people even owned computers.

Like Ibirama's German settlers, the *confederados* have a long tradition of literacy and reading. This, along with ease of travel and the proximity of major cities, means that people in Americana have been much less isolated than have the residents of our four main research sites. Several of Potter's informants mentioned reading when he asked them "What American values have you inherited?" This value was confirmed during interviewing. Unlike our other field-workers, Potter often had trouble finding space on our printed form to write down all the answers to our questions about books and magazines, because his informants had so much print exposure. Both Americana and Santa Barbara have at least two semi-daily newspapers. Their bookstores and magazine shops offer many publications. Newsstands in Americana even stock the weekly Latin American edition of *Time* in English.

What about perceived effects of television? (This matter is explored at greater length in later chapters.) As in Ibirama, our informants in Santa Barbara said that because of TV, people stay home more, but family members don't talk as much. They said that TV affects scheduling of activities. For instance, men don't go to bars until after the *telenovela* is over. They also schedule local sports events around *novelas*.

Along with the people of Ibirama, those of Americana–Santa Barbara gave the most negative evaluations of television and its effects. To an extent this reflects their greater wealth and longer length of exposure, compared with Gurupá, Cunha, and Arembepe. I explain this relationship in Chapter 9. However, this negative view of TV also reflects longstanding cultural differences between communities. German and American settlers brought to Brazil their traditions of literacy and reading. In the Brazilian communities they formed, as among many contemporary Americans, the value of print is expressed through hostility toward television.

CHAPTER NINE

Television's Social Impact

> While basic attitudes and behaviors are quite seldom affected by single programs or informational campaigns, the mass media may be far more effective in conveying *generalized information* to the mass audience than studies following traditional research designs have so far suggested. (Hirsch 1979:270)

Although rural Brazilians' knowledge of the contemporary world may be nonacademic, it is certainly greater now than it was before TV. By the mid-1980s, as a direct result of exposure to television, villagers had become much more world-wise. Children in Arembepe, like those in the studio audiences of dance-along TV shows throughout Brazil, imitated Michael Jackson, whose videos are shown on *Fantástico*. We discovered in a 1984 survey that Brazilians could identify a photo of Michael Jackson as readily as a photo of the Pope, and more easily than Ronald Reagan, or than photos of the major Brazilian presidential candidates at that time.

Although international stars such as Jackson, Madonna, Julio Iglésias, and George Michael are well known in Brazil, Brazilian TV does more to spread national than international culture. By training villagers in national norms, television makes it easier for them to deal with the outsiders they meet, almost all of whom are other Brazilians. It is difficult for Americans to appreciate this role of television as facilitator of social interaction because we so rarely encounter anyone who was not raised in the daily presence of the mass media. Here is where, as Marcus and Fisher point out, cultural anthropology can make a powerful contribution to knowledge. "In using portraits of other cultural patterns to reflect self-critically on our own ways, anthropology disrupts common sense and makes us reexamine our taken-for-granted assumptions" (Marcus and Fisher 1986:1).

SOCIAL NAVIGATION

Most Americans will never have a chance to observe directly, through before–after comparison of individual cases, the dramatic effects that television can have on (1) stimulating curiosity and a thirst for knowledge and (2) increasing skills in social navigation and communication with outsiders. As illustration of these effects, consider Sonia, a woman in Arembepe. In July 1984, during pilot testing of our questionnaires, I interviewed our next-door neighbor, Sonia. At that time she was an excellent example of a *media-deprived person,* someone who was barely literate and had spent a lifetime without TV, although she did have a radio, on which she listened mostly to music. Still in her twenties, Sonia had accompanied her husband, a caretaker for a summer home, to Arembepe in 1981. They came from a rural community much more distant from the state capital than is Arembepe.

Although she had been in Arembepe for three years, Sonia lived in substantial isolation from the local social system. She dared visit just one of her neighbors. She even let her husband do most of the shopping. Sonia found interactions with strangers, including most Arembepeiros, threatening. She and her husband didn't let their three young sons play in the street, even during the day, because they were afraid of problems with neighbors.

Sonia found it difficult to converse with strangers. As I interviewed her, I found myself feeling guiltier and guiltier as I inflicted my standard set of questions on her. Sonia responded reluctantly. Tears occasionally streaked her face, for instance when she said that she had no friends and when she lamented that she missed her mother, the most important person in her life—more so than her husband and her sons. Sonia longed for a home of her own. She said that she would build one (and feed her family better) if she won the lottery. Sonia knew virtually nothing about Rio or São Paulo and found it difficult to imagine what life was like in those places. My impression was that Sonia was a terrible informant, unaccustomed to and uninterested in talking with strangers. My interview with her had been like pulling teeth, an unpleasant experience for me and a terrifying one for her.

No doubt some of Sonia's behavior reflected her individual personality and class position. A member of class D (lower working), she had little personal contact with elites, particularly men. Her life experience provided absolutely no clue about why someone like me would want to talk to her for more than a minute—particularly to elicit her opinions. Whenever I encountered her that year, Sonia displayed the obsequious, eye-averting, voice-lowering, limp-handed demeanor that is often adopted by poor rural Bahians when they deal with perceived social superiors. For Sonia, that meant virtually everyone she met.

However, there is also reason to conclude that some of this fearful and obsequious behavior reflected Sonia's lack of media exposure. In July 1985, a year after the disastrous interview, I returned to Arembepe to do formal interviewing. In the meantime Sonia's family had acquired a black-and-white TV set, which they watched constantly. I soon noticed a change in Sonia's demeanor. She was no longer the shy, quiet person she had been in 1984. She now visited her neighbors, conversed with my wife, usually looked me in the eye when we talked, sang as she worked, and even made a few jokes. This time she proved an average respondent when we formally interviewed her again.

These changes were obvious to my wife and me. However, for Sonia and for the people who saw her each day, they had happened gradually, unspectacularly, and without any obvious relationship to television. Although Sonia could say that she was happier in 1985 and that she felt more at home in Arembepe, she couldn't conclude that television had changed her life. But it had.

I have no doubt that, at least partially, such changes in demeanor and social behavior as those that took place in Sonia exemplify important effects of televiewing. It familiarizes provincial folk with urban–national norms. It makes them less reluctant and less uncertain in dealing with strangers, including representatives of higher social classes. Far from isolating Sonia, television had increased her social skills and connectedness.

HAS TELEVISION CHANGED YOUR LIFE?

When directly asked "Has television changed your life?" most of our respondents, like Sonia, said no.[1] On the other hand, people were twice as likely to answer yes when asked "Can TV change someone (else)'s life?" They were also much readier to admit that TV had affected their community than themselves, as we discovered when we next asked "Has TV changed life here in ——?" They also seemed better to understand the idea being queried, and they gave fuller answers to our follow-up question of "How so?" We routinely used that open-ended question to elicit our informant's personal opinions about TV effects.

Hirsch raises the following questions about media effects on the individual American televiewer:

> Does exposure to certain types of *content* . . . lead audience members to measurably alter their *behavior* (become more aggressive, change their vote); and does exposure alter their *attitudes* or opinions on specific topics (the U.N., smoking, Presidential candidates)? [emphasis added] (Hirsch, 1979:268)

He concludes that:

> there is overwhelmingly little evidence that people's *basic attitudes* or behavior patterns are changed in direct response to exposure to individual programs, new stories, and short term information campaigns. [emphasis added] (Hirsch, 1979:268)

However, Hirsch bases this conclusion on research about short-term effects. It is not surprising that basic opinions don't change in the short run. (This is implied in the meaning of *basic*.) The most profound effects of television on viewers are massive and take place gradually, over a long period. They may well be imperceptible to individual natives (and to researchers as well) at a given time.

Fortunately, in addition to our use of a questionnaire (interview schedule) to gather quantifiable information about television's effects on Brazilians, our research project also had a qualitative dimension. We were doing ethnography as well as survey research. We knew our respondents, having firsthand contact with them not only during our interviews but in less formal contexts as well. I, for example, had been visiting Arembepe for several years. I could compare my personal observations and impressions of Arembepeiros across time. I systematically gathered quantitative survey information (in 1985, as I had previously done in 1964). However, I was also developing a more qualitative, case-based impression of the effects of televiewing, as Sonia's case exemplifies.

This qualitative perspective is often as enlightening as statistical results, and it helps us make sense of the numerical data. As another illustration, consider my encounter with Olga, one of the first people I interviewed in Arembepe in summer 1985. Olga was a 55-year-old woman I had known in the 1960s, who expressed delight to see me again. Unlike Sonia, she was eager to talk to me and to answer my questions. However, to my surprise after such a warm welcome, she turned out to be as difficult an informant as Sonia had been.

Olga lived with her daughter and grandchild in downtown Arembepe and had never owned a TV set. She was an avid participant in *candomblé* (Afro-Brazilian religion) and in local festivities, and rarely bothered to watch television in neighbors' homes. Olga reminded me of the older unmarried women I had known in Arembepe during the 1960s. Her exuberance stood out against the more demure and "proper" behavior of married women.

As we went through the questionnaire, Olga displayed none of Sonia's shyness. However, she failed to understand certain questions that most Arembepeiros (particularly those exposed to television) answered easily.

What did she think of a homosexual relationship?

"Just fine," said Olga, obviously never having heard the term, although probably familiar with cases of homosexual behavior.

Did she agree that "a friend of a friend is also a friend"?

"That's right. Friends are good."

"What's more important—what you learn in the streets, what you learn from your family, or what you learn in school?"

"Yes," responded Olga, "what you learn at school is important."

"Is it more important than what you learn in the streets?"

"Yes, what you learn in the streets is very important."

"Is it more important than what you learn in your family?"

"Oh yes, what you learn in your family is very important."

"What's the most important one of them all?"

"They're important, all right. That's right."

From this and similar early interviews, our field team soon became sensitive to "Olga-type respondents"—as we dubbed people who were so unfamiliar with the kind of information processing our survey called for that they had difficulty with opinion questions and with answers that came naturally to most villagers. The Olga types were almost always people with little television exposure.

Another interesting, but quite different, case was Paulo, a fairly wealthy, although illiterate, fisherman who loved to watch his giant color set and listen to his modern stereo system. Paulo still found time to manage and occasionally captain his fishing boat, and to support three wives and two families. (He was Arembepe's best-known polygynist.) Paulo got most of his information about the outside world from TV. He was a news addict, much better informed about political issues than were most Arembepeiros. (Paulo was probably also better informed about current national and international matters than are most middle-class Americans.) An eager participant in external systems, Paulo worried that he might not be able to vote in upcoming elections because he had never learned to read and write.

Another TV addict, but literate and better educated, was Jaime, a skilled factory worker. Jaime said that he often bought books (including an encyclopedia set he proudly pointed out to me) to learn more about stories he had seen reported on television.

HOW WE ANALYZED TV EFFECTS

This simple paragraph is basic to understanding many of the results discussed in the rest of this book. For many of our statistical analyses we used a technique called **multiple regression.** This measures the separate effects (and the combined effects) of several potential predictors on a dependent variable. For example, to predict risk of heart attack (the dependent variable), potential predictors include gender, age, family history, weight, blood pressure, serum cholesterol, exercise, and cigarette smoking. Each one would make a separate contribution, and some would have more impact than others. However, someone with many risk factors (particularly the most significant ones) would have a greater risk of heart attack than someone with few predictors.

For our TV impact study we used a standard set of nine predictor variables and examined their effects on many dependent variables. Our nine predictors were gender, age, skin color, class, education, income, religiosity, length of home TV exposure, and current televiewing level.

Note that our research design permitted us to examine the predictive value of two TV variables: current viewing level and length of home exposure. We could do this because our sample includes people who have had television in their homes for different lengths of time. American research must rely on current viewing level as the main potential predictor of TV impact. This is because there is little variation in length of home exposure, except for variation related to age. Most Americans aged 40 and below have never known a world without TV.

Sometimes, age is used as an indirect measure of TV's cumulative effects in the United States. The assumption is that TV will have influenced older people (up to a point, around age 40) for a longer time period than younger people and thus will have had a cumulatively greater effect. However, this approach has difficulty distinguishing the effects of length of TV exposure from the effects of other aspects of aging. However, our Brazilian research sample included people of the same age who had been exposed to TV for different lengths of time. This allows us to separate years of home TV exposure from aging per se. It also permits us to compare the impact of *current* viewing habits with *cumulative effects* associated with length of home exposure.

STAGES OF TV IMPACT

One of the most important findings to emerge from our research in Brazil is that TV impact should be interpreted as a phenomenon that occurs in stages. There is an initial stage (Stage I—now in progress in Gurupá) of strangeness and novelty, when gazes are usually glued to the set. The medium rather than the message is the mesmerizer.

Becoming more accustomed to and comfortable with television, people—against the backdrop of the cultural systems in which they participate—enter Stage II. They begin a process of selective acceptance and rejection, interpretation, and reworking of TV messages. The community experiences a 10–15-year period of maximum immediate receptivity. Because TV saturation is still only partial, many statistical correlations between viewing and other factors are obvious.

Analyses of our questionnaire data (for example, Appendix 2) suggest that, in a later stage (Stage III), as community saturation and length of exposure increase, clear statistical correlations between televiewing and other variables diminish. To review our field sites, Gurupá, where TV penetration occurred during our study period, remains in Stage I. There were fewer correlations between current viewing time and other variables, because it takes time for specific effects to occur. Arembepe and Cunha are in full Stage II. Ibirama is in late Stage II, in transition to Stage III. Americana and Niterói are full Stage III.

Televiewing produced the strongest correlations in the Stage II communities of Arembepe and Cunha. The latter has the largest number of statistically significant correlations between televiewing and other variables. Cunha may be especially receptive to TV influence. As a traditional county seat in the rural area between Rio and São Paulo, it is much more like the usual settings of the 6 o'clock *novela* than are our other field sites.[2]

In the early stages, television allows an increasing number of formerly isolated villagers to embark on an adventure of instantaneous national participation. Initially, particularly among media-deprived people, attitudes toward TV are overwhelmingly positive. (Tables 9.1 and 9.2 summarize, respectively, attitudes toward television by community and by income groups.) Unlike typical academics and intellectuals in many nations, the unsophisticated Brazilians we studied had an overwhelmingly favorable opinion of television. This positive attitude was obvious during informal ethnography. We also confirmed it statistically by responses to a series of opinion questions about television and what it conveys:

What do you think of TV?

Do you think that television conveys information, knowledge?

Does it entertain?

Is it addictive?

What else does TV do?

Does TV do anything bad? What?

Negative attitudes toward television increased with higher income and with years of exposure. Many comments we heard in Ibirama and Americana, as discussed in Chapter 8, illustrate this relationship. Another strong correlate of an anti-TV attitude was religiosity. (Brazil's religious programming is sparse. There are no indigenous televangelists. The American TV pastor Jimmy Swaggart was dubbed in Portuguese and broadcast on Sundays [not on Globo]. He attracted a small audience, as did the few other regularly scheduled religious programs.) Our statistical analyses show that the correlates and effects of religiosity and of television usually run in opposite directions.

We found that representatives of organized religion were among TV's most consistent opponents. Many Brazilian Protestants (particularly fundamentalists and evangelicals) taboo such activities as drinking, dancing, and televiewing, and therefore lack sets. Catholic priests also opposed television. For example, Ibirama's priest said that he doubted the value of our study, because he already knew TV's effects—they were harmful.

It isn't surprising that churches and elites (along with schools, parents, and the print media) perceive television as a threatening rival and label it harmful. Three decades ago Klapper (1960) summarized American TV research through the 1950s, thereby covering a period in which television had penetrated the United States to roughly the same extent as it now pervades Brazil. Klapper's study is relevant here for that reason. Klapper found communications researchers to be much less likely than parents, educators, and free-lance writers to express fears about television's detri-

TABLE 9.1 *Attitudes Toward Television by Research Site*

RESPONDENT EVALUATION OF TV EFFECTS	COMMUNITY							TOTAL CASES
	GURUPÁ	CUNHA	AREMBEPE	IBIRAMA	NITERÓI	AMERICANA		
Negative	14	50	17	42	22	67		212
	8.7%	15.0%	5.9%	13.8%	10.0%	32.2%		14.0%
Neutral	7	31	10	33	31	40		152
	4.3%	9.3%	3.5%	10.9%	14.0%	19.2%		10.0%
Positive	140	252	259	229	168	101		1149
	87.0%	75.7%	90.6%	75.3%	76.0%	48.6%		75.9%
Total cases	161	333	286	304	221	208		1513
	100.0%	100.0%	100.0%	100.0%	100.0%	100.0%		100.0%

TABLE 9.2 *Attitudes Toward Television by Income Group*

	HOUSEHOLD INCOME			
EVALUATION OF TV	LOWEST	MIDDLE	HIGHEST	TOTAL CASES
Negative	66	56	90	212
	12.4%	9.9%	22.0%	14.1%
Neutral	34	44	74	152
	6.4%	7.8%	18.1%	10.1%
Positive	431	465	245	1141
	81.2%	82.3%	59.9%	75.8%
Total cases	531	565	409	1505
	100.0%	100.0%	100.0%	100.0%

mental effects, particularly on children. Many contemporary Americans continue to believe that media values differ from traditional ones, and therefore harm children. However, research findings have failed to substantiate many everyday assumptions about the effects of the media. Still earlier in American history there had been comparable suspicions of radio and comic books. Popular opinion has linked all these media to varied social ills, including juvenile delinquency.

In the United States, Brazil, and probably throughout the world, elites tend to be more negative about television than are the masses. However, Brazilians of all classes are much less suspicious of TV than Americans are. Our Brazilian informants again and again made the point that TV brings knowledge (*conhecimento*) of the outside world. As one young man in Arembepe put it, "You sit here in this little place and learn about the whole world because you have TV." Awareness of national and global events *is* much greater among viewers than among unexposed people. Regular viewers have more general knowledge and can recognize and interpret more information from outside—both images and ideas.

Widespread naivete and curiosity about the external world preceded television in rural Brazil. Wagley, the original ethnographer (in 1949) of Gurupá, has told me how much villagers used to enjoy looking through his picture magazines, although they had difficulty interpreting the images they saw. (I also remember this interest in photo journals from my own fieldwork in Arembepe in the early 1960s.) Once, as Wagley's informants tried to comprehend magazine photos of the United States, a villager asked him if the Empire State Building was his home.

Tables 9-1 and 9-2 confirm that negative attitudes toward television develop over time, especially among people of higher SES (socioeconomic status). People reject ordinary television as its novelty declines and its status-differentiating value diminishes. In Stages I and II, however, TV enhances social status in two ways. First, it is a possession, a token of conspicuous consumption of material goods. Second and more subtly, it is a source of privileged information. About the status value of TV as a possession, Pace made the following observations in Gurupá:

> Possession of a television was a status symbol which clearly placed one among the upper echelon affluent of Gurupá. For many people who had gone through the financial hardship of buying a television, it was important to reap prestige by showing off the apparatus at every opportunity. To this end, it was common to see television sets on and the owners sitting in their doorways, *with their backs to the set,* watching people pass by on the street. [emphasis added] (Pace n.d.:15)

About the second point, Costa concluded that high-SES people in Ibirama watch TV attentively and frequently because it brings them special information. By disseminating this, they gain prestige and authority.

During Stage III (community saturation), once TV has reached most homes in a locale, statistical measures of its impact become less obvious and accurate.[3] This is because as a phenomenon pervades a community, its presence differentiates less and less among residents. However, this third stage—during which TV impact is apparently least, in terms of a standard set of statistical measures—actually has a subtle, though powerful, impact. Its legacy is a fourth stage—represented by Americans of the baby boom generation and younger.

Stage IV encompasses the continuing and lifelong impact of televiewing on full-grown natives who have spent their entire lives in a national culture pervaded by television and the mass phenomena it spawns. During this fourth phase the more profound and long-term sociocultural effects of television become discernible. I discussed some of them in Chapter 1. Meyerowitz (1985) also describes a series of Stage IV effects, although he does not use that term for them.

TELEVISION'S EFFECTS ON SOCIAL BEHAVIOR

Stages I and II occurred decades ago in the United States but still may be studied in Brazil. Certain differences in TV's contemporary impact in Brazil as compared with the United States are due to stage. We may contrast Stage IV United States with multi-stage Brazil.

However, other differences in television's impact in the two nations are fundamental, dramatic, and probably enduring. First, compared with Brazil, a much longer and greater exposure to print media and radio has mediated television's impact in the United States. Brazil, which actually outlawed printing presses until the 19th century, has never been particularly reading oriented. The contrast in cultural traditions about reading is apparent in many everyday settings.[4]

For example, it is easy to identify foreigners (particularly Americans) on the beach in Rio. They're the ones with books. Brazilians occasionally take newspapers, but rarely books, to the beach. They go there to socialize. Many *cariocas* sit in the same place, with the same friends and relatives, from week to week, throughout their lives. The paucity of reading lamps in Brazilian hotel rooms and homes also illustrates the cultural difference involving reading.

Brazilians view reading as anti-social. They relegate books to a sphere beyond humane, personal society. Books belong to the public world of school, formal education, work, and the rules and records of the bureaucratic state. Books belong to the outside, impersonal world of street and work rather than the inside, intimate world of home and family (DaMatta 1987).

Given Brazil's print media history and attitudes about reading, most Brazilians were truly media-disadvantaged when television reached them. In the United States, television may be the mass medium *par excellance,* but it is nevertheless one among many familiar media that have been available for decades. Compared with other media, television's infiltration of the home has been much more exclusive in Brazil. Furthermore, its most popular presentations, *telenovelas*, help bridge the outside–inside dichotomy. They do this by using family matters as content and domestic settings as backdrop, for portrayals of issues involving relationships among house, street, community, and nation. Thereby, for most Brazilians television has become the primary, often exclusive, conduit to regional, national, and international information. Especially for nonelites, it is the only gate to the global village.

Brazilians do not perceive either television or radio, both of which may be used socially (see below), as being as antisocial as print. Although radio was widely available in Brazilian cities and county seats by the 1950s, its penetration of such rural communities as Arembepe and Gurupá is more recent. Small transistor radios became a fad in these isolated areas in the early 1960s. By the mid-1960s one of the most ubiquitous status symbols of successful fishing boat captains and other men with disposable cash in Arembepe was a portable radio. They purchased these in Salvador (the state capital) or Rio (if they had fished there commercially). Showing their radios off and so that others might listen—that is, *using radio socially*—these men carried their sets around the village. They tuned in soccer games, music, and news—including international reports from the Voice of America, broadcast in Portuguese.

At that time, Arembepeiros had little exposure to print media. The literacy rate was very low. The most educated local schoolteacher had only a fourth grade education, and almost no one read for pleasure. Many Arembepeiros did enjoy picture magazines brought back from the city, and a few occasionally read pamphlet versions of regional ballads.

Television in Society

Our research in Brazil confirms that television per se is not an isolating device. Like radio, TV has a social function there. However, the matter of whether TV promotes or hinders social interaction, like many of its other effects, depends not only on the culture to which it is introduced but also on stage—the extent of saturation of homes. In Brazilian towns and rural areas, an initial TV effect (Stages I and II) is to *promote* social contact. Television brings people from different households together to watch. This occurs in homes (or through the windows) of people with sets, and in public places.

Often, when I told educated Brazilians about my intention to do research on television's impact on rural life, they responded with essentially the same story. They told me about some interior town they had visited where a set was set up in a central square, and to which townsfolk flocked each evening to watch *telenovelas*. This scene was already familiar to me. I had seen it dramatized in the commercial film *Bye, Bye Brasil*, which focuses on the impact of mass communications, including television and international popular culture, on traditional life in the Brazilian backlands.

At the time of our study, comparable scenes could still be seen in Gurupá. Townspeople there were attracted to homes with sets during the evening hours when the town generator was running. Gurupá researcher Pace even observed that the local social hierarchy was manifest in nightly placement of people around sets. The local elites were the first to buy TVs and the powerful antennas needed to pick up a still weak signal from the city of Belém. The more important visitors (including Pace) got chairs in the living room, whereas others stood near the door or watched through the window. I remember a similar nightly scene from Arembepe in 1973. Villagers lined up outside a house in the central square to view an early *telenovela*. Its weak black-and-white signal flickered on the screen of a small battery-operated set, Arembepe's first television.

A quote from a paper by Pace nicely illustrates the social role of television in Stage I Gurupá:

> Whether or not people are allowed to enter homes to watch television, there is a definite cultural rule which stipulates that television viewing should be accessible from the outside of the house for everyone. There is social pressure applied to those who do not conform. I discovered this rule after a few months in Gurupá. As part of the research project, I had purchased and transported a television and antenna to my house. For a month the television was turned on and displayed in front of our window. Friends were invited in and many passersby watched from the window. However, the reception was poor, with the picture fading every five minutes or so. Growing tired of this nuisance, I disconnected the television and packed it away and began closing the shutters of my windows at night (for privacy and to keep mosquitoes out). A few weeks later during a religious festival, a young man unknown to me, who had a

few drinks to bolster his courage, approached me on the street and sarcastically commented, "It's real nice to close your shutters at night and watch television all by yourself, isn't it." Upon realizing that I was being chastised for "hoarding" a scarce "public" form of entertainment, I tried explaining that the television did not work properly and was not being used. To prove my point, I left my shutters open for the next few evenings, clearly demonstrating that the television was not in use. (Pace *n.d.*:13–14)

In each of our four main research sites, set ownership and hours of operation correlated strongly with number of household visitors. (This was no longer true in the Stage III communities of Niterói and Americana–Santa Barbara.) Expectably, large color sets attracted more people than small black-and-white ones. Usual daily household TV hours was the best predictor of the number of visitors a household had.[5]

On the other hand, in Stages III and IV, with set ownership widespread, people tend to stay home to watch their own sets—behavior that the people of Ibirama and Americana lamented. TV ownership in (Stages III and IV) São Paulo appears to be strengthening the nuclear family and the household at the expense of general community life.[6] Even Stage II Arembepeiros had already noticed the beginning of such likely long-term effects. When queried about how TV had changed local life, some villagers responded that it keeps people indoors, with their immediate families, off the streets. Some said that it detracts from activity in the central square. (For a complete list of responses to the question "How has television changed life in your community?" by site, see Appendix 3.)

Marriage, Family, and Social Distance

TV-impact research should be aware of both the *cultivation effect* (the influence of content on heavy viewers) and the *behavioral effects of the medium* per se and its social repercussions in communities. (Of course, social and behavioral effects would be expected to increase when content is culturally appropriate and therefore popular.) Both these aspects of TV impact are potentially important—for example, in producing changes in marriage and the family. In addition to the effects of content, which varies cross-culturally, we must consider the possibility of a more generalized, cross-national behavioral effect. This is the home set's magnetic role in keeping viewers inside with members of their immediate family and household.

Our evidence suggests that both content and viewing circumstance affect Brazilians. Given the characteristic instability of *telenovela* marriages (see Chapter 5), we would predict (from content) that heavy viewing might tend to devalue the marital relationship. On the other hand, *telenovelas* usually end in a succession of marriages. Thus, we might also predict (from content) that legal marriage and the wedding ceremony would gain in value.

Our statistical findings on these matters have been inconsistent. Heavier (current) viewers *were* less likely to agree with the statement that "marriage is important."[7] However, another set of queries, calling for a ranking, produced different results. We asked respondents to rank the relative importance of their children, parents, siblings, and marital partner.[8] Length of home TV exposure *was* significantly associated with a higher ranking of spouse and a lower ranking of parents. This finding supports the magnetic role of the TV set in strengthening nuclear family and household. In addition to the (perhaps countervailing) effects of content, this finding thus seems to reflect a behavioral effect linked to stage of TV penetration (Stage III and beyond).

A ranking of spouse above parents would fit the hypothesis that televiewing eventually augments the value of the immediate domestic unit. That is, long-term home viewing strengthens the nuclear family of procreation (an individual's marriage and the family) over his or her parents and siblings (the family of orientation). This also seems to have been a TV effect in the United States. This finding therefore may exemplify a social-behavioral effect of TV as medium rather than as message.

On the other hand, ubiquitous *telenovela* conflicts between parents and children (particularly teenaged and young adult children) suggested a content-based hypothesis about social relations. We predicted that heavy viewers would tend to see their parents as more unlike themselves than would lighter viewers. To investigate such perceptions, we queried the extent to which Brazilians considered various social categories (including parents) to be different from themselves. (We used a scale from 3, most different, to 0, least different.) The predicted TV bias *was* apparent in the answers of heavy viewers. They considered their parents more different from themselves than did the lighter viewers. Current viewing level turned out to be the number-one predictor of perceived distance from parents.[9] (Issues of causal direction raised by such correlations are discussed in Chapter 12.).

Another finding also illustrates the impact of content on perceptions. When we asked about the extent to which "*telenovela* characters are different from you," heavy viewers considered them more similar than did light or medium viewers.[10]

We found no consistent evidence that TV in Brazil either increases or decreases perceptions of social distance, isolation, or alienation. Long-time viewers saw their friends as closer to themselves than did shorter-term viewers.[11] However, our TV variables did not correlate at all with a composite social-distance index that we constructed.[12]

Contact, Solitude, Alienation, and the Issue of Telepassivity

The initially positive effects of TV on visiting and of home exposure on feelings of closeness to friends are two of several statistical indications we found that television is not inevitably a social isolating mechanism.

Televiewing also correlated strongly and consistently with our index of total external contact.[13] We thus found statistical support for a conclusion I had already reached from qualitative ethnography in Arembepe: Televiewing both *expresses* (preexisting) and *fuels* (new) hunger for external contact and information.

I remembered the time (the early 1960s, more than a decade before TV arrived in Arembepe) when villagers had interrogated me about such matters as foreign travel and the animals found in the United States. I knew that Arembepeiros had always been hungry for external information. I was not surprised to find that their average daily televiewing hours were highest (tied with Niterói—Table 9.3) among our field sites.

Contradicting a common sense opinion often expressed in the United States, our results suggest that heavy televiewing is associated not with inward-looking social isolation, but with an *external orientation*.[14] In Arembepe specifically, in Brazil generally, and I suspect in the United States as well, heavy televiewing may well be linked to a general thirst for information beyond that which is locally and routinely available. Televiewing plays on this tendency and strengthens it.

In assessing television's impact cross-culturally, we should also consider the following hypothesis. *In a culture where people like to be alone, TV may contribute to greater isolation. However, in one where people like to be with others, it may lead to greater social interaction.* DaMatta (personal communication) sees a fundamental difference between Brazil and the United States involving the value of solitude. On certain occasions (sadness, grief, hurt, disappointment) Americans are likely to say "I want to be alone." On those same occasions Brazilians are apt to say "Don't leave me." This cultural contrast helps us understand why Brazilians are suspicious of books and print. Reading is "an essentially solitary, contemplative activity."[15] However, televiewing can easily be done with others.

TABLE 9.3 *Year of TV Arrival and Current Average Daily Individual Viewing Hours by Field Site*

COMMUNITY	YEAR[a]	MEAN HOURS	STANDARD DEVIATION	CASES
Gurupá	1984	.8	1.3	127
Cunha	1977	1.3	1.5	250
Arembepe	1976	2.7	2.4	183
Ibirama	1970	2.2	1.5	248
Niterói	1960	2.7	1.8	138
Americana	1955	2.4	1.3	83
Overall		2.0	1.8	1029

[a]*Year sets arrived in significant numbers.*

Brazilians tend to stigmatize reading as antisocial, although making social use of radio and television. I see two cultural reasons why Americans, in contrast, assign a higher value to reading. First, Americans tend to be more solitary and individualistic than Brazilians. Second, we think that reading demands more *active participation* than do the other media.[16] The *doing* orientation of American culture assigns a high value to activity. "Passive" is a potent negative label. (Reflecting this mentality, American culture now derides heavy televiewers as vegetables, "couch potatoes.")

Cultural values bias opinions about the media. Many common sense assumptions and conclusions have little research support. For example, one early before–after study in Great Britain found no evidence that television makes children passive. However, there was some evidence that viewing *increased* the diversity of children's interests.[17]

In a systematic, comparative, before–after study of three Canadian communities, television initially cut into the use of records, radio, movies, and comic books (Williams 1986). However, it did not affect leisure use of print media or children's visits to the library. Nor was TV related to verbal IQ and vocabulary scores.

Despite such findings, assertions in the popular press about telepassivity persist. These are illustrated in the following discussion of TV's potential negative effects on social interaction (Bernikow 1986:5–6):

> A lot of people . . . think of watching television as something they do by default or as a sign of defeat. If their ability to participate in life and relate to others fails, they watch TV. . . . A young Los Angeles housewife . . . home all day with an infant . . ."coped" by watching soap operas. . . . Her husband left her, and she joined the Displaced Homemakers Network, which referred her to an office-job-training program. "What I'm learning most," she says today, "is how to be with people. I just didn't know how."
>
> The danger television presents to the lonely is that it can keep them passive, reducing whatever stirring they might have to bring more people into their lives or deepen the connections they have. . . . Like any addictive substance, television allows people to escape instead of confront their problems. . . .
>
> Soap operas are very popular among lonely people [who] have pseudo-relationships with the people on the soaps that are very much like real-life relationships.

However, the same article also notes positive effects:

> Some television shows address and assuage this sense of being a pariah. To help people feel "I am not alone in this; others have similar experiences"—whether or not solutions are offered—is a tremendously reassuring aspect of the best of television's talk shows. Even more important is the sense of community that television can provide. Since

lonely people feel they are not part of anything larger than themselves and have no sense of belonging, television can give them a common language and a common set of references at times. . . .

Whenever cataclysmic events have befallen us—the Kennedy assassinations or the shuttle disaster—television has brought us together. On such occasions, it matters less what is being said than that we are all participating, sharing the grief and horror of the nation. . . .

Our Brazilian findings strongly challenge the notion that television is necessarily or fundamentally an isolating, alienating instrument. Televiewing can enhance social interaction in several ways: It provides topics for conversation. It can stimulate visiting. It can teach skills in social navigation. We found these effects in Brazil, but American research has also shown that media supply topics for conversation and thus provide a common ground for social intercourse (Klapper 1960:176). Many listeners looked to soap operas, the serials that dominated American day-time radio in the 1930s and 1940s, for help and advice about real-life problems (Klapper 1960:181). A study in the 1950s of the role of comic strips in the daily lives of low-income American males with limited educations showed something similar. These men used comic characters as descriptive archetypes and plot developments as analogies for real-life situations (Klapper 1960:180). Similarly, rural Brazilians routinely use *telenovela* characters to summarize personality traits of co-villagers.

Some studies in the United States a generation ago suggested that televiewers did less visiting than did nonviewers, and possibly also than they themselves had done before getting a set. However, televiewing neither increased nor decreased the probability that children would take up new pursuits (Klapper 1960:239). We sought comparable data for Brazil. We asked about visiting patterns and frequency of contacts with outsiders, including neighbors and relatives. We found some apparent (previously discussed) differences with the United States. Some of these contrasts are related to stage of TV penetration. Thus, during Stages I and II, social networks are wider, and extradomestic interactions more frequent, in Brazilian households with television.

In our study, televiewing variables neither predicted nor even correlated with "yes" answers to the question "Do you like to be alone?"[18] We also explored variation in social networks and group activities outside the home with questions about membership in professional groups, unions, clubs, and teams. Again, televiewing had no inhibiting effect on membership in such groups.[19]

Televiewing's Effects on Reading

There is a corollary of the link we did find between Brazilian televiewing and an external orientation. Our findings contradict the usual assumption that televiewing has a negative effect on reading. Viewing level correlates consistently with greater use of print media. This was particularly noticeable in the three Brazilian communities that had received television most recently.[20] Confirming my ethnographic conclusion that televiewing is stimulating Arembepeiros to read more was the strong statistical correlation there (as in Cunha) between number of books in the home and daily TV hours. Only education was a stronger predictor than televiewing of scores on our reading index. This measures use of books, magazines, and newspapers.[21] It is *current* TV hours, rather than years of exposure, that correlates very strongly with reading. As hypothesized then, heavy televiewing is associated with general information hunger. Given literacy and the availability of print media, heavy viewers are precisely the people who are also most apt to devour books, magazines, and newspapers.

In the print-saturated United States, it has been difficult for media researchers to disentangle the relative impact of the press and of television. Reflecting this problem, a controversial 1987 article in *TV Guide* attracted widespread media attention. It purported to show that many long-assumed television effects are spurious and that newspapers really set the agenda for television. However, that article failed to convince me that its conclusion was true for the United States. It is even less likely to be true for Brazil, where people read much less, so that TV effects are more exclusive and direct.

There is, nevertheless, a relationship of mutual reinforcement operating in Brazil. Because televiewing stimulates reading, it increases exposure to the press. It hooks people on information and stimulates curiosity, which motivates many Brazilians to read more. One study of Brazilian TV programs designed for children and made from works of literature showed that TV in the classroom stimulated reading (Távola 1984).

American programs routinely stimulate sales of the books on which they are based, and even the writing of new books based on TV (for example, *Star Trek*) characters. By virtue of the television roles they play, such venerable TV stars as Bill Cosby and Carl Sagan write guaranteed best sellers. Critics often cite television as a prime reason that Americans don't read more. However, McDowell (1986) points out that public television has given rise to a highly competitive book publishing business tied to its series.

In discussions of television's educational role, academics and intellectuals in the United States, Brazil, and other countries often focus on the ideal rather than the actual. They ask how TV might be used to teach kids what society says they should know. They might better investigate what TV actually teaches children.

The foremost student of Brazilian television content, Artur da Távola, illustrated this tendency in one newspaper column. He posed the following questions: If (Brazilian) TV is so powerful, molding so much, introducing so much conformity, shouldn't it be used to educate the country by dispersing information, instructing, offering culture, showing major works of drama, and teaching how to analyze and interpret? Given the strength of television, Távola asks, shouldn't it be for the modern world what the (French) encyclopedists were in the past?

The point that Távola misses here is that television does serve these functions. It *has* brought informal educational benefits to Brazil (and to other countries), often in ways that are not immediately apparent. To people who were once isolated from daily contact with external forces, television *has* brought a wider world (a "global" universe, as the Globo network phrases it).

To summarize, our study reveals several positive effects of television in Brazil. It has helped rural folk deal with outsiders. It hones information processing skills and abilities. It stimulates a thirst for knowledge. Additional effects are discussed in Chapter 10.

CHAPTER TEN

Television's Impact on Attitudes, Fears, Values, Images, and Consumerism

Many everyday assumptions and common sense conclusions about how television affects us are supported neither by cross-cultural evidence nor by research findings in the United States. We asked Brazilians several questions designed to test both the usual assumptions and the United States-based research findings.

MEASURING TV EXPOSURE

Our research project used three ways of measuring different degrees of exposure to television: length of site exposure, length of respondent exposure, and current viewing habits.

1. A significant number of television sets with clear and reliable reception reached our field sites in different years (1955, 1960, 1970, 1976, 1977, 1984), providing a continuum of exposure among the six communities.[1] (Refer to Table 9.3.)

2. Our respondents started watching television at different times (either outside or in their homes).

3. The individuals and households we studied had different current viewing habits. In some households the set remained on almost all day, whereas in other homes sets were absent, broken, or rarely turned on. Some people were heavy viewers; some watched rarely, others not at all.

In our interviews we asked each respondent when he or she had begun watching television at home, and anywhere. We explored TV saturation with questions about each household's number of current sets and the viewing habits and preferences of each resident. We determined how many hours each set was normally on each day.[2] We asked each individual interviewee (1032 cases) how many hours he (454) or she (498) custo-marily watched television weekdays and Sundays (the only day Globo's schedule is markedly different).[3] We added together hours watched yesterday, Sunday, and five times usual weekday hours, obtaining a weekly total, which was divided by 7 to give a daily average. This figure served as our main measure of that individual's current television exposure.[4]

In our total sample, the average household kept its set on 4.7 hours per day, with our average individual respondent watching 2.0 hours.[5] As a rough approximation of an individual's TV saturation, we multiplied cur-rent viewing hours by the period during which that person had been watching TV at home. We also used that figure ("life TV hours") to derive "lifeshare," the percentage of the person's life (assuming 24-hour days) spent watching television. Our informants had watched between zero and 82,000 hours of TV and had spent up to 33 percent of their lives in front of a set.[6] Women were 50 percent more TV-exposed than were men, with the average woman having spent 3.4 percent of her life in front of a set (versus a man's 2.2 percent).

For quick analysis and easy presentation, we also grouped average daily viewing hours by individuals into three viewing levels. Our cutoffs were light (0–.99 hour), medium (1.0–2.59), and heavy viewing (2.6+). House-hold viewing levels required higher cutoffs—light (2 hours or less), medium (2 to 6 hours), and heavy (more than 6).[7] In each case, our cutoffs produced three groups with approximately equal numbers.

MEASURING ATTITUDES

We assessed relationships between extent of televiewing and attitudes in a variety of ways. First, we tested a preliminary version of our questionnaire through a 1984 pilot study in Arembepe. Certain kinds of questions work well in the United States, within a national culture permeated by informa-tion processing. We discovered that many of those questions weren't very useful, or had to be modified so that rural Brazilians could understand them. Most of our informants had little conception of such statistically based ideas as frequency and probability. American researchers had asked two samples of schoolchildren the following: "*How often* is it all right to hit someone if you are mad at them? Is it almost always all right or almost never all right?" (Gerbner et al. 1978:195–196). Such abstract evaluations of frequency (how often, almost always, almost never) were unfamiliar to many of our informants. We therefore elicited Brazilians' opinions of physical responses by asking "Is it sometimes necessary to hit a child?" "Is it sometimes necessary to hit a person?" and "Have you ever hit someone?" Given the low violence content of Brazilian entertainment programming, we didn't expect to find much of a TV effect with respect to these ques-tions.

Our results were inconsistent. Heavier viewers were *more* likely to admit that they had hit someone. However, longer-exposed viewers were somewhat *less* apt to say that it's sometimes necessary to hit a child.[8] TV had no effect on the answer to whether it's sometimes necessary to hit an adult. All in all, the effects of TV on hitting were slight, as we had expected.

The United States is a society that offers constant training in information processing, including discriminations of quantity and degree. Because of this, American respondents have an easier time making such distinctions than do Brazilians. Consider one example of such a response scale format that works well for Americans but not for poorly educated, barely literate or illiterate Brazilians. This is a seven category scale running from "delighted," through "pleased," "mostly satisfied," "mixed," "mostly dissatisfied," "unhappy," to "terrible" (Andrews 1984). During pilot testing, we found it futile to try to get our informants to draw distinctions among more than three or four categories. Accordingly, most of our opinion variables used a three- or four-point scale (such as, yes, maybe, no; or very much, somewhat, a little bit, not at all).

For example, we posed the Gerbner-derived question, "Do you think the world is a dangerous place?" (to which Brazilians often responded "It's not the world that's dangerous, but people who are dangerous"). We elicited responses about degree of danger (of the world) on a four-point scale from "very dangerous" to "not at all dangerous." Next we asked how dangerous the community was.

Appendix 2 summarizes the most significant correlations[9] between *current* viewing hours and other variables and indices.

Viewer Demographics

The demographic and socioeconomic characteristics of heavy viewers in Brazil set them off rather dramatically from American heavy viewers. In the United States, the heavier viewers tend to be children, the elderly, lower-income people, blacks, and females.

Our Brazilian heavy viewers, in contrast, scored higher on most socio-economic measures than did lighter viewers. Average televiewing increased with national class, local class, household income, and urban residence. However, as in the United States, females were heavier viewers than males, particularly in the upper-income group.

A Scary World?

Gerbner and Gross (1976a, 1976b) found that adult heavy viewers in the United States tended to perceive a scary world. They saw the real world as more dangerous, violent, and untrustworthy than did light viewers. In order to assess the impact of televiewing on Brazilians' fears and perceived dangers, we asked a series of questions about crime, fears, and cautionary behavior. We also gathered background information, including personal experiences with crime. This permitted us to separate television's influence on fears from other causes. Was a newspaper, radio, or television the informant's main source of news about crime? Did the respondent regularly listen to a crime program? (Such programs are confined to radio. Local and national news are the main sources of crime information on television.)

More often than light viewers, heavy viewers in the United States say that they would be afraid to walk alone "in a city" or "around here" at night. (Gerbner et al. 1978). Pursuing such issues, we asked:

Are you afraid to walk in the streets at night? During the day?

Do/would you let your children play outside at night? During the day?

Are you sometimes afraid of being assaulted or robbed (again)?

What (else) are you afraid of?

Do you think that [name of community] needs more police? Why?

Do you lock the doors of your home
  During the day?
  At night?
  When there's no one at home?
  When there's someone at home?
  Always?

In our data analysis, we looked for correlations between responses to these questions and televiewing variables. (Recall that our two primary TV variables were current viewing hours and length of home exposure.) We constructed a perceived danger index[10] and a fear index.[11] The latter is the sum of positive responses to the following six questions:

Is there anything you're afraid of?

Are you afraid to walk in the streets at night?

Are you afraid to walk in the streets during the day?

Do you lock your doors during the day?

Do you lock your doors at night?

Do you lock your doors when there's no one home?

Finally, our fear-danger index is the sum of the fear index and the perceived danger index.[12]

As I have already noted, research in the United States has found heavy viewers to be more fearful, that is, more likely than lighter viewers to say that the world is a dangerous place. (It seems reasonable to suspect that circular and reinforcing causality is operating here. Inherently fearful people stay home more and watch more television. Given the characteristic American crime and violence-saturated content, this viewing increases their perception of external dangers.) However, televiewing in our field sites, which are safe compared with Brazilian cities, did not seem to cause, or even to correlate consistently with, increased fears and fearfulness. Neither of our main TV variables predicted fear–index scores.[13] Current viewing[14] was associated with a very slight increase in fear–danger index scores. However, neither TV variable influenced the perception that the world was dangerous. Length of home exposure (but not current viewing) *was* associated with an increased perception of danger in the community.[15] Neither variable predicted fear of the streets.[16] Nor did viewing produce any statistically significant difference in door-locking patterns. We found no evidence that televiewing promoted gun sales.[17] However, current viewing level did turn out to be the number one predictor of the opinion that one's community needed additional police. We also found evidence that fearful people (indeed, people with good reason to be fearful) were especially attracted to television: Daily televiewing hours were higher among crime victims.

Consistently, Brazilians' fears correlated more strongly with radio listening than with TV, and there is an inverse correlation between hours spent listening to radio and hours spent watching TV. (Thus, although televiewing tends to stimulate interest in print media in Brazil, television tends to displace, rather than supplement, radio.)

Trust

Gerbner and Gross found American heavy viewers to be "less trustful of their fellow citizens" (1976:41). We asked several questions and, during analysis, devised various indices to test cross-culturally in Brazil the hypothesis that trust diminishes and social alienation increases with heavier viewing (Gerbner et al. 1978:195). However, we found very slight evidence for such relationships. Specifically, we asked people about the degree of confidence they had in various categories: your parents, your children's school, your family, your friends, the priest, your neighbors, the government, local leaders, and what you see and hear on TV. One of our indices added together informants' expressions of degrees of confidence in *close* members of their personal networks. Another index assessed trust in more *distant* people and institutions.[18]

What did we find? Surprisingly, our TV measures had absolutely nothing to do with the amount of confidence people said they had in the information they heard on television.[19] However, length of home exposure turned out to be the strongest predictor of negative trust in government.[20] *This was the strongest TV effect we measured on any aspect of trust.* Still, TV did not affect the likelihood of voting (in a country where voting has been mandatory for literate people, but irregular because of dictatorship).[21]

When we added our two trust indices together to assess total trust,[22] we found the predicted negative relationship between heavy viewing and overall trust in just one of our six sites (Cunha). This negative relationship also showed up in a sample of low-income people compiled from all the sites.[23] In other words our evidence suggests that TV cultivates a lack of trust among poorer Brazilians.

Overall, however, our analyses show no consistent contribution of TV to trust, except for lower trust in government.

Liberal Sex–Gender Views

Televiewing did correlate consistently and *strikingly* with liberal sex–gender views on social issues, as assessed in an index derived from ten questions. This was one of our strongest and clearest statistical confirmations of television's impact on attitudes. We constructed our liberal sex–gender index—to assess liberal–modern (high scores) versus conservative–traditional views on certain sex–gender issues—by adding together positive responses to each of the following questions:

Should a woman work outside the home when her husband doesn't make much money?

Should she work outside when her husband is a good earner?

Should a pregnant woman work outside the home?

Is it proper for a woman to smoke?

Is it proper for women to go to bars?

Should men cook?

Should men wash clothing?

If a woman likes a man, it okay for her to go after him?

Do you think that a married woman's place is in the home?

Is family approval necessary for a marriage?

Statistical analysis showed that Brazilian television strongly influenced sex–gender views.[24] Considering either our index of sex–gender views—or virtually any one of its component questions individually—heavier viewers are *strikingly more liberal.* They are much less traditional in their opinions about such social issues as whether women belong at home, should work when their husbands earn well, should work when pregnant, should go to bars, should leave a husband they no longer love, should pursue men they are interested in, and about whether men should cook and wash clothes, and whether parents should talk to their children about sex.

Supporting the cultivation hypothesis, as applied to Brazil, all these questions elicit TV-biased answers. The world transmitted by Brazilian television (particularly Globo's *telenovelas*) draws on an urban–modern reality in which sex roles *are* less traditional than in small communities. This liberalization was also one of our strongest pan-Brazilian effects, with little variation among field sites. However, we shall soon see that Brazilian TV effects are much less obvious in gender-based job stereotypes. (Still, this finding also fits the cultivation hypothesis, because employed people and workplace/public settings are so much less common on Brazilian than American TV.)

The contemporary Brazilian Portuguese language contains another striking demonstration of a liberalizing TV effect. Traditional Brazilian culture expected children to use the formal (respectful) "you" pronouns when addressing parents and elders.[25] On Brazilian TV, lower-middle class-characters (including adults) tend to use the formal "you" with their parents. However, elite characters, including kids, almost always use the informal term with their parents. This nontraditional usage has therefore become the prestige norm, and ordinary Brazilians are emulating it. Both current viewing level and length of home TV exposure predicted informal "you" terms.[26]

Values: Family, Education, Love, Honor, Ability, Luck, Hard Work

We used many other questions (including open-ended ones) to explore the impact of *telenovela* content. For instance, we asked "What's most important: what you learn in the street, at school, or from your family?"[27] Home TV exposure correlated positively with the value of street learning and negatively with the value of school learning. We had hypothesized such an effect, because education is so unimportant on Brazilian TV.[28]

We also asked our informants to rank a series of values (self-fulfillment, honor, love, family, and education) compared with each other. (*Telenovelas* routinely mention all of these, except education.) For this entire set of questions TV had just one effect: Years of home exposure contributed slightly to the value assigned to the family.[29]

Telenovelas pay little attention to mobility through education, achievement, hard work, and professionalism. We therefore expected the TV-biased responses of Brazilians about these matters to contrast with those of people in more doing-oriented cultures. England, for example, is a more doing-oriented culture than Brazil, albeit more being-oriented than the United States. In one before–after study in Britain (Himmelweit et al. 1958), TV made viewers more ambitious in their expected job choices and aspirations (Klapper 1960:224). I would suspect the same to be true for the United States.

Our work index summed positive responses to several questions about the value of work. As we had predicted, given the low value of work in Brazilian TV content, television had absolutely nothing to do with our work index.[30]

Occupational Prestige Ratings and Aspirations

We sought to determine the extent to which Brazilian televiewing had affected occupational prestige ratings, job aspirations for children, and employment stereotypes based on gender. Given its content, Brazilian TV would be less likely than American TV to produce either higher aspirations for children, or nontraditional gender stereotypes about jobs. The role of Brazilian TV in spreading liberal sex–gender views *has* been much more prominent for *social* issues (see earlier section) than employment issues. Brazilian TV women often speak their minds and act independently in the context of home, family, and marriage. It is much less common to see them vying with men in the work force or in traditionally male professions.

As expected, our data show that nontraditional sex–gender views are *much less obvious* in occupations than in social issues. We assessed this matter with an index derived from responses to questions about whether certain occupations were "good for men," "good for women," or "good for both."[31] Length of home TV exposure *did* predict nontraditional job stereotyping more accurately than did any other variable (including respondent's sex, age, skin color, education, household income, class, or religiosity).[32] However, as predicted, the TV link was much weaker here than with social issues.[33] Furthermore, current viewing hours, which correlated strongly with liberal social views, played no role in gender-based job stereotypes.

We also looked at relative job prestige by asking our informant if he or she considered certain occupations good (3), okay (2), or bad (1). The following list is ranked in order of overall prestige rating (averaged across all respondents) in our national sample of 1032 cases.

engineer	2.88
physician	2.86
large landowner	2.84
industrialist	2.77
performer	2.73
lawyer	2.69
writer	2.68
businessperson	2.62
teacher	2.58
nurse	2.52
paid driver	2.38
factory worker	2.27
small farmer	2.25
mason	2.23
politician	2.20
fisherman	2.08
domestic (paid)	2.04
numbers game ticket seller	1.65

Our index of attributed job prestige adds the scores for a standard list of 16 of those professions. Here, Brazilian TV had anti-work effects, with heavy viewers scoring lower on this index.[34] That is, overall respect for occupations declined with viewing. Given the focus on work in American TV content, we would predict the opposite effect in the United States (that is, appreciation of occupations probably increases with viewing level). In Brazil, performer was the only occupation that increased significantly with viewing level. The occupations that declined were business, industrialist, domestic (maid's work), engineer, lawyer, and fisherman.[35]

Results were similar and also antiwork as predicted in responses to "If you won the lottery would you stop working?" As we expected, because nonworking rich people are common on Brazilian TV, we got more yeses from heavy viewers. As predicted, current viewing level was an important predictor of a "stop work" response.[36]

To investigate professional and status mobility aspirations for children, we asked, "Do you think there's a chance your children will attend college?" As hypothesized, given that education is not valued in Brazilian television content, our TV variables played no detectable role in educational aspirations for children.[37]

The nonworking young people in Brazilian *telenovelas* pose contrasts with traditional work roles of rural Brazilian children. This is particularly true in farming communities such as Gurupá, Cunha, and Ibirama. In our study, both current viewing level and length of home exposure influenced opinions about the age (older) at which children should begin working.[38] Light viewers said that children should start working at an average age of 11.6 years, versus 12.9 years for medium viewers, and 13.5 for heavy viewers.[39]

TELEVISION AND CONSUMERISM

Brazilian television advertising is both direct (commercials) and indirect (consumer goods are introduced as part of entertainment program content). One way in which *novelas* spur consumerism is by having characters chat about their wishes for products. For instance, two young middle-class men discuss their hopes of eventually being able to purchase a home and a car, and to have meat on the table ("as rich people have"). Two women extol a new corn-popping machine. As mentioned previously, Globo is straightforward in its within-program promotion of consumerism. Outdoor locales may include a branch of a sponsor bank, in front of which characters stop to talk, with the bank logo easily visible.

As a result of television, therefore, information about products (their existence, appearance, function, availability, and current price) directly and regularly reaches people in small communities and remote areas. Although televiewing had no discernible statistical impact on answers to "Does TV (do TV ads) influence the products you buy?"[40] effects are very obvious to the ethnographers who originally worked in our research sites a generation ago. New consumer patterns show up in hairstyles, diet, and clothing (for example, sneakers versus sandals).

One of our questions designed to elicit information on consumerism was "If you won the lottery, what would you do with the money?" Most people replied that they would place it in a savings account. We also asked all our respondents (many of them rural people who had been notably bank-wary when first studied ethnographically) if and when they had opened a savings account. TV constantly advertised this investment option during our fieldwork period. No one in Arembepe had had a savings account in the mid-1960s, but many did by the mid-1980s. Current viewing level proved an excellent predictor of whether our informants had savings accounts.[41] (Better roads and bus service also provided villagers with easier access to banks, and made participation in a consumer economy less difficult.)

However, the decision to open a savings account was not just TV-conditioned behavior. It was also a rational response to a very attractive use of surplus money. A savings account offered both interest and "monetary correction" (additional guaranteed monthly interest *equaling* the inflation rate). Savings accounts have been popular in Brazil because they have offered a risk-free investment in an international economy that is far from risk-free.

The existence of millions of savings accounts with monetary correction (and, therefore, TV's impact on economic behavior) has helped fuel the inflation for which Brazil is famous. Advertising (both TV and print) also perpetuates inflation (running 300 percent annually in 1987, 900 percent in 1988). Commercials state only the amount of monthly installment payments for appliances, rather than their actual price (when someone pays "cash").

In addition to spurring savings accounts and installment purchases, Brazilian TV has honed viewers' wishes to own a home—and to be upwardly mobile. We have seen that *subir na vida*, "to rise in life," is one of the main *telenovela* themes, and home ownership is a constantly expressed goal of lower-middle-class *novela* characters.

Despite its overwhelmingly commercial nature, Brazilian television contrasts dramatically with the United States in its few automobile ads. This scarcity reflects Brazil's shrinking domestic new car market, due to the rising cost of cars relative to lower-level salaries. A diminishing proportion of the population can afford an automobile. This explains why production of the Volkswagen bug, VW's cheapest car and for many years a best seller among Brazil's lower-middle and working–class population, was halted in 1987.[42]

Because Brazilian TV aims at the middle class (rather than the very rich or the very poor), there are few ads for expensive products. In 1983–84, when a videocassette recorder sold for more than $1000 in Brazil, I never saw an ad for that product on TV, or even in a newspaper—except when VCR prices were slashed.

A final example of TV impact on consumers' behavior is a widespread correlation and probable negative public health effect. With its fashionable society women and powdered milk ads, Brazilian television promotes early weaning and bottle feeding. Both our main TV variables correlated negatively with breastfeeding.[43] In Cunha, for example, the average female heavy viewer had nursed her last infant just 8 months, versus 13 months for medium viewers, and 18 months for light viewers. On the whole, heavy viewers tended to breastfeed less (or to wean earlier) than did other Brazilian women.

The public health effect is likely to be negative because (1) babies who are nursed acquire antibodies and immunities from mother's milk, (2) mother's milk is often richer in nutrients than is a combination of powdered milk and locally available supplements, and (3) powdered milk is sometimes mixed with polluted water, which causes infantile diarrhea and other illnesses.

URBANISM AND RURAL–URBAN MIGRATION

Because of its predominantly urban content, Brazilian television brings the city to the country and the metropolis to smaller urban centers. Life in such overpopulated, polluted, crime-ridden megacities as Rio and São Paulo is dramatically different from daily existence in Brazil's villages, towns, and small cities. Globo's *telenovelas* characteristically present images of urban glamour and sophistication. Videocameras caress the natural and architectural attractions of Rio and São Paulo, ignoring their more sordid aspects. On the other hand, news programs, which are also popular, convey more negative images of the city, particularly about crime. This raises the possibility that television may affect rural–urban migration, which is often seen as an impediment to rural development. Does Brazilian television (because its messages are contradictory) encourage or discourage urban migration?

After determining whether each informant had visited Rio, São Paulo, and the state capital, we asked several questions designed to assess TV-generated images of Brazilian cities.[44] Because TV transmits contradictory images, with *telenovelas* positive and news negative about urban life, it is not surprising that our TV variables had no clear directional effect on images of city life. Our respondents viewed Rio (the setting of most *novelas*) more positively than São Paulo. However, our TV variables did not serve to predict the image score of either city.[45] Similarly, we found no discernible effects of television on responses to "Would you like your children to live in a big city?"[46]

Our project is examining many other aspects of TV's varied cultural, social, economic, and psychological effects in Brazil. Those results (and elaborations on many of the findings reported here) will be given in future publications. I recognize, of course, that it is not just through the electronic mass media that rural and small-town Brazilians participate in nation and world. There are many other sources of exposure to external institutions and the currents of social change. These include seasonal, temporary, and permanent rural–urban migration and improved transportation (particularly bus), which permits people to shop in cities and to visit emigrant relatives. City and nation also increasingly invade local communities in the guise of tourists, development agents, government and religious officials, and political candidates.[47] Such linkages, of course, are prominent components of the larger-scale (regional, national, and international) systems of politics, economics, and information that increasingly affect the people and places traditionally studied by anthropology. The study of such linkages and systems is a prominent part of the subject matter of modern anthropology.

CHAPTER ELEVEN

🌀 Festivals, Celebrations, and Gift-Giving

Television has influenced the ways in which Brazilians celebrate certain occasions, including Carnival, Christmas, and birthdays. Televiewing promotes gift-giving, as one manifestation of consumerism. In particular, television increases the popularity of collective holidays, such as Christmas and Carnival, which is the Brazilian equivalent of Louisiana's Mardi Gras. Brazilian television has aided the national spread of Carnival beyond its traditional centers—Rio de Janeiro and the northeastern cities of Salvador (Bahia) and Recife. However, local reactions to TV images of Carnival and other celebrations are not simple or uniform responses to external stimuli. Rather than direct adoption of Carnival, or rote imitation of it, local Brazilians have responded in various ways. These reactions (discussed later in this chapter) include processes called "stimulus diffusion" and "reactive opposition." Communities are modifying their traditional *local* festivities, sometimes to fit (stimulus diffusion), sometimes to avoid (reactive opposition) Carnival images and associations.

DaMatta points out that public celebrations such as Carnival must be interpreted in terms of the opposition between home and street that is so prominent in Brazilian society (1987:164). Brazilians think of home, the primary domain of their society, as a realm of family and friends, of relationships based on blood and hospitality. The street, which is an entrance to the public world beyond the home, is a domain of professional groups and categories, markets and competition, crime and punishment. Different rules and values (domestic/internal versus public/external) apply to relations and behavior in these two domains. According to DaMatta (1987:165), things are different in the United States because there is no such split between the moral and ethical rules of home and those of the outside world.

How is nationhood forged and maintained in such a family-oriented society as Brazil? As DaMatta observes, *public celebrations, particularly Carnival, bridge the normally separate domains of the Brazilian social universe.* They temporarily unite home, street, and the larger external world.

Like Carnival, soccer also promotes social identities beyond the family. Thus, Brazilians are identifying with a nonkin group when they make such a common statement as "I *am* Fluminense [a soccer team]." Similarly, they may assert "I *am* Mangueira [one of the clubs or samba schools that performs in Rio's Carnival parade each year]." Americans likewise identify with clubs or teams of which they are members. They do this by saying "I am an Elk," "I am a Moose," "I am a Wolverine," or "I am a Golden Gopher." In the United States, only team members normally make such a statement. Fans properly say "I'm a Wolverine (Dodger, and so on) *fan.*"

The typical American belongs to dozens of nonkin-based groups. These include churches, political parties, clubs, teams, occupational groups, organizations, associations, and committees. In Brazil, where home and extended family hold their own so vigorously against the external world, nonkin associations are fewer. When such associations are rarer, they may well be more precious. This probably explains why identification with a soccer team is more direct, personal, and intense in Brazil than is fandom in the United States. The lifelong Flamengo fan feels that he or she "is Flamengo" just as much as are the players, who come and go.

The *telenovela* also extends Brazilians' horizons beyond the home. However, unlike a samba club membership or a team loyalty, the expression "I am Globo" does not differentiate among Brazilians. This is because the Globo network is nationwide, whereas festivals and soccer loyalties are more regional or local. This makes television particularly significant in forging external social identities. In contrast to soccer clubs and samba schools, it is a *common,* rather than a sectarian, bridge between home and outside, between family and nation. Operating as such on a daily basis, it has become the main mechanism whereby alien images, and people who are neither relatives nor friends, enter the home. It introduces otherwise unfamiliar settings and types of people. For example, country people glimpse urban life; city dwellers meet rural folk. Given massive illiteracy and lingering rural isolation, Brazilian television is a key mediator. For millions it is the sole source, rather than one among many, of exposure to global information and social interactions involving strangers.

The *novela*, soccer, and Carnival are alike therefore because they link the home and the external world. They are also similar in that they originated as urban phenomena, then became national ones. First radio, then television, helped spread *novelas*, soccer, and Carnival to the countryside. Through radio, soccer became a staple of Brazilian national popular culture in the 1950s, as did, through photo magazines, the Miss Brazil and Miss Universe contests.[1] However, in contrast to soccer's steady popularity, public interest in beauty contests has declined, for two reasons. First, Globo does not televise these contests. Second, women who are more attractive, glamorous, talented, and interesting than beauty contestants now appear daily in Globo *telenovelas*.

Before television's national spread, people saw beauty contestants in photo magazines comparable to *Life* and *Look*. Rural people who visited the city brought such magazines home. They used them to discuss how state beauties compared with those from other areas of Brazil. Television seems to have diminished rural Brazilians' interest in photo magazines—except for magazines about TV. Moving images are more enticing than still ones. Similarly, in the United States *Life* and *Look* declined in popularity as TV entered the home.

CARNIVAL: LOCAL OR NATIONAL, STIMULUS DIFFUSION, REACTIVE OPPOSITION

According to DaMatta (1981), who is its best-known academic student, Carnival introduces unity, equality, and democracy to Brazil's normally hierarchical and divided (between house and street) social world. It dispenses with the divisions and multiple codes that permeate normal Brazilian life.

> Carnival represents a movement toward an egalitarian utopia, toward a society of equals similar to that of American daily life: everything happens simultaneously, everyone has the same rights, everyone talks with everyone else, everyone is able to live, act, and think in a "coherent" way. (DaMatta 1981:137)

Brazilian intellectuals often argue about whether Carnival is a truly national or merely a regional–urban event. Those who hold the former view point out that nationwide, even in small towns, there are dances and balls during the four days of Carnival (Saturday through Tuesday). (Thereafter come 40 days of Lent, leading up to Easter in the Roman Catholic calendar.) Those who hold the latter view point out that Carnival is celebrated most enthusiastically, with public displays—lavish floats, parades, and dancing in the streets—in Rio de Janeiro. The assumed *carioca* identity of Carnival became very clear in 1983. That year, Rio de Janeiro (state) Governor Leonel Brizola, not himself a *carioca*, drew criticism concerning the construction of a new arena *(sambádromo)* to which Rio's Carnival was moving. One charge was that there was too wide a space along Samba Avenue before the finale in Apotheosis Square. This mistake was attributed to the fact that he was not a *carioca* and therefore did not understand the space requirements of Carnival flow patterns.

For decades the most enthusiastic celebration of Carnival *has* been in Rio, which has the main samba schools. These schools, which compete annually for prizes based on their Carnival performance, are nonkin-based voluntary associations. They usually have their headquarters in lower-class suburban neighborhoods (for example, Mangueira), but they attract people from all over the city and from varied walks of life. Samba schools are unique in Brazil in that they bring together, in direct interpersonal relations and common egalitarian activity, thousands of unrelated people. Their main connection is their common objective: samba work. Jointly they organize their school's entry for the lavish competitive Carnival parade. Annually each school prepares an original display consisting of score, music, rhythm, dance, floats, and costumes. For instance, in 1984 the school called Portela, whose performance won second place, fielded 43 sections, each with 60 people—a total of about 2500 singers, dancers, musicians, and float performers.

The Carnival parades for which Rio de Janeiro has become internationally famous feature performances by a dozen such schools. This culminates a year of hard communal work. Members have developed ideas for innovative shows. They have discussed and prepared floats, costumes, songs, and dance formations. There is similar preparation, though on a smaller scale, in the northeastern cities of Recife and Salvador. The activities in those three Brazilian cities have done much to create an annual national festival transmitted by television.

Given its policy of sticking to its normal nightly *telenovela* schedule no matter what, Globo does not always offer national Carnival coverage. It has sometimes suffered as a result. In 1984, for example, Globo's regular shows were badly beaten (in Rio de Janeiro but not nationally) by rival network Manchête's Carnival coverage. Since then Globo has offered more Carnival coverage, but usually (except for flashes) not in prime time.[2] Globo's strategy seems appropriate, because Carnival has yet to attain the nationwide popularity of either the *telenovela* or of a World Cup soccer game. Carnival therefore does remain more of a local–regional concern than either of these, although its national influence is growing.

This is shown in Table 11.1, which tabulates responses to the question "What is the most important festive occasion of the year for you?" (There are more responses [2563] than respondents [1032] because people could give more than one response. They gave up to six.) We see that interest in Carnival does increase in proportion to televiewing. Still, Carnival does not match the popularity of Christmas. The top-ranked occasions were Christmas, the main local festival, birthdays, New Year's Day, Easter, and Saint John's Day (a June festival).

Case Analysis: A National Sex Symbol of Carnival

Carnival is most popular in Rio de Janeiro, where most of Brazilian television also originates. In the case analysis that follows, I show how and why one of Brazil's top sex symbols, a native of Rio, symbolizes Carnival and the cultural values it encapsulates. This case parallels the discussion of *Star Trek* in Chapter 7. It demonstrates once again that popular media content expresses values that are prominent in many other domains of culture, including a national holiday.

For the past few years, one of Brazil's top sex symbols has been an attractive young woman named Roberta Close, whom I first saw in a television commercial for office furniture. Roberta, whose physical appearance reminded me a bit of the young Natalie Wood, ended her pitch with

TABLE 11.1 *Responses to "What Is the Most Important Festive Occasion of the Year for You?" by Viewing Level*

CELEBRATIONS BY RESPONDENT	TELEVIEWING LEVELS			TOTAL CASES
	LOWEST	MIDDLE	HIGHEST	
Christmas	138	255	240	633
	20.5%	26.7%	27.8%	25.4%
Main local	186	104	69	359
	27.6%	10.9%	8.0%	14.4%
Birthdays	60	159	139	358
	8.9%	16.6%	16.1%	14.4%
New Year	45	138	130	313
	6.7%	14.5%	15.1%	12.6%
Easter	37	103	79	219
	5.5%	10.8%	9.2%	8.8%
June festivals	37	59	97	193
	5.5%	6.2%	11.2%	7.7%
Minor saints' days	60	44	22	126
	8.9%	4.6%	2.5%	5.1%
Easter related	45	16	17	78
	6.7%	1.7%	2.0%	3.1%
Parents/Kids day	15	15	21	51
	2.2%	1.6%	2.4%	2.0%
Carnival	5	17	22	44
	.7%	1.8%	2.5%	1.8%
Religious parties	20	15	6	41
	3.0%	1.6%	.7%	1.6%
Civic dates	10	16	6	32
	1.5%	1.7%	.7%	1.3%
Weddings	4	10	10	24
	.6%	1.0%	1.2%	1.0%
Others	11	4	5	20
	1.6%	.4%	.6%	.8%
Total cases	673	955	863	2491
	100.0%	100.0%	100.0%	100.0%

an admonition to prospective furniture buyers to accept no substitute for the advertised product. "Things," she warned, "are not always what they seem."

Nor was Roberta, I soon learned. This petite and incredibly feminine creature is actually a man. Nevertheless, despite the fact that he—or she (to speak as natives do)—is a man posing as a woman, Roberta Close has won a secure place in Brazilian mass culture. Her photos decorate the major magazines. She travels throughout Brazil making public appearances. From time to time she is a panelist on the amateur-hour portion of a popular weekly variety show. She has starred with an actor known for his supermacho image in a stage play in Rio. Roberta even inspired a well-known, apparently heterosexual, fortyish singer to record a single and make a video honoring her. In the video, Roberta pranced around Rio's Ipanema Beach in a scant bikini, showing off her ample hips and buttocks. The female derriere has the same positive cultural value in Brazil that breasts do in the United States. Roberta's breasts, though less noteworthy than her lower body, are also feminine. Although the matter of whether Roberta has undergone genital surgery is not publicly discussed, no one would ever spontaneously identify her as a man.

The subject matter of the video, which became an overnight success, was appreciative male reaction to Roberta's beauty. It showed men falling off ladders as she passed by, and ogling her out of bus windows. One heterosexual middle-aged Brazilian man told me that he had once traveled on the same airplane as Roberta and had been struck by her looks and femininity. Another man said he'd like to have sex with her.

Here, it seemed to me, were some striking cultural contrasts. Would a middle-aged North American heterosexual male tell me that he would like to go to bed with a transvestite? I doubt it. Yet in Brazil, a Latin American country noted for its machismo, heterosexual men did not feel that admitting attraction for a transsexual blemished their masculine identities.[3]

How different, I thought, from the United States, where transvestism has a stigma, and transsexualism, although legal, is not exactly mainstream. Never, to my knowledge, has *Seventeen* featured a male cover girl. Never has a transsexual judged at a Miss America pageant or served as a panelist on a network TV show.

Yet when I have told all this to my university colleagues in the United States—even to anthropologists—a frequent response is: "But don't you see. We have the same thing. What about Michael Jackson? He's androgynous, too."

Were my friends right? Did Roberta Close and Michael Jackson play similar roles in their cultures of origin? I started rethinking the matter.

Even in Brazil in 1983–84 one could not escape Michael Jackson's meteoric rise to international renown, to rival Pope John Paul II as the most famous man in the world. Jackson's records played incessantly on Brazilian radio. His videos showed up on TV, and kids throughout the nation imitated his dance steps. Jackson's success began in the United States, then spread overseas. Michael Jackson followed in the footsteps of other decade-dominating singers. These were Frank Sinatra in the 1940s, Elvis Presley in the 1950s, and the Beatles in the 1960s. Like my university colleagues, many of the experts who have written about Jackson have focused on his androgyny. What, however, did androgyny have to do with Michael Jackson's success, and what does this tell us about American culture, in which his popularity began?

Jackson's consummate showmanship is a major factor in his success, but this does not permit us to ignore the role of his culture in propelling him to the top. Key cultural figures often become that because they dramatically mediate (help reconcile by uniting) oppositions or contrasts that are significant in their culture. I believe that a large part of Michael Jackson's continuing success is due to the fact that he mediates not just one but several oppositions considered important in American culture. These oppositions extend beyond male–female. Jackson also mediates between black and white, good and bad, fantasy and reality, and (most important I think) childhood and adulthood.

All these oppositions are problematic in contemporary American culture. Because our culture places such a high value on youth, people fear growing old and do all they can to avoid it. American culture raises males and females to be different, but our ideology of equality also tells them they should be the same. Overlooking obvious physical differences, our culture requires us to use the term *black* to describe people of many physical types. Some of those people have light skin, blue eyes, and blond hair. Another contradictory feature of contemporary American culture is that millions of people regularly seek fantasy escape through such outlets as television, films, and pilgrimages to Disney shrines. They also constantly admonish their children to "work hard" and "be realistic."

Michael Jackson's persona helps resolve these fundamental contradictions of contemporary American culture. His public presence incorporates elements of male and female, child and adult, black and white, fantasy and reality, public exuberance and private reclusiveness. By the contrasts he incarnates, and therefore helps mediate, Michael Jackson has enjoyed wide appeal, particularly in 1984. That year, riding the success of history's most popular record album "Thriller," he became not just an individual but a summary representation of a culture. Such symbolic summation is a key attribute of figures who dominate their cultures at particular times, as Michael Jackson dominated American culture the year Roberta Close became popular in Brazil.

It is wrong, I have concluded, to single out androgyny as the most important factor in Michael Jackson's success. Even more significant in the cultural explanation of Jackson is that he is childlike. True, Michael Jackson has a high voice. Yet how can one say for sure whether his voice is feminine or preadolescent? In his youthfulness (now a bit forced), Michael

Jackson is like the Beatles and the high-voiced Bee Gees previously. All these stars have distilled essences of that precious American commodity—carefree, exuberant, premarital youth.[4] We long to hold onto our youth, even as, increasingly, our North American work ethic and our contemporary full-work economy force us to abandon youth for adult responsibilities.

The search for the Fountain of Youth is a prominent American cultural theme. It is not so pervasive in Brazil. Middle-class Brazilian men are more content to let their heads turn to gray as their wives turn to Clairol, and their bellies swell with beer as their wives' do with babies. All this signals maturity, leisure, the good life. The middle-aged man's beer belly is a status symbol. It tells others its bearer doesn't have a job that demands hard physical labor. However, in a perpetual youth oriented culture like the United States, such public figures as Michael Jackson embody our fantasy that we can escape the constraints of normal time. Through such symbolic mediators as Michael Jackson and Peter Pan, we can fantasize that there is a Never-Neverland where responsibilities are absent and aging stops.

My colleagues were therefore off the mark in equating Michael Jackson with a Brazilian transvestite. A more accurate view is that the singer personifies and melds multiple social contrasts that American culture considers important. In particular, he appeals to wishes for perpetual youth, which Americans feel more intensely than do Brazilians.

Aside from mediation, another way of dramatizing key cultural themes is *symbolic inversion*. The nature of something may be clearer once we see it momentarily as its opposite. Roberta Close is not a mediator but an inverter. She does not bring masculine and feminine closer together, but she dramatizes the differences between them by carrying them to extremes. Roberta Close stands at one end of a Brazilian cultural scale that runs from extreme femininity to extreme masculinity, with little in between.

Another Brazilian cultural contrast, which is related to the masculine–feminine one, is between active (masculine) and passive (feminine). This contrast pervades Brazilian sexual life, even providing a model for male homosexuality. Brazilians think of male homosexuality[5] almost completely with reference to the contrast between active and passive anal sex. One man is supposed to be the active (inserting) partner, the other the passive one. Brazilian culture assumes these preferences to be permanent and part of an individual's identity. For example, newspaper reports about a sensational 1984 robbery–murder case described the victim as a "passive homosexual." An effeminate passive homosexual is derided as a *bicha* ("intestinal worm"), but little stigma attaches to the inserter (particularly the occasional one). Brazilian culture permits poor boys to preserve their masculine identities while they earn money as active partners in anal sex with passive men.

Brazil has been rather tolerant of homosexuality, which has never been illegal there. Before AIDS became a public health concern,[6] supposed homosexual and heterosexual love affairs were regular fodder for gossip columns.[7] In addition to male homosexuals there are a few public lesbians in Brazil. Some of them exaggerate masculine behavior. However, the male-dominated media don't pay much attention to masculine women, and most Brazilian lesbians retain more than a semblance of traditional Brazilian femininity. Judging by their public appearance and behavior, they don't want to be men, or to be like men. On the other hand, as Roberta Close and dozens of similar men–women in the public eye demonstrate, it is much more common for a man to want to be, and to become, a woman, and to be appreciated by the public as a result.

In Brazil the male–female contrast in rights and behavior is much stronger than in the United States. Brazilian men confront a more rigidly defined masculine role. They have fewer alternatives than do North American men. If Brazilian men choose homosexuality, their culture tells them they must define themselves either as active, which is still an ultramasculine role, or as passive. In the latter case this has usually meant joining the stigmatized category of the effeminate *bicha*. However, there is one other choice: to escape homosexuality (man–man sex) altogether by becoming a woman. That is what Roberta Close and others like her have done. In these cases, the cultural demand of ultramasculinity yields to a performance of ultrafemininity. These men–women have created and occupy one extreme end of a more stretched-out sex–gender identity scale than the one that operates in contemporary American culture.

Despite the fact that homosexual practice traditionally has been more rigidly prescribed in Brazil than in the United States, pre-AIDS Brazil was known internationally as something of a paradise for gay men. Gay tourists from Europe and North America still flock to Rio at Carnival time. They can participate in the ambience of inversion, which is the most striking characteristic of Carnival. In the culturally accurate words of the American popular novelist Gregory McDonald, who sets one of his books in Brazil at Carnival time:

> Everything goes topsy-turvy . . .
> Men become women;
> women become men;
> grown-ups become children;
> rich people pretend they're poor;
> poor people, rich;
> sober people become drunkards;
> thieves become generous.
> Very topsy-turvy. (McDonald 1984:154)

Most notably, *men become women.* Even small rural villages such as Arembepe have the tradition of men dressing as women at Carnival time.

This occasion of socially permitted inversion reveals and expresses tensions and conflicts that are normally hidden. Normal social life is inverted, turned upside down. *Reality is illuminated through dramatic presentation of its opposite.*

This, then, is the final key to the cultural meaning of Roberta Close. Roberta's image emerged in a city where male–female inversion is an accepted part of the year's most popular festival. Transsexuals such as Roberta are the *pièces de résistance* of Rio's Carnival balls, where they dress as scantily as real women. They wear postage stamp bikinis, sometimes with no tops. Photos of real women and transformed ones like Roberta vie for space in *Manchête*, Brazil's most popular *Life–Look* imitator. It is often impossible to tell the born women from the hidden men. Roberta Close, the inverter, is a permanent incarnation of Carnival. She is a year-round reminder of the spirit of Carnivals past, present, and yet to come. She, like Carnival itself, has become a national symbol of Rio's *carioca* values and life-style.

Roberta Close is the creation of a Latin culture with sex roles and sexual preferences that contrast strongly with those of the United States. From small village to massive city, Brazilian males are public, and Brazilian females, private creatures. Streets, beaches, and bars belong to the men. Although bikinis adorn Rio's beaches on weekends and holidays, there are many more men than women there on weekdays. The men revel in their primate displays. As they sun themselves and play soccer and volleyball, they regularly stroke their genitals to keep them firm. They are living publicly, assertively, and sexually in a world of men.

Brazilian men work hard at this public image, at this *representation* of their culture's definition of proper masculine behavior. It is no accident that the Brazilian word for acting is *representaçao*. Brazilian public life is a play in which the only strong roles go to men. Women, on the other hand, get the good parts in the private sphere. Roberta Close, of course, is a public figure. Given that Brazilian culture defines the public world as male, we can perhaps now understand why the nation's number one sex symbol is a man who excels at performing in public as a woman.

FESTIVALS, LOCAL CULTURE, AND THE WORLD SYSTEM

Television helped make Roberta Close, who is a symbol of Carnival's dominant inversion, a national celebrity. More generally, the mass media have made Carnival more of a national phenomenon than it used to be. However, this has not been a matter of simple stimulus and response. Nationwide broadcasting of Carnival and its trappings does not always stimulate automatic and direct local imitation. Just as often, Carnival's national propagation leads to *stimulus diffusion*. In this process, communities do not take up Carnival itself, but they do modify their own local festivities to fit images and patterns of Carnival. The local response may also be *reactive opposition*. In this process, people consciously and deliberately reject or avoid Carnival. Sometimes they do this by celebrating their traditional local festivities on a previously unimagined scale.

As Marcus and Fisher observe "The penetrations of a world economy, communications, and the problems of identity and cultural authenticity . . . have increased markedly among most local and regional cultures worldwide" (1986:37). Some believe that contemporary technology, including television, is killing off traditional cultures by homogenizing products in order to reach more people. Others, including cultural critic Walter Benjamin (who predeceased television's worldwide diffusion), have forecast a role for modern technology in allowing social groups to express themselves and in disseminating particular subcultures (Marcus and Fisher 1986:122). Today's voracious American media establishment, for example, constantly brings local events, concerns, and initiatives (for instance, a chicken festival in Iowa) to the attention of a larger public. American television plays a key role in stimulating local activities of many sorts. Similarly, in many parts of Brazil, traditional celebrations and performances are being transformed in response to tourism and television, as local events draw the attention of outsiders.

There is reason to ask how television has affected festivities in small Brazilian communities. Brazil's national Carnival coverage seems more often to inspire stimulus diffusion than direct borrowing through simple imitation. That is, outside of Rio, Salvador, and Recife, community groups work hard not on Carnival per se, but on incorporating Carnival elements and themes in their own local ceremonies. Some of these seem to have grown in scale, in imitation of Carnival celebrations shown on national television.

Both Carnival's national exposure and its stimulus–diffusion effects have been spreading as a result of television. However, local reactions can also be negative, even hostile, as in Arembepe. Carnival was never very important in Arembepe. This is probably because of its calendrical closeness to the major traditional local festival honoring Saint Francis, which is held in February.

In 1985 we discovered the full extent of Arembepeiros' reactive opposition. Not only do they reject Carnival, they are growing increasingly hostile to their own once-favored local festivity as well. Again and again Arembepeiros told us that they resent the fact that Saint Francis has become "an outsiders' event." It draws thousands of tourists to Arembepe each February. Commercial interests and outsiders have appropriated Saint Francis. In reaction, many Arembepeiros now say that they like and participate more in the June festivals honoring Saint John, Saint Peter, and Saint Anthony. These were celebrated on a much smaller scale than was Saint Francis during the 1960s. Arembepeiros celebrate them now with a new vigor and enthusiasm, as they react to outsiders and their celebrations, real and televised.

However, external attention to another traditional Arembepe event has generated a more favorable local reaction. Here TV coverage has stimulated participation in a traditional annual performance, the *Chegança*. This is a fishermen's dance-play that reenacts the Portuguese discovery of Brazil. For the first time in 1985, Arembepeiros traveled to a suburb of Salvador to perform the *Chegança* in front of television cameras. This was part of a program featuring traditional performances from many Bahian communities. Here one sees television's potential role in allowing social groups to express themselves and in disseminating particular subcultures.

One reason Globo's Sunday night variety program *Fantástico* is so popular in rural areas is its inclusion of footage showing such local events. (National and international celebrities such as Roberta Close and Michael Jackson also appear on *Fantástico*.) In several towns along the Amazon River, I discovered that annual folk ceremonies are now staged more lavishly for TV cameras. In the Amazon town of Parantins, for example, boatloads of tourists arriving at any time of year are shown a videotape of the town's annual Bumba Meu Boi festival. This is a costumed performance mimicking bull-fighting, parts of which have been shown on *Fantástico*. This pattern, in which communities preserve, revive, and intensify the scale of traditional ceremonies in order to perform for television audiences, appears to be growing.

TELEVISION, GIFT-GIVING, CONSUMERISM

Studies in many societies have demonstrated that major religious ceremonies usually have functions and consequences that extend well beyond the domain of constituted religion. In state-organized societies in particular, religious activity has important political and socioeconomic implications. For the subsistence-oriented peasants of rural Madagascar, for example, ceremonial expenses are even more important than taxation in stimulating participation in the cash economy (Kottak 1980). People work for cash mainly in order to buy supplies for their ancestral ceremonies. Like religion, television also promotes gift-giving and the need for cash (sometimes borrowed) and its use in exchanges.

Christmas and Birthdays

In bringing images of Carnival to the nation, Brazilian television has affected traditional community performances and celebrations in various ways. Furthermore, television, that preeminent handmaiden of consumerism, is also transforming the Brazilian Christmas. Particularly in cities and among the consuming classes, television has promoted the notion of Christmas as an occasion for spending large sums of money on gifts and feasting. Our statistical results confirm that Christmas gift-giving rises with televiewing level.[8] Table 11.1 shows a steady increase in Brazilians' ranking of the importance of Christmas as their televiewing rises.

Nowadays, as Christmas approaches, a barrage of Brazilian TV ads appears, hawking such appliances as television sets and stereo systems. Santa Claus (Papai Noel) has become almost as ubiquitous a commercial figure at tropical Christmastime as in North America. One department store chain, for example, uses a team of trampoline-jumping, hand-clapping Santas to advertise summer clothes. Brazilians who can afford to do so give costly imported Christmas baskets containing liquors, jellies, nuts, olive oil, caviar, and other delicacies. Locally packed baskets are available for those with smaller budgets.

Given a predominantly Christian population to start with, Christmas offers an excellent mass gift-giving occasion for a consumer society. Consumerism favors collective holidays over occasions focusing on individuals, as birthdays and weddings do. This is because it is easier for manufacturers to plan products to appear at a particular season than to stagger production and distribution. Also, fads, which stimulate sales, are easier to sustain for a few weeks than a year. Consequently, the importance of Christmas seems to be growing in tandem with Brazil's consumer economy.

I initially hypothesized that Christmas might be spreading at the expense of the birthday celebration, which is traditionally important in Brazilian society. Our results (Table 11.1) indicate, however, that this is not so. The importance of birthdays also increases with viewing level. Thus, *Brazilian television stimulates a higher level of gift-giving in general.* Christmas gifing is in addition to, rather than in replacement of, birthday obligations.[9]

When birthdays are more important than collective, seasonal holidays such as Christmas, gift-giving is staggered throughout the year. The pile of bills that Americans (and many contemporary Brazilians) associate with Christmas did not come rolling in when the birthday was the major event. Members of the focal individual's extended family attended the traditional birthday party. The occasion marked that person's entrance into, and ongoing membership in, a kin group. For each member, it reinforced and symbolized the continuity of the Brazilian family.

However, because of Brazil's current high rate of population increase, there are more and more birthdays to celebrate. Even as a Brazilian's own nuclear family of procreation is growing, he or she must also celebrate the birthdays of other children within the extended family. Each birthday provides an occasion for the extended family to get together. The web of birthdays creates a never-ending string of social obligations throughout the year. This is one reason that many contemporary Brazilians have less leisure time to spend with nonfamily members than they did in the past.

The combined forces of increasing population (hence increasing kinship obligations) and consumerism may eventually force a contraction of the extended family. This may push Brazilians away from birthdays and toward Christmas. Focusing on Christmas, a one-day event, rather than a series of birthday parties throughout the year permits Brazilians to satisfy kin obligations by buying smaller presents for several children in the extended family. They can restrict their participation in birthday parties to the most important ones.

The Evolution of Christmas

A personal case comparison between the United States and Brazil can illustrate the relationship between traditional cultural celebrations and contemporary forces. My mother-in-law was born and raised in Brazil long before the advent of television. She has strong opinions about fundamental differences between traditional Brazil and the United States, where she has lived for 50 years. One key difference involves Christmas, which she insists was unimportant in Brazil during her childhood. For her, the traditional Brazilian Christmas stands in sharp contrast to the overblown festivities she sees in the United States. It is hard for my mother-in-law to understand why Christmas is so important to Americans. Birthdays, she says, were most important to Brazilians. "When I was a child in Brazil, we didn't give Christmas presents. We had a nice lunch, then went to the beach. We only gave presents for birthdays."

Not only older Brazilians, but even Americans who grew up before World War II, may have difficulty understanding today's Christmas, with its conspicuous consumption and media-manufactured seasonal memories. For most Americans, today's Christmas is more of a cultural than a religious holiday. For many of us it retains its religious significance as birthday of the Christ Child. However, for almost all of us, Christmas has become the year's main gift-giving festival, a holiday with huge commercial significance. As the familiar carol was parodied in an old album by Bob Newhart:

> Angels we have heard on high.
> Tell us to go out and buy.

Anthropologists know that a festival's origin is a different matter from its current context, content, and consequences. Along with Easter, Christmas is one of the most sacred days in the Christian calendar. However, nations with predominantly Christian populations celebrate Christmas in many different ways. The manner of celebrating reflects not just differences between sects and denominations, but also distinctive social, economic, and climatic conditions. The American Christmas has become progressively more elaborate with the growth of a consumer economy and with changes in the organization of work and family.

The American Christmas, which many of us believe to be as old as the Pilgrims, was actually a "conscious and deliberate invention" of the middle 19th century (Coy 1984:D1, D11). The celebration of Christ's *mass* had been banned by the Puritans, including the Pilgrims. They deliberately spent their first Christmas in Massachusetts working hard all day. They wished to avoid a celebration associated with the Church of England and Roman Catholicism.

In the United States Christmas first became a legal holiday in Alabama, in 1836. During the Civil War 13 other states gave it this status. The holiday grew in importance after the Civil War, for several reasons. One was massive immigration of German, Irish, and Italian Catholics, among whom the holiday was traditional.[10] Another reason for the increasing importance of Christmas was probably the labor movement, whose aims, realized mainly during the twentieth century, included shorter working hours. One result was an increase in the number of legal holidays.

Only gradually has Christmas acquired its status as our culture's most important symbol of enduring family ties. Its evolution into a commercial potlatch, fueled by the media, has taken several decades and has depended on the growth of consumerism. The origin of the word *potlatch* is a public ceremonial display among American Indians of the North Pacific Coast. Native potlatches were giveaways of food and wealth to relatives and acquaintances from other villages. Potlatching often entailed the destruction of property, including blankets and canoes. Sometimes the host even burned down his home. As one year's hosts became next year's guests, potlatching linked people together within a regional economy, and it leveled out wealth differences among individuals and communities.

The contemporary American Christmas doesn't entail any direct or obvious destruction of property, but it does fuel the trade deficit. (Gifts as different as Nintendo and Cabbage Patch Kids are now imported from the Orient.) Thus, Christmas, like potlatching, plays a role in a larger economic system—an international economy. It levels out surplus wealth that may accumulate during the course of the year.

Indeed, for many Americans Christmas creates debts that last much of the year. Each May we hear about Freedom from Taxes Day. (Because our average total tax burden exceeds one-third of our annual income, we retain less than two-thirds of what we earn. Thus, we work more than four months just to pay our taxes.) Considering our opportunities to overspend at "the most wonderful time of the year," it's a wonder that no one has yet invented a Freedom from Christmas-Indebtedness Day. Two weeks before Christmas 1988, *The New York Times* was offering many intriguing holiday debt enhancers. There was a Brooks Brothers crew neck sweater for $325, a champagne opener for $135, a Bergdorf mink coat "on sale" for $9500, Tiffany ear clips for $5950, and a kilogram of Bloomingdale's beluga caviar for $1500. All this was enough to make a cynic proclaim "Read my lips; no new gifts."

Festive Participation and the Efflorescence of Giving

Within the highly developed consumer economy of the United States, many people give gifts or send cards for Christmas, birthdays, Mother's

Day, Father's Day, and Valentine's Day. More recent additions include occasions such as Sweetest Day, Grandparents' Day, and National Secretaries' Week. (These are blatantly commercial inventions of the greeting card, telephone, florist, and candy industries. We might wonder how far away are Pets' Day and My-Friend-the-Computer Week.)

With consumerism less developed in Brazil, television there uses seasonal advertising to hype just the older mass gift-giving occasions: Mother's and Father's Day and Christmas. Commercial television also has its way of encouraging gifts on the individual-focused occasions—birthdays, weddings, and anniversaries. Brazilian TV promotes birthday and anniversary gifts by inserting occasional reminders in regular programming, dramatized through particular individuals. Forgotten anniversaries and birthdays cause hurt and embarrassment on *telenovelas*.

Our research project included a set of questions concerning religion,[11] holidays, celebrations, and festive participation. We asked the following questions concerning ceremonial participation, gift-giving, and consumerism:

> What events/celebrations do you celebrate/commemorate?
>
> What's the most important festive occasion of the year for you? How do you celebrate it?
>
> What's the most important festive occasion that happens here in your community? With whom and how do you celebrate this local event?
>
> What's most important to you (and rank): Carnival, Christmas, or the main local festive occasion?
>
> What's most important: Christmas or your birthday?
>
> Where, how, and with whom do you spend Christmas? Do you give Christmas presents? To whom? Do you receive Christmas presents? From whom?
>
> Where, how, and with whom do you spend your birthday? Do you give birthday presents? To whom? Do you get birthday presents? From whom?
>
> Are there other occasions on which you give or receive presents? (Name them and indicate whether you give, receive, or both.)

What were the main results? Table 11.2 lists the occasions most often celebrated in each community. Table 11.1, discussed throughout this chapter, has listed such occasions by TV viewing levels. One obvious contrast related to television, shown in both tables, is that the (inter)national holidays tend to be favored by the heavy viewers. Tables 11.1 and 11.2 both demonstrate that televiewing correlates dramatically with celebration of (inter)national holidays at the expense of local ones. Local celebrations, including many minor saints' days, decline with viewing level.

TABLE 11.2 *Responses to "What Is the Most Important Festive Occasion of the Year for You?" by Community*

CELEBRATIONS BY RESPONDENT	COMMUNITY						TOTAL CASES
	GURUPÁ	CUNHA	AREMBEPE	IBIRAMA	NITERÓI	AMERICANA	
Christmas	41 16.5%	95 21.2%	103 21.7%	228 29.2%	112 32.0%	74 28.5%	653 25.5%
Main local	137 55.2%	121 26.9%	102 21.5%		1 .3%	1 .4%	362 14.1%
Birthdays	10 4.0%	51 11.4%	19 4.0%	170 21.7%	79 22.6%	43 16.5%	372 14.5%
New Year	4 1.6%	36 8.0%	46 9.7%	84 10.7%	90 25.7%	60 23.1%	320 12.5%
Easter	3 1.2%	5 1.1%	5 1.1%	175 22.4%	12 3.4%	28 10.8%	228 8.9%
June festivals	9 3.6%	11 2.4%	135 28.5%	4 .5%	27 7.7%	13 5.0%	199 7.8%
Minor saints' days	28 11.3%	25 5.6%	31 6.5%	43 5.5%		1 .4%	128 5.0%
Easter related	2 .8%	59 13.1%	6 1.3%	8 1.0%	1 .3%	3 1.2%	79 3.1%

T A B L E 11.2 (Continued)

CELEBRATIONS BY RESPONDENT	GURUPÁ	CUNHA	AREMBEPE	COMMUNITY IBIRAMA	NITERÓI	AMERICANA	TOTAL CASES
Parents/Kids day	3 1.2%	6 1.3%	2 .4%	24 3.1%	6 1.7%	13 5.0%	54 2.1%
Carnival		7 1.6%	17 3.6%	1 .1%	15 4.3%	6 2.3%	46 1.8%
Religious parties	1 .4%	18 4.0%		23 2.9%			42 1.6%
Civic dates	8 3.2%	5 1.1%		9 1.2%	3 .9%	9 3.5%	34 1.3%
Weddings		7 1.6%		10 1.3%	4 1.1%	5 1.9%	26 1.0%
Others	2 .8%	3 .7%	8 1.7%	3 .4%		4 1.5%	20 .8%
Total cases	248 100.0%	449 100.0%	474 100.0%	782 100.0%	350 100.0%	260 100.0%	2563 100.0%

There is also a striking decline in the perceived importance of the main local festival in proportion to the length of community exposure to TV. Thus, in Gurupá, the most recently exposed site, 55 percent of our respondents said that a traditional local celebration was most important to them. This declined to 27 percent and 21 percent respectively in Cunha and Arembepe. In the still longer-exposed communities of Ibirama, Niteroi, and Americana, no local ceremony retained much significance. There was a similar drop in the importance of minor saints' days from Gurupá to Americana. However, the importance of Christmas and New Year's rose with length of community exposure.

We found that length of home TV exposure was the key statistical predictor of a low ranking of local celebrations.[12] Also as predicted, we confirmed statistically that long home exposure did increase the importance attributed to Carnival.[13] We found no evidence that Christmas giving caused a decline in birthday gift-giving. Rather, televiewing was positively correlated with gift-giving and receiving in general. Thus, Brazilian commercial television, like its North American analog, stimulates gift exchange in general, as one among many expressions of consumerism.

CHAPTER TWELVE

❧ Television and Modern Life

Let me summarize the most innovative aspects of the research project from which this book has emerged.

1. We combined survey research and ethnography across a range of Brazilian communities. We used a detailed questionnaire to gather comparable quantitative data, which we analyzed statistically. In each community, we also gathered qualitative data through participant observation. Each researcher did an ethnographic study of local social life and of the thoughts, opinions, and actions of people in the community setting.

2. Our cross-cultural approach expanded perspectives derived from U.S.-based research with an appropriate cross-national case.

3. We were able to consider and to distinguish between two key TV variables. First was current viewing level, which is routinely used in American correlational research. Second and more important was length of home TV exposure. We were able to study groups of people of the same age exposed to television for different times for reasons beyond their (or their family's) control.

There are compelling reasons for doing TV research outside the United States, in countries such as Brazil. When television is virtually everywhere, as it has been in America for decades, researchers can only observe how people behave when it is present. However, in many Third World nations, including Brazil, many households still lack sets. In such settings we can study effects of both length and degree of exposure. Our project began in time to locate and interview many Brazilians with virtually no exposure to television.

To assess the impact of television we used a standard set of nine potential predictor variables. We examined their effects on hundreds of dependent variables (only some of which have been discussed in this book). Our nine predictors were: gender, age, skin color, social class, education, income, religiosity, length of home TV exposure, and current televiewing level.

Again I emphasize that our research design permitted us to examine the predictive value of two different TV variables. These were length of home exposure and current viewing level. We could use the first measure because our sample included people with television in their homes for different time periods. In contrast, American research must rely on current viewing level to measure TV's influence, because there is little variation in length of home exposure, except for variation based on age. Americans aged 45 and younger have never known a world without TV.

Some American researchers have tried to use age as an *indirect measure* of TV's effects. Their assumption is that viewing has a cumulative effect, its influence increasing (up to a point) with age. However, this approach has difficulty distinguishing the effects of TV exposure per se from other aspects of aging.

Our Brazilian sample included people in the same age groups but exposed to TV for different times. We could therefore separate length of home TV exposure from aging. Years of age and years of home exposure were two separate potential predictor variables. We could also compare the correlates of current viewing habits with cumulative effects associated with length of home exposure.

Table 12.1 summarizes the effects (or correlations) of length of home exposure. Table 12.2 lists the correlations associated with current viewing level.

TV impact research should consider both the cultivation effect (the influence of content on heavy viewers) and the behavioral effects of the medium per se and its social repercussions in communities. Length of home TV exposure provides the best, most direct measure of the cumulative effects of television. However, it generally has not been possible to use this measure in the United States. In our Brazilian study, home exposure predicted more dependent variables (and predicted them more strongly) than did current viewing level.

Thus, longer home exposure was one of the top two predictors of the following 11 dependent variables:

greater use of print media

reading widely

nonsexist job stereotyping

"liberal" (less sexist) views on social issues

having more household possessions

having a favorite performer of the same skin color

having less trust in government

assigning a lower value to local festivals

considering school learning less important

less corporal punishment of children

less fearful about kids

On the other hand, current viewing level (average daily hours) was one of the top two predictors of just 7 dependent variables. They were:

TABLE 12.1 *Summary of the Effects[a] of Long-Term Exposure to TV at Home*

BRAZILIANS WITH LONG-TIME HOME EXPOSURE ARE MORE LIKELY TO:

Be skin-color conscious
> say they have a favorite performer of their own skin color*[b]

Be liberal
> have "liberal" views on social issues*
> do less sexist job stereotyping*
> use informal "you" terms
> let their children address them informally

Consume
> have many household possessions*
> give birthday gifts
> give and receive presents

Value (inter)national holidays and the external world
> say they like Carnival
> say they value "what you learn in the street"

*Use print media**

Devalue work
> say they would stop working if they won the lottery
> say kids should wait to start working until they are older

Focus on the nuclear family of procreation
> value spouse over parents

Perceive danger
> score high on the danger index
> consider their town dangerous

LESS EXPOSED BRAZILIANS ARE MORE LIKELY TO:

Trust
> trust government*
> score high on the trust index

*Value local festivals**

*Value school learning**

*Use corporal punishment**

*Fear for their children**

Focus on the family of orientation and the extended family
> value parents over spouse
> value siblings

[a]*Statistically significant separate and independent effects as assessed through stepwise multiple regression analysis.*
[b]*Asterisk (*) indicates that home exposure was one of the top two predictors (among nine potential predictors) of this dependent variable.*

T A B L E 12. 2 *Summary of Correlates[a] of Current Viewing Level*

CURRENT HEAVY VIEWERS ARE MORE LIKELY TO:

Be skin-color conscious
>   say they have a favorite performer of their own skin color*[b]

Be liberal
>   have "liberal" views on social issues*
>   let their children address them informally
>   use informal "you" terms

Consume
>   have household possessions
>   give Christmas gifts

*Have savings accounts**

Consider their siblings important

*Have many visitors**

Devalue work
>   say they would stop working if they won the lottery*
>   say children should wait to start working until a later age

Admit hitting someone

Worry about safety
>   have a high fear–danger index score
>   say that the community needs more police*

Read
>   use print media generally
>   read widely*

*Say that TV has changed their life**

LIGHT VIEWERS ARE MORE LIKELY TO:

Consider TV addictive*
Trust members of their personal network
Say they consider family important
Say they value "what one learns in the family"
Say they consider marriage important

[a] *Statistically significant separate and independent effects as assessed through stepwise multiple regression analysis.*
[b] *Asterisk (*) indicates that the TV variable was one of the top two predictors (among nine potential predictors) of this dependent variable.*

reading widely

having visitors

having a favorite performer of the same skin color

having savings accounts

thinking the town needs more police

thinking that TV has changed one's life

not considering TV to be addictive

Television's most profound effects on people, society and culture take place very gradually. They may well be imperceptible to natives, and researchers, at a given time. However, our research design (studying a gamut of communities and people exposed to television for varying lengths of time) did reveal many effects.

The demographic and socioeconomic profile of the typical Brazilian heavy viewer differs substantially from his or her American counterpart. In the United States, correlates of heavy viewing include being a child, elderly, black, female, and having a lower income. Brazilian heavy viewers, in contrast, scored higher on most socioeconomic measures than did lighter viewers. Only the gender correlation was the same. Brazilian women were 50 percent more TV-exposed than were men.

Our project confirmed that TV impact occurs in *stages*. There is an initial stage (Stage I—now in progress in Gurupá) of strangeness and novelty. The medium (the set) rather than the message (content) is the mesmerizer. Stage II (Cunha, Arembepe) is a 10–15-year period of maximum receptivity. People accept, reject, interpret, and rework TV messages. Because TV saturation is still only partial, many statistical correlations between viewing and other factors are obvious. Televiewing produced the strongest correlations in the Stage II communities of Arembepe and Cunha.

Ibirama is entering, and Americana and Niterói are fully in, Stage III. Once TV has reached most homes in a community, measures of its impact become less obvious. This is because as an innovation pervades a population, its presence differentiates less and less between people.

However, this third stage—during which TV impact *appears* to be least—has a subtle, though powerful, legacy. Stage IV, exemplified by Americans of the baby boom generation and younger, encompasses the cumulative effects of TV on full-grown natives who have spent their lives in a society pervaded by television and the behavior patterns and mass culture it spawns. During this fourth phase the more profound and long-term sociocultural effects of television—those that led me to this study, as discussed in Chapter 1—become obvious.

Opinions about television vary with social class and with stage. Brazilian elites are more negative about TV than are the masses (which is probably true throughout the world). People of higher socioeconomic status reject ordinary television as its novelty declines and its status-differentiating value diminishes. Long-exposed people are more disparaging than are novices. However, Brazilians of all classes tend to have more favorable impressions of television and more positive assessments of its effects than do comparable Americans.

Fears about harmful effects of television are most typical of traditional information brokers and moral guardians. These include elites, intellectuals, educators, writers, and the clergy. In Brazil we found representatives of organized religion to be the most consistent opponents of television. In most of our statistical associations, religiosity and TV exposure ran in opposite directions.

Television's infiltration of the home has been more exclusive and revolutionary in Brazil than in the United States, where there has always been greater use of print media. For most Brazilians, television is the main gateway to the global village. By fueling information hunger, television fosters media use. It can therefore encourage reading and promote literacy.

Our findings thus contradict Americans' usual assumption that televiewing hurts the reading habit. (Many such common sense assumptions and conclusions have little research support.) A relationship of mutual reinforcement operates in Brazil, where televiewing stimulates reading by hooking people on information and stimulating curiosity.

Brazilian televiewing *expresses and fuels* hunger for contacts and information. Heavy viewing is part of an external orientation, a general thirst for information and contacts beyond those that are locally and routinely available. Many of our respondents regarded television very positively for bringing information about national and global events. Although rural Brazilians' knowledge of the world is nonacademic, it is much greater now than it was before TV. Regular viewers can better recognize and interpret information, images, and ideas from outside the local setting. Our village studies confirmed that television can (1) stimulate curiosity and a thirst for knowledge, (2) increase skills in communicating with outsiders, (3) spur participation in larger-scale cultural and socioeconomic systems, and (4) shift loyalties from local to national events.

Brazilian TV does more to spread national than international culture patterns. It familiarizes rural people with urban and national norms. It facilitates social interaction by making provincial folk more comfortable dealing with strangers, including representatives of higher social classes. TV exposure can reduce fearful and obsequious behavior.

TV is neither necessarily nor fundamentally an isolating, alienating instrument. The medium has varied effects on social life and behavior. Brazilian televiewing enhances social interaction in several ways. It provides topics for conversation, stimulates visiting (in the early stages at least), and teaches skills in social navigation.

TV's role in promoting or hindering social interaction depends on the culture it enters. It also depends on stage of community saturation. An initial effect (Stages I and II) is to promote social contact, by bringing people from different households together to watch. In Stages I and II, set ownership and hours of operation correlate very strongly with number of household visitors. However, in Stage III, with set ownership widespread, people stay home to watch their own sets.

Besides the effects of content, which varies cross-culturally, we must also consider the possibility of a more generalized, cross-national behavioral effect of television. This is the set's magnetic role in keeping people home with members of their household, often a nuclear family. There was an increased tendency to rank spouse above parents among long-term Brazilian viewers. This fits the hypothesis that viewing augments the value of the immediate domestic unit.

That is, long-term home viewing strengthens the nuclear family of procreation (an individual's marriage and the family) over his or her parents and siblings (the family of orientation). This may also have been a TV effect in the United States. This finding may therefore exemplify a social–behavioral effect of TV as a medium, rather than through particular content.

Does television eventually alienate people from their fellows and increase perceptions of social distance? Televiewing in Brazil does not keep people from joining and attending meetings of professional groups, unions, clubs, or teams. Furthermore, our televiewing variables correlated *not at all* with a social distance index we developed. Religiosity was the best predictor of stated feelings of *closeness* to parents, relatives, and network members. Education, the second best predictor of perceived social distance, had opposite effects from religiosity. *Education—but not television—increases perceptions of social distance among Brazilians.*

Do heavy viewers in Brazil, as in the United States, tend to perceive a scary world? That is, do they tend to view the real world as more violent, dangerous, and untrustworthy than do light viewers? We found some, but not a lot of, evidence for this relationship. I suspect that circular and reinforcing causality operates to produce such statistical associations. That is, inherently fearful people are more likely to stay home, watch more TV, and choose programs addressing their concerns and fears. In the United States particularly, given the heavy dose of crime and violence in content, heavy viewing may well sharpen already overdeveloped perceptions of external dangers.

Televiewing did not correlate consistently with fears and fearfulness in our field sites, all of which have very low crime rates. Our TV variables did *not* predict increased fear of the streets at night. Current viewing level, but not length of exposure, predicted an increase, but a very slight one, in fear–danger index scores. This finding would seem to support the hypothesis that heavy viewing merely correlates with fears, rather than causing them.

Current viewing level was also the number one predictor of the opinion that the community needs more police. Again, however, we had no reason to conclude that this was an effect rather than simply a correlation. Brazilians' fears correlated more strongly with radio listening (particularly to the daily hour-long crime reports) than with TV.

For the American finding that trust diminishes with heavy viewing, we also found some support. Heavy viewers expressed less trust in members of their personal social networks. Longer-exposed Brazilians had slightly lower average scores on our trust index. Finally, lower trust in government correlated strongly with years of home exposure.

Some of the most consistent content-related correlates of Brazilian televiewing are antiwork, antiachievement, and antieducation opinions and attitudes. *Telenovelas* pay little attention to mobility through education, achievement, hard work, and professionalism. In full accordance with the cultivation hypothesis (given the unimportance of education in Brazilian TV content), length of home exposure did correlate with attributing *less* importance to education. Heavier viewers granted less prestige to our standard list of occupations than did lighter viewers. Results were similar and also antiwork in responses to "If you won the lottery would you stop working?"

The nonworking young people in *telenovelas* contrast strongly with traditional work roles of rural Brazilian children. Length of home exposure influenced opinions about the age (older) at which children should begin working.

Brazilian television spreads both positive (*telenovela*) and negative (news) images of big city life. It is probably because of these contradictory images that our TV variables did not correlate with images of city life. Our respondents did tend to view life in Rio (where most *novelas* are set) more positively than life in São Paulo. However, we found no discernible TV effects on responses to "Would you like your children to live in a big city?"

INTERNAL VARIATION: TV IMPACT AS A PROCESS

Attention to cultural, political, and economic variation *within* towns, regions, and nations, as well as between nations, is vital in understanding the effects of technology on human behavior. With television, cultural variation intervenes in determining: (1) specific aspects of program content, (2) program preferences, and (3) how people interpret and are affected by televised messages.

Content is part of the culture of the creators. Brazilian creators belong primarily to the urban elite. However, ordinary people can influence content, because creators monitor audience reactions to a given *telenovela* during its course.

Program preferences, interpretations of content by audiences, and impact are all *processes*. TV impact is not a matter of simple, automatic, programmed responses to irresistible, omnipotent stimuli. Viewing, interpretation, and impact all take place within the context of the prior culture(s) of audiences.

Viewers are not passive victims. They are not the couch potatoes who populate contemporary American conversations. Instead, they are human beings who make discriminations about and use television in ways that make sense to them. They watch to validate beliefs, develop fantasies, and find answers to questions that the local setting discourages or condemns. People use TV to relieve frustrations, build or enhance images of self, chart social courses, and formulate daring life plans. Sometimes the interaction between viewer and set leads to unrealistic plans, false hopes, disappointment, and frustration. However, the process of TV impact is not one in which an all-powerful Big Brother zaps a defenseless zombie.

We take prior culture(s) and subcultures into account when we consider why different programs attract different audiences. Program choices and preferences reflect preexisting social categories and contrasts, power differentials, and variant predispositions within the local culture. Audiences use television in varied ways. They go on watching because they find meaning in its images and content. In Ibirama, for instance, Costa (n.d.) concluded that women and young adults of both sexes were particularly attracted to *telenovelas*. Through his participant observation and general ethnography he found that these relatively powerless social groups use Globo's *telenovelas* to challenge conservative local norms.

Thus, besides varying *between* nations, audience preferences also vary with local (and regional and national) cultural contrasts and categories. Since the beginning of this book, I have insisted that there is a reciprocal relationship between television and culture. Preexisting cultural categories and views influence indigenous creations and audience behavior.

Long-term exposure to messages feeds back on social reality, gradually changing old beliefs, attitudes, and behavior. This process contributes to a changing (mass) culture. Unifying themes may emerge, but the result is not simply homogenization. New differences and divisions may also arise, and preexisting distinctions and conflicts may be reinforced or even intensified.

An example from our findings may clarify these matters. The world that Globo creates and transmits has its genesis in an urban–modern reality in which sex and family roles are markedly less traditional than in small communities such as our field sites. Brazilian televiewing correlates consistently with liberal views on social issues. Aspects of liberalization provided some of our strongest pan-Brazilian correlations, with little variation among the communities. This showed up in views about sex, gender, and social issues, and in language. Usage of the informal "you" pronoun with parents is nontraditional. However, it is the prestige norm in *telenovelas*. As we expected, ordinary Brazilians are emulating it.

Are these effects or just correlations? That is, does Brazilian TV make people more liberal, or do already liberal people, seeking reinforcement for their views, simply watch more television, particularly *telenovelas*? Do they look to TV and its urban elite world view for moral options that are missing, suppressed, or disapproved of in their own, more traditional towns?

I have concluded that liberalization is both a correlation and an effect. There is a strong *correlation* between liberal social views and *current* viewing hours. Liberal small-town Brazilians may well watch more TV, to validate personal views that the local setting suppresses (Costa n.d.). However, confirming that long-term TV exposure also has an *effect* on Brazilians' attitudes, there is an even stronger correlation between years of home viewing and liberal social views.

It is difficult to separate effects of televiewing from mere correlations when we use current viewing level as a predictor variable. However, *effects* are more obvious when length of home exposure is the predictor. We can compare, logically, this predictor and its processual impact to education and its effects. If the cumulative effects of formal education increase with years of schooling, then it seems reasonable to assume a similar result with years of home exposure to television.

Thus, heavy (*telenovela*) viewers are probably predisposed to liberal views. However, over time, content—entering Brazilian homes on a daily basis—reinforces those views. TV-biased and TV-reinforced opinions and attitudes spread in the community as televiewers take courage from the daily validation of their unorthodox local views in national programming. More and more townsfolk encounter nontraditional views and come to accept them as normal.

In a larger context, TV impact is one highly significant part of a more general process of urbanism, nationalism, and state solidification, with many mutually reinforcing aspects. That *telenovela* characters tend to belong to the national elite, enjoying the good life of wealth, power, and leisure, encourages local-level acceptance of the external messages. Townspeople mine the world of *telenovelas* for patterns and values that eventually influence local prestige norms. More and more people emulate them. Over time, Brazilian TV gradually aids a national process of social liberalization. This is one of its many effects (Table 12.1), all of which, I suspect, develop in a similar processual manner.

HOW IMPORTANT IS TELEVISION FOR UNDERSTANDING MODERN LIFE?

A unique perspective has emerged from this research project in Brazil. Our results have convinced me that television's social and cultural significance is much greater than I imagined when I started planning the study. This conclusion is confirmed by considering the relative predictive value of our TV variables compared with such traditional social indicators as education, income, gender, and social class. Recall that we used a set of

TABLE 12.3 *Summary of the Predictive Power of Nine Variables*

	DEPENDENT VARIABLES[a] PREDICTED	AVERAGE RANK
Education	7	2.0
Years of home TV exposure	10	2.6
Gender	10	2.6
Skin color	12	2.8
Household income	9	2.9
Social class	10	3.3
Religiosity	8	3.5
Age	10	3.7
Current average daily viewing hours	5	5.2

[a]*Of 17 considered for this particular comparison.*

nine (potential) predictor variables and examined their effects on hundreds of dependent variables. Our nine predictors were gender, age, skin color, class, education, income, religiosity, length of home TV exposure, and current televiewing level.

Table 12.3 shows how well each of the 9 fared as a predictor of the following 17 dependent variables and indices:

    considers the world dangerous
    considers the community dangerous
    danger index
    fears for kids' safety
    fear index
    fear–danger index
    trusts close network members
    trust index
    prefers (inter)national holidays to local ones
    gift-giving and receiving index
    sodality index (membership in clubs and associations)
    would like to live in a big city
    urban image index

nonsexist job stereotyping (index)

liberal views on social issues (index)

print index

inventory of household possessions (index)

Length of home TV exposure was a much more potent predictor than was current viewing level. Furthermore, *home exposure was one of our very best predictors.* Its average rank as a predictor (first, second, third, and so on as best predictor of a dependent variable) was 2.6. Only education had a higher average predictive rank (2.0). However, education predicted only seven of the dependent variables, compared with ten for home TV exposure.

Home TV exposure and gender tied as predictors, both in number and in rank. Skin color predicted the largest number of dependent variables (12), but with a weaker average correlation (2.8) than the variables just mentioned. Social class and age each predicted ten dependent variables, but they had much weaker explanatory power. Religiosity, age, and current viewing hours were the poorest predictors. (Appendix 4 lists the dependent variables associated with each predictor variable.)

These findings convince me that no serious study of modern society can ignore the long-term effects of television. I became interested in TV because I saw all around me evidence of its effects. They seemed comparable to those of humanity's most powerful traditional institutions—family, church, state, and education. I went to Brazil for a cross-cultural perspective on the social context and impact of television. I chose Brazil because it was a major nation permeated, but still incompletely, by commercial television. There I could carry out a research project of a sort that is no longer possible in the United States. The results of that project have led me to a firm conclusion: In today's world, the home TV set has joined education, gender, skin color, income, class, religiosity, and age as a key indicator of what we think and what we do.

Epilogue: Stage V – The Couch Potato Strikes Back

Even in Stage IV settings in Brazil (the major cities), network TV—and a single network to boot—still dominates as none has ever done in the United States. If a mass medium is supposed to give most natives what they want, Globo does it better than the American networks do. Indeed, network inadequacies in holding the mass audience are a prime reason for the tremendous increase in cable and videocassette use in the United States.[1] Of course, the job of attracting and holding audiences is tougher in the United States: More diverse than Brazilians, Americans offer a much more differentiated pool of target markets.

During the 1950s and 1960s, even into the 1970s, Americans were network loyalists. However, the era of *I Love Lucy, Roots,* and *M*A*S*H* has ended. The American commercial networks' combined share of the prime-time audience has been falling consistently, from 90 percent in 1980 to 75 percent in 1986, and 68 percent in 1989 (Rothenberg 1989). As one observer put it:

> A new challenge faces [America's] . . . broadcast-television industry. Threatened as never before by competition from cable, videocassettes and independent stations, network TV operates in an environment of shrinking audiences, weakening advertising revenues, and predatory outsiders who see profit in taking over and streamlining a high-cost business. (Time 1986:69).

Simultaneously, an electronic revolution has forged myriad new links between American homes and the outside world. Rotating antennas and satellite dishes, but especially cable channels and videocassette recorders (VCRs), provide more options than ever in our use of television. The hallmarks of this latest phase of TV impact, Stage V, are diversity and activity, in the form of audience–TV interactions. New technology is permitting the ordinary viewer to seize control of the means of production, distribution, and consumption of TV content.

One of the most striking contrasts between television in the United States and other nations is the viewing diversity and alternatives that cable provides. The number of Americans homes with cable doubled between 1985 and 1988, and cable TV's share of the prime-time audience rose from 13 percent to 22 percent (Rothenberg 1989:45). Americans can choose among channels specializing in headline news, regular news, weather, sports, foreign movies, intellectual movies, old movies, new movies, health, exploration and discovery, ethnic fare, religion, country music, and pop-rock music. Cable makes superstations and independent stations, which show films, sports, syndicated programs, and local news, as accessible as the networks. The superstation share of the prime-time audience rose from 3 percent in 1982 to 5.5 percent in 1988, as the independent channel share increased from 11 percent to 14.6 percent (Gerard 1989).

In an increasingly differentiated nation, American television is striving as much for segmental as for mass appeal. In this sense Stage V TV is becoming more like our other media. The movies, radio, and magazines all gear their topics, formats, and subjects more toward particular homogeneous segments of the population (that is, interest groups) than toward a mass audience (Hirsch 1979:260). Similarly, cable TV and the videocassette have helped direct television away from the networks' cherished mass audiences toward particular viewing segments.

During the mid-1980s the VCR, a key element of Stage V, became one of the fastest-selling domestic appliances in history (Waters 1988:85). Less than 8 percent of American homes had a VCR in 1984, compared with 60 percent by fall 1988.

The VCR has modified television's aspect as a calendrical and instantaneous medium that can schedule human activity. Before the recorder, television content was for one emission. People had to rush home to catch an episode of *Roots* if they didn't want to wait for a later rebroadcast, which they might very well miss again.

Stage V technology permits us to have much more control over television and to be more interactive with it than we were previously. We interact with TV through the new technology whenever we work out to a Jane Fonda tape, play a videogame, use a computer, or monitor several channels simultaneously with a remote control device—another instrument of viewer liberation.

The VCR allows people to manipulate messages and to do their own programming and scheduling. It allows us not simply to choose but also to create personally meaningful content. With videocameras and camcorders people can record aspects of their own lives. We can compile precious video memory scrolls to be handed down across the generations, as scrapbooks and family Bibles once were.

Using VCRs actively and creatively, Americans amass collections of films by favorite actors and collect all the epiosodes of *Star Trek*. The students in my current seminar, "Television, Society, and Culture," bring examples of programs they are analyzing to class, so that others can view them and offer commentary, interpretations, and advice. At the airport I recently saw some new adoptive parents videotaping their babies' arrival from Korea. Weddings are recorded to remember and to share with people who missed the first run. I've seen dozens of dads taping their kids' sports achievements. Coaches record athletic performances to reveal strengths and weaknesses and guide improvement. Social scientists use videocassette recorders to study social interactions.

The VCR also affects our use of theatrical films. People can watch varied fare at home. This includes X-rated movies, previously accessible only in seedy movie houses, which the VCR is also helping destroy. Rental clubs offer recent movies for less than one pays for a ticket to a theater. The typical TV screen has expanded as the movie screen has shrunk. The difference between family room and theater has diminished.

The movie palaces of the past, with their CinemaScope and Todd-AO-sized screens, have become rarities. Soon the cinematic spectacles that enthralled my generation may be preserved only in museums and amusement parks. For example, the Naturemax theater at the American Museum of Natural History in New York City shows huge-screen movies, such as one shot in space by astronauts. Disney World features (in Tomorrowland) a mammoth circle-vision theatre. There is also Michael Jackson's Captain Eo at Disney's Epcot Center.

The VCR has even made inroads in Brazil, where viewers initially used recorders the way people generally start using innovations—not to change their habits, but to maintain them. For example, during the elections of 1985 and 1986 the government forced the networks to simulcast political programming in prime time. This delayed Globo's most popular *telenovela* from 8:25 until after 9 P.M. Brazilians who could afford to do so responded by buying videocassette recorders. Some of them rented films to watch during the political broadcast. Others videotaped their favorite *telenovela* to watch the next day at its accustomed time, during the political programs.

The prestige value of a possession, including an electronic appliance, depends on its scarcity. In Brazil, not only VCRs but even color televisions are still sufficiently uncommon to be prestigious. Brazil's consumer economy lags a few decades behind that of the United States. For Americans, the color TV, once a status symbol, has become too ubiquitous to differentiate between high-quality people and run-of-the-mill people.

Reflecting this difference in availability in the two countries, elite Brazilians at least tolerate television, whereas high-status Americans delight in putting down the tube, labeling it a lowbrow medium. During the days of commercial network domination, "cultured" Americans often chose the "quality" programming of PBS, which was of limited distribution and also rare (because so few people ever watched it). More recently, upscale Americans have turned to the VCR. However, as that apparatus becomes inexpensive enough to be generally available, it will also fall in esteem.

Stage V technology may be having subtle mental and behavioral effects besides those I have described. As more and more people get used to recording programs and life events, they may develop an illusion of omnipotent creative control. They may start imagining that they can freeze, fast forward, and reverse not just video images but also reality. Have you ever thought about rewinding and editing a real-life sequence that didn't work out as you had hoped? Have you ever pointed a remote control device at some real person and pushed the Mute or the Off button?

Television is more pervasive than we usually realize. All those people we see every day in front of computer monitors are actually watching, and interacting with, television. Stage V television, as computer monitor and through videogames, has also become a tutor and playmate of American children.

Television is fundamental in an electronic, statistical, information-loaded, consumer society. We even have TV look-alikes in our kitchens. Take a look at an appliance store ad in your local newspaper. Notice how much the microwave ovens resemble the television sets. If the villagers I studied in Brazil and Madagascar, who know about TV sets but not microwave ovens, walked into an American kitchen, they might very well get the idea that we cook in our TV sets. Considering the huge impact of television on modern life, that would not be a particularly outlandish conclusion.

Appendices

APPENDIX 1 *Statistical Comparison of Field Sites*

VARIABLE	OVERALL	GURUPÁ	CUNHA	AREMBEPE	IBIRAMA	NITERÓI	AMERICANA
Indiv. interviews (*n*)	1032	127	250	183	251	138	83
Household (HH) interviews (*n*)	847	121	197	140	186	125	78
Total interviews (*n*)	1879	248	447	323	437	263	161
First HH TV	1978[a]	1985	1981	1981	1976	1971	1969
Indiv. life TV hrs.	7721	632	4332	7288	8584	15825	13776
Yrs. home expo.	8.2	.8	5.0	5.8	9.8	16.7	15.8
No. HH TVs now	.9	.3	.6	.7	1.2	1.5	1.6
Daily indiv. TV hrs.	2.0	.8	1.3	2.7	2.2	2.7	2.4
Daily HH TV hrs.	4.7	.9	3.2	7.1	4.9	6.1	6.9
HH income units	6.8	.7	3.6	3.7	5.9	15.7	21.2
Education (years)	6.0	3.6	4.6	5.2	7.1	8.3	9.1
Local class	2.8	1.7	2.6	2.7	3.4	3.4	3.4

[a]*All remaining figures are averages, overall and by community.*

APPENDIX 1 (Continued)

VARIABLE	OVERALL	GURUPÁ	CUNHA	AREMBEPE	IBIRAMA	NITERÓI	AMERICANA
National class	2.4	1.1	2.4	1.9	2.9	3.0	3.4
Skin color (1 = light)	2.0	2.6	1.7	3.3	1.2	1.9	1.3
Sex (1 = M, 2 = F)	1.52	1.54	1.5	1.5	1.52	1.59	1.59
Age	37	38	41	35	33	34	43
Community danger	.8	.5	.7	.9	.2	1.5	1.9
Godchildren	5.0	7.0	9.2	3.5	4.1	1.1	2.5
Mos. nursing	11	15.4	14.9	11.0	9.4	6.3	7.0
INDICES							
Outside contact	10.7	6.5	8.3	9.7	12.1	13.5	18.2
HH possessions	21.8	12.0	17.1	16.9	27.2	29.3	33.2
Print exposure	5.3	3.7	3.7	5.1	5.6	6.4	10.3
Reading	2.8	1.8	1.8	2.6	3.6	3.4	4.8
Liberal	10.5	8.4	9.2	10.1	11.1	12.7	12.6

APPENDIX 2 *Significant Correlations Between Current Daily Televiewing Hours and Other Variables and Indices by Income Group and Community*[a]

	TOTAL SAMPLE		COMMUNITIES (FIELD SITES)					
CORRELATED VARIABLE OR INDEX	LOW INCOME	HIGH INCOME	GURUPÁ	AREMBEPE	CUNHA	IBIRAMA	NITERÓI	AMERICANA
Possessions*	+	+	+	+	+	+	+	
Likes soaps	+	+		+	+	+	+	+
Overall external contact*	+	+	+	+	+	+		
Literate household head	+	+	+	+	+	+		
Local class	+	+	+	+	+		+	
Urban vs. rural area	+	+	+	+	+			
Exposure to print media*	+	+	+	+	+			
Lived in a city*	+	+			+	+	−	
Household income	+		+	+	+			
National class	+	+		+	+			
Has TV changed your life?	+	+		+	+		+	
Was crime victim	+	+	+		+	+		
Liberal sex-gender views*	+	+			+	+		
Breastfeeding duration	−	−		−	−			
No. years exposure	+	+			+			
Age kids should start work	+	+	+					
Candomblé ("voodoo")*	+	+	+					

APPENDIX 2 (Continued)

CORRELATED VARIABLE OR INDEX	TOTAL SAMPLE		COMMUNITIES (FIELD SITES)					
	LOW INCOME	HIGH INCOME	GURUPÁ	AREMBEPE	CUNHA	IBIRAMA	NITERÓI	AMERICANA
Radio hours*	+		+	+				+
Different from parents	+		+		+			
Likes to be alone	+	+				+		
Trusts institutions*	−				−		+	
All gift exchanges*	+	+			+			
Gift giving*	+			+	+			
Gift receiving*	+				+			
Likes news	+				+			
Number of books				+	+			
No. visitors				+	+			
Community is dangerous		+						
Trusts townsfolk*	−				−		−	
Overall trust*	−				−			
Danger index*		+					−	
Fear–danger index*		+					−	
Age girl should marry		+					+	
Importance of Carnival					+	+		
Church going*	−					+		

Devoutness*		−				+		
Female		+						
Light skin color				+				
Siblings' importance				+				
Considers TV addictive	−							
Readiness to hit*								+
Gun/police*					+			
Fears for children*					−			
Importance of local celebration					−			
Likes collective holidays					+			
No. of godchildren								+
Frequency of leaving community								−
Believes TV does something bad								−
Total correlations	30	25	12	17	30	10	10	6

a Significant correlations (Pearson r) are at the .001 confidence level. Items with an asterisk are indices. Pluses and minuses indicate significant correlations between current televiewing level and the variables (and indices) listed to the left. Pluses indicate a positive correlation. For example, people who watch more TV also have more possessions, more external contact, and higher social class. Minuses indicate negative correlations. For example, people who watch more TV breastfeed, trust, and go to church less.

APPENDIX 3 *Responses to "How Has Television Changed Life in Your Community?" by Field Site*

	COMMUNITY						
	GURUPÁ	CUNHA	AREMBEPE	IBIRAMA	NITERÓI	AMERICANA	TOTAL CASES
Violence in general		2 .9%	1 .5%		1 2.9%	1 .8%	5 .7%
Children learn bad behavior					1 2.9%	3 2.5%	4 .5%
Bad influence on teens		3 1.4%	3 1.6%	3 1.9%			9 1.2%
Telenovelas bad				2 1.3%			2 .3%
Bad behavioral changes	1 1.8%	6 2.8%	2 1.1%	9 5.7%	1 2.9%		19 2.5%
Teaches bad habits	1 1.8%	13 6.2%	1 .5%	13 8.3%	1 2.9%	4 3.3%	33 4.3%
Bad in general	1 1.8%			2 1.3%			3 .4%
Decreases social interaction	2 3.5%	12 5.7%	6 3.3%	22 14.0%	5 14.7%	30 24.6%	77 10.1%
Alienates				1 .6%			1 .1%
Disturbing news reports	1 1.8%						1 .1%

	C1	C2	C3	C4	C5	C6	C7
Spreads distortions				1 / .6%			1 / .1%
Harms mental health		1 / .5%					1 / .1%
Manipulative		1 / .5%	1 / .5%	1 / .6%		1 / .8%	3 / .4%
Addictive	1 / 1.8%	9 / 4.3%		8 / 5.1%		5 / 4.1%	24 / 3.1%
Sets agendas						6 / 4.9%	6 / .8%
Steals time		8 / 3.8%	2 / 1.1%	1 / .6%		7 / 5.7%	18 / 2.4%
Advertising bad						1 / .8%	1 / .1%
Enslaves economically	1 / 1.8%	1 / .5%	2 / 1.1%	1 / .6%			5 / .7%
Homogenization		1 / .5%		1 / .6%			2 / .3%
NEUTRAL overall influence	4 / 7.0%	19 / 9.0%	14 / 7.7%	27 / 17.2%	10 / 29.4%	15 / 12.3%	89 / 11.7%
People go out	1 / 1.8%	5 / 2.4%		2 / 1.3%			8 / 1.0%
People stay home	4 / 7.0%	21 / 10.0%	15 / 8.2%	14 / 8.9%	1 / 2.9%	19 / 15.6%	74 / 9.7%

APPENDIX 3 (Continued)

| | COMMUNITY | | | | | | | |
	GURUPÁ	CUNHA	AREMBEPE	IBIRAMA	NITERÓI	AMERICANA	TOTAL CASES
POSITIVE: overall influence	1 1.8%	1 .5%		2 1.3%			4 .5%
Entertains	8 14.0%	29 13.7%	22 12.1%	4 2.5%		2 1.6%	65 8.5%
Beneficial habit change	2 3.5%	7 3.3%	15 8.2%	2 1.3%		1 .8%	27 3.5%
Development, progress	4 7.0%	31 14.7%	37 20.3%	5 3.2%	4 11.8%	4 3.3%	85 11.1%
Educates	3 5.3%	1 .5%	8 4.4%	6 3.8%	3 8.8%	3 2.5%	24 3.1%
Informal teaching	1 1.8%	5 2.4%	1 .5%	7 4.5%		4 3.3%	18 2.4%
Information	13 22.8%	17 8.1%	31 17.0%	16 10.2%	4 11.8%	10 8.2%	91 11.9%
Informs kids		4 1.9%	5 2.7%	1 .6%			10 1.3%
Culture, civilization		4 1.9%	3 1.6%	2 1.3%	1 2.9%	2 1.6%	12 1.6%
Enhances vocabulary			1 .5%				1 .1%

Raises consciousness		2 .9%	1 .5%				3 .4%
Work models				2 1.3%			2 .3%
Sex education			1 .5%				1 .1%
Increases social interaction	8 14.0%	6 2.8%	6 3.3%	1 .6%	2 5.9%	2 1.6%	25 3.3%
Good for health				1 .6%			1 .1%
Birth control			4 2.2%				4 .5%
Good for economy						2 1.6%	2 .3%
Religious benefits		2 .9%					2 .3%
Total cases	57 100.0%	211 100.0%	182 100.0%	157 100.0%	34 100.0%	122 100.0%	763 100.0%

A P P E N D I X 3 (Continued)

HOW TV HAS AFFECTED YOUR COMMUNITY	COMMUNITY						
	GURUPÁ	CUNHA	AREMBEPE	IBIRAMA	NITERÓI	AMERICANA	TOTAL CASES
Negative	8	57	18	65	9	58	215
	10.7%	19.4%	8.0%	26.2%	6.6%	45.0%	19.4%
Neutral	25	125	70	134	113	41	508
	33.3%	42.5%	31.3%	54.0%	83.1%	31.8%	45.9%
Positive	42	112	136	49	14	30	383
	56.0%	38.1%	60.7%	19.8%	10.3%	23.3%	34.6%
Total cases	75	294	224	248	136	129	1106
	100.0%	100.0%	100.0%	100.0%	100.0%	100.0%	100.0%

APPENDIX 4 *Explanatory Power of 9 (Potential) Predictors of 17 Dependent Variables and Indices.*

EDUCATION PREDICTS (7 dependent variables—average rank 2.0)

Rank as
Predictor

1	prefers international holidays to local ones
1	liberal views on social issues index
1	higher sodality index (clubs and associations)
1	higher print index
2	lower trust index
2	higher gift-giving and receiving index
7	larger inventory of household possessions index

YEARS OF HOME TV EXPOSURE PREDICTS

Rank as
predictor

1	less fear for kids
1	liberal views on sex–gender social issues
2	liberal job sex-gender stereotyping
2	higher print index
2	larger inventory of household possessions
3	perception that community is dangerous
3	negative trust
3	greater appreciation of international holidays
4	higher gift-giving and receiving index
5	higher danger index

FEMALE GENDER PREDICTS (10 dependent variables—average rank 2.6)

Rank as
predictor

1	considers the world dangerous
1	higher fear index
1	higher fear–danger index
2	liberal job stereotyping index
2	lower sodality index
3	higher danger index
3	liberal views on social issues index
4	lower trust of network members

4	considers the community dangerous
5	higher gift-giving and receiving index

DARKER SKIN COLOR PREDICTS (12 dependent variables—average rank 2.8)

Rank as
predictor

1	would like to live in a big city
1	higher urban image index
2	considers the world dangerous
2	less fear for kids' safety
2	prefers local holidays to international ones
2	higher danger index
3	lower trust of network members
3	higher fear index
3	higher fear–danger index
4	lower trust index
4	smaller inventory of household possessions
6	considers the community dangerous

HOUSEHOLD INCOME PREDICTS (9 dependent variables—average rank 2.9)

Rank as
predictor

1	higher danger index
1	perception that community is dangerous
2	higher fear–danger index
3	considers the world dangerous
3	liberal job stereotyping index
3	higher print index
3	larger inventory of household possessions
4	higher fear index
6	liberal views on social issues index

LOCAL CLASS PREDICTS (10 dependent variables—average rank 3.3)

Rank as
predictor

1	larger inventory of household possessions
1	higher gift-giving and receiving index
2	perception that community is safe
3	higher sodality index
4	less fear for kids

4	lower urban image index
4	lower danger index
4	higher print index
5	lower fear index
5	fear–danger index

RELIGIOSITY PREDICTS (8 dependent variables—average rank 3.5)

Rank as
predictor

1	trusts close network members
1	higher trust index
3	lower urban image index
3	greater fear for kids' safety
3	higher gift-giving and receiving
5	traditional social views
5	higher sodality index
7	lower danger index

OLDER AGE PREDICTS (10 dependent variables—average rank 3.7)

Rank as
predictor

2	higher fear index
2	more trust of close network members
2	would not like to live in a big city
2	lower urban image index
4	higher fear–danger index
4	higher sodality index
5	higher print index
5	higher trust index
5	considers the community dangerous
6	higher danger index

CURRENT VIEWING LEVEL PREDICTS (5 dependent variables—average rank 5.2)

Rank as
predictor

4	liberal views on sex-gender social issues
5	less trust of close network members
5	larger inventory of household possessions
6	higher print index
6	higher fear–danger index

Notes

CHAPTER ONE

1. For studies of activities that accompany "watching television," see Gunter and Svennevig (1987:11–15).

2. The survey was conducted by the D'Arcy Masius Benton & Bowles advertising agency.

CHAPTER TWO

1. See Gerbner and Gross (1976a); Gerbner et al. (1979); Gerbner et al. (1980); Hawkins and Pingree (1980); Hawkins and Pingree (1982); Signorielli, Gross, and Morgan (1982).

2. Previous review studies had included (1) the report of the Surgeon General's Scientific Advisory Committee on Television and Social Behavior (1972); (2) a Ford Foundation report (1976) concerning research on television and children; (3) and 1980 report (Withey and Abeles) of the SSRC-supported Committee on Television and Social Behavior, whose subtitle (Beyond Children and Violence) suggests its contributors' intent to broaden the focus on violence, aggression, and children that had dominated previous reports. Other relevant studies include Comstock et al. (1978), Tannenbaum (1980), and Adler (1981).

3. See, for example, Arens and Montague (1981); Kottak (1982).

4. An important exception, based on decade-long research involving intercommunity comparison among Canadian Indians, is Granzberg and Steinbring (1980). Williams (1986) reports on another systematic comparative study, with a before–after component, in three Canadian communities. Murray and Kippax (1978, 1979) did a relevant comparative study in the Australian outback.

5. Carey (1989) and others (for example, Thorburn 1988) are promoting a "cultural studies" approach for the discipline of communications, which they oppose to the "stimulus–response" models that previously dominated. This cultural studies approach draws heavily on interpretive and symbolic anthropologists, such as Geertz (1973, 1983) and Turner (1974).

   The movement to pay greater attention to culture within communications should be applauded. However, its advocates should also consider that the interpretive model is far from being the only one that anthropology offers. Of growing prominence in "modern anthropology" is the multi-site, multi-level, "cultural linkages" research model (village, region, nation, world) that orients this book (see Marcus and Fisher 1986).

   One point that the cultural studies school seems to miss as it attempts to incorporate anthropology into the communications field is that *comparison,* particularly cross-cultural comparison, is an essential part of the anthropological perspective. A true cultural studies approach to television and society must contrast the context, meaning, and effects of television across cultures. Furthermore, cultural studies, as understood in anthropology, attempt not only to "diagnose human meanings" but also to "predict human behavior" (quotes from Carey 1989: 56). All these are goals of *Prime-Time Society,* which approaches television from the viewpoint of cultural anthropology, rather than communications.

6. See Wolf (1982) for related interests, within a precolonial, colonial, and immediately postcolonial time frame.

7. See Lang and Lang (1953) and Williams (1975).

8. In Nigeria a local soap opera called *The Mirror in the Sun* played to mass audiences between 1984 and at least 1987 (Gutis 1987).

9. Pertinent previous studies of content analysis of television include Krippendorff (1980); Smythe (1954); Holsti (1968); Signorielli, Gross, and Morgan (1982), which reviews the basis of the violence profile and other content indices developed by the Gerbner Annenberg group); Greenberg (1982, 1980); Roberts (1982); Berger (1980); and Newcomb (1974).

CHAPTER THREE

1. Personal communication; see also Távola (1984).

2. The agency Dentel was charged with applying authoritarian state regulation to Brazilian television.

3. Similarly, a 1986 editorial in *The Kenya Times,* owned by the government party, proclaimed that "Our youth need to be protected from corrupting foreign cultural influences that glorify violence and other attendant social vices that are slowly but effectively eroding our social values."

4. Gallup has a Brazilian branch, but it is overshadowed by IBOPE (Instituto Brasileiro de Opinião Pública e Estatística).

5. The assistance of various IBOPE representatives, of Maxim Castelnau, Director of Audimarket, and of Otavio da Costa Eduardo, is gratefully acknowledged. I am especially grateful to Cid Pacheco and Lucia Ferreira Reis for many hours of conversation, enlightenment, and assistance.

6. We developed a standard stepwise multiple regression equation examining the effects of nine predictor variables (chosen to reduce problems with multicollinearity among predictors) on a set of dependent variables. The statistical results are discussed throughout this book, mainly in Chapters 9–12.

   The nine potential predictors whose effects are examined in our formula include two television variables—average current daily televiewing hours (ATVHOUR) and years of television exposure at home (HOMEEXPO).

   The other variables in the formula are local social class (LCALCLS—estimated by the field-worker at the end of each interview), household income (TTLHHINC—in multiples of the Brazilian minimum salary), age (AGE), sex (SEX—male 1, female 2), skin color (COLOR—on a light-to-dark scale coded 1 to 5, as perceived and recorded by field-workers, after joint training), religiosity (CHURCH—an index derived from church attendance and statements about the importance of religion in one's life), and years of education (EDUC).

   In this case, each dependent variable was a positive response to a question about whether the respondent liked a particular program type (*telenovela,* news, humor, and variety).

Not surprisingly, ATVHOUR was positively correlated with all program preferences. That is, people who like TV programs tend to watch more. The other variables that helped determine program preferences were as follows (in order for each dependent variable):

For *telenovelas* (mean of 1.8 on preference scale of 1–3): sex (female), age (younger), class (lower), and education (less). Final multiple R = .48.

For news (mean of 2.4): education (more), sex (male), and age (older). Final multiple R = .34.

For humor (mean of 1.6): sex (male), age (younger), education (more), skin color (darker), class (lower). Final multiple R = .29.

For variety (mean of 1.9): income (less), skin color (darker), age (younger), religiosity (more). Final multiple R = .39.

7. This is the conclusion of the contributors to *Anos 70, #7: Televisão,* Rio: Europa.

8. Avancini, quoted in Kehl (1981b:19).

9. Herz (1987) is a recent analysis of Globo's strategy for dominance; see also Ramos (1986).

10. Personal communication and in virtually all of Távola's writing.

11. Personal communication; interviews with Lucia Ferreira Reis and Paulo Alberto Monteiro de Barros (Artur da Távola).

CHAPTER FOUR

1. *David Copperfield,* for example, was written in 19 monthly installments, each 32 pages long, between May 1849 and November 1850.

2. Carey (1989:42) contrasts a "ritual view of communication" with perspectives that focus on communication in terms of persuasion, attitude change, behavior modification, socialization through information, influence, and conditioning. Carey seems to believe that the basic questions of the first (ritual) view cannot connect with those of the second (study of media effects).

   Communications scholars, of course, can set their own goals. However, I believe that anthropology's job is not simply to discover and interpret "meaning" within messages and texts (see Carey 1989:43, 93–94), but to study cultural effects as well. Anthropologists know full well that rituals have not only context and meaning, but multiple effects. The study of all those aspects of ritual is essential to the inclusive cultural pictures that anthropologists seek to paint.

CHAPTER FIVE

1. This is true despite the fact that the creators of Brazilian programs tend to be members of the middle and upper classes.

2. A late 1985 Census Bureau report (see *Ann Arbor News* 1985a) apparently contradicted our growing tendency to live with strangers. The report stated that more young adults (20–24) were either remaining with their parents, or moving back in with them. A census statistician blamed this on the 1981–82 recession and on an increase in the divorce rate.

Later age at marriage in the United States is obvious and indisputable. Three-quarters of young men 20–24 were single in 1980, compared with 55 percent in 1970. About half (52 percent) of the men 20–24 were living with their parents in 1980, versus 43 percent in 1970.

What happens, however, when we determine who was living with relatives in 1970 and 1980 by adding together the married men and those living with their parents? In 1970 88 percent of young men were either married (45 percent) or living with their parents (43 percent). That figure fell to 77 percent (25 percent + 52 percent) in 1980.

Therefore, despite the suggestion that more Americans are living with their families, the statistics show that more are actually living with strangers, as I contend.

3. In a 1986 survey, lawyers ranked low when Americans were asked which profession they respected most. Only 5 percent picked lawyers, compared with 30 percent for the clergy, 28 percent for doctors, 19 percent for teachers, and 3 percent for executives and journalists.

However, when people were asked what profession they would recommend for their child, 12 percent opted for law. Business (at 36 percent) and medicine (at 24 percent) were the top choices. Just 8 percent wanted their children to become teachers. Only 3 percent would suggest joining the clergy (Marcus and John 1986).

4. As has been discussed at length by DaMatta (1981), Chapter 4.

5. Long ago, Sir Henry Sumner Maine, in *Ancient Law* (1861), his well-known treatise on the evolution of law and society, characterized the transition from primitive to modern society as the movement from status to contract. This parallels the distinction between being (status) and doing (contract). A related opposition is that of ascribed versus achieved status.

6. For a historical explanation of these contrasts, see Harris (1964).

7. As reported in Wagley (1952).

8. In prime time, blacks were loyal to programs featuring black actors. However, black performers were not absolutely essential for popularity among blacks, who also particularly liked night-time soaps, action–adventure, and Steven Spielberg's *Amazing Stories* (Morgan 1986).

9. In one survey *The Cosby Show* got a 34.9 rating overall and 48.7 among blacks (Morgan 1986).

CHAPTER SIX

1. Examples of continuing series include *thirtysomething, L.A. Law, St. Elsewhere.*

2. Examples of miniseries are *Roots, Shogun, The Winds of War, War and Remembrance.*

3. Examples of docudramas are *The Burning Bed, Something about Amelia, Baby M.*

4. Average number of sets per airing (300+ airings for the national news and each of the three Globo *telenovela* time slots versus 52 for the weekly *Fantástico*).

5. Note that films, humor, and variety programs do air daily on some channel at some time.

6. Table 6.4 lists average number of sets per time slot for Brazil, single broadcasts for the United States.

7. Their viewers were probably being diverted to cable movies.

8. For obvious climate reasons, the 1988 Winter Olympic figure was 6 to 0.

9. What of sports televiewing among Brazilians in our six research sites? Fewer than 7 percent listed sports among the programs they watched usually (6.6 percent) or yesterday (3.0 percent); 7.2 percent listed sports as their favorite program type (see Tables 6.1, 6.2, and 6.3).

10. In Brazil, although rivalries between "free-world" and "communist" athletes are not emphasized as they are in the United States, Olympic coverage is even more nationally oriented.

11. Coverage in Latin American editions of *Time* and *Newsweek,* August 3, 1984, and in the Brazilian journals *Veja* and *Isto E.*

12. Analysis of media coverage of the 1984 Summer Olympics is based on *Time* and *Newsweek* accounts, compared with treatment of some of the same stories and events by Brazilian television and by *Veja* and *Isto E,* Brazil's most popular weekly newsmagazines. I was not a firsthand witness to American TV treatment of the 1984 Games (being in Brazil at the time). This is why my analysis is mainly based on written accounts and my study (through videotape) of the American motion picture *Sixteen Days of Glory,* an account of the Los Angeles Games. In Brazil, I did see ABC film, which was the basis of TV coverage there, as throughout the world.

13. The same share pledge was not met during the 1988 Winter Olympics.

14. Facts, figures, and quotes from *Isto E* 1984.

15. Facts, figures, and quotes from *Veja* 1984c.

16. Facts, figures, and quotes from *Newsweek,* August 13, 1984.

17. This belief is linked to the interest in suspense revealed in so many American genres. Because of different degrees of fascination with the unexpected, Americans make suspense, adventure, horror, and fantasy movies, whereas Brazilians make repetitive *novelas* with urban domestic settings.

18. Despite the doing–being opposition, neither Americans nor Brazilians are blind to some of the physical (ascribed) features that contribute to athletic success. Thus, although Canadian swimmer Alex Baumann proclaimed, "I think I won [first to Ricardo Prado's second place in the 400 IM] because I had more self-confidence," *Veja* pointed to an ascribed status difference: body build—Prado is 20 centimeters shorter than Baumann—and said that technique had enabled Prado to get as far as he did. All over the world, the press agreed that West Germany's outstanding swimmer Michael Gross benefited from a physical anomaly: the huge arm span that earned him the nickname of the "albatross." Mary Lou Retton also had physical advantages for her sport: a "low center of gravity" and stocky legs (*Newsweek* 1984:32–33).

19. Facts, figures, and quotes from *Veja* 1984d:48.

20. Some other examples: Mary Lou Retton underwent a knee operation six weeks before the games—a fact that wasn't publicized until she had the gold medal. Wrestler Jeff Blatnik, 27, who had a cancerous spleen removed in 1982, won a gold medal in 1984.

21. Facts, figures, and quotes from Axhelm 1984b:7.

22. Anthropologist James Clifton, editor of the Wadsworth Modern Anthropology Library, dubs this obsession with numbers the Numerical Index Pattern (NIP). He considers it a key American metaphor (personal communication).

23. One example of the kind of suspect research done in a less statistically oriented society was a newspaper article (Sunday, December 18, 1983) about Brazilians' sexual fantasies; reporters just went out and asked people in the street what their sexual fantasies were.

CHAPTER SEVEN

1. The degree to which informants said that they got their crime information from a newspaper was highest in the communities (Niterói, Arembepe, and Americana) located near major cities, which have ready access to the press.

2. On our scale measuring reliance on alternative media as sources of crime information, newspapers scored 1.2, versus 1.8 for radio and 1.8 for television. Television exceeded radio in all sites except Gurupá.

3. Roberto DaMatta (1987) and personal communication.

4. This refers to a study by Neil Malamuth, Chairman of Communications Studies at the University of California, Los Angeles, and Edward Donnerstein of the Communications Arts Department of the University of Wisconsin, Madison, reported in Smith (1985).

5. Sources I consulted disagreed about the date (either 1621 or 1623) of the first Thanksgiving—the one featuring about 90 Indians and 40–50 Pilgrims (only about half the original settlers). The feast apparently lasted a few days and consisted of maize, barley, peas, and other crops, plus fowl, including wild turkeys (shot by four Pilgrim musketeers) and meat (venison hunted by five Indians). The next Thanksgiving took place in *February* 1630, and celebrated the arrival of a shipload of provisions from England, which helped feed a Puritan population that apparently had not been very adept at extracting its livelihood from the land.

6. Berger (1988) is obviously right in noting that Kirk represents superego and civilization—specifically Anglo–American civilization.

CHAPTER EIGHT

1. This research has been supported by three agencies, in addition to the University of Michigan (through a sabbatical leave), to all of which I express my gratitude: (1) the Wenner-Gren Foundation for Anthropological Research, for a grant to study the electronic mass media and social change in Brazil (1983–84); (2) the National Science Foundation for a research grant (NSF-G-BNS 8317856–Kottak) to study the social impact of television in rural Brazil in the states of Bahia, Pará, Santa Catarina, and São Paulo (6/84–11/86); and (3)

the National Institute of Mental Health for a research grant (DHHS-PHS-G-5-R01-MH38815-03–Kottak) to investigate television's behavioral effects in Brazil, supporting field team research and data analysis in six Brazilian rural communities (1/1/85–12/31/88).

2. Later, to round out the national-level component of the research, in summer 1986 Straubhaar of Michigan State University's Department of Telecommunication, whose previous research had also focused on Brazilian television, worked with Rio-based project consultant Lucia Ferreira Reis gathering additional data in Rio and São Paulo. They obtained data from the major Brazilian public opinion and media research organizations. These data were gathered for the cities transmitting the television signals received in each project community—for the period during which research was being done in the communities—to be compared with the community data to provide a regional- and national-level perspective on television diffusion and impact, and to permit rural–urban contrasts.

3. The Department of Social Anthropology of the National Museum, a division of the Federal University of Rio de Janeiro, cooperated in this project by offering me an institutional affiliation in Brazil and by providing field researchers Rosane Prado and Alberto Costa and Brazilian liaison Roberto DaMatta. To all of these project participants I offer my deepest gratitude, which I also extend to researchers Celeste DaMatta, Iraní Escolano, Betty Kottak, Pennie Magee, Richard Pace, and Edward Potter.

4. Alberto Costa worked in Ibirama, Rosane Prado in Cunha, Richard Pace in Gurupá, and four field-workers in Arembepe (Iraní Escolano, Pennie Magee, Betty Kottak, and Conrad Kottak).

5. For more on networks, see Burt (1980).

6. We used many PRE (proportionate reduction of error) and nonparametric statistics in data exploration and analysis.

7. The bulk of fieldwork (in Arembepe, Gurupá, and Cunha) was completed by February 1986, but interviewing continued through March 1986 in Ibirama and in two sites added later to broaden our understanding of television's effects. Throughout the project, there were very few problems, probably because the researchers had been carefully chosen. All had graduate social science training and all are fluent in Brazilian Portuguese.

8. Iraní Escolano and Celeste DaMatta did the research in Niterói, and Edward Potter worked in Americana–Santa Barbara.

9. An additional 14,000 people are widely dispersed in Gurupá's sparsely populated rural zones.

10. In Wagley's 1949 sample of 256 households, 5 percent included someone who had been to Belém, the state capital.

11. One favored program that year was the now classic Globo *telenovela, O Bem Amado,* which eventually became a popular weekly series.

12. Even in 1965, describing the nearby rain forest, Shirley could assert that to travel around Cunha was to travel back in time 400 years to the very opening of the country, to Brazil's original rain forest.

13. See Shirley (1971:26). Cunha's main experiment in cash cropping was cotton cultivation on a limited basis during the American Civil War.

14. Average household income in Cunha's rural area was 4.3, compared with 2.9 standard units *(salários mínimos)* in our urban sample. The rural sample had higher standard deviations for all socioeconomic measures. This reflects great contrasts between large landowners and migratory day workers in the rural zone.

15. As Prado and Costa have argued, gossip is a characteristic feature of social life in small Brazilian communities. Gossip simultaneously expresses a strong network of personal relationships and an equally strong mechanism of social control of individual behavior in such communities. Gossip is an aspect of local social life that people use to contrast themselves with the external world presented by TV. Prado and Costa constantly heard the claim that privacy should be respected—which echoes the worldview transmitted by Brazilian *telenovelas*. Gossip, and the *telenovela* characters that fuel it, was strongly criticized by townsfolk in Cunha and Ibirama. However, people who criticized gossip also engaged in it. In Ibirama and Cunha, gossip was a point at which new ideals pressured traditional cultural patterns. Through gossip a complex process of cultural reproduction and transformation was taking place.

CHAPTER NINE

1. The mean response to the question "Has television changed your life?" was .7 on a scale from 0 for no to 2 for yes.

   Appropriately, current viewing level turned out to be the best predictor of the opinion than TV had changed one's own life. Current viewing hours (ATVHOUR) was the first of two predictor variables entered in our standard multiple regression equation, with a "yes" response to "Has TV changed your life?" as the dependent variable. Darker skin color was the other predictor. Current viewing hours produced an R^2 change of 2.5 percent, and a final beta of .16. (The final multiple R was .18.) We got the highest percentage of yeses in Arembepe and Americana, the two communities in which average daily household TV hours were greatest.

   Interestingly, the opinion that TV is addictive was negatively correlated with current viewing hours, which was again the first variable entered in our standard regression formula, with a final beta of –.09.

2. Similarities between Cunha and Globo settings and characters are discussed in Rosane Prado's larger ethnographic study (1986) of reactions by the women of Cunha to the women portrayed in *telenovelas*.

3. This is particularly true of Americana, where there were few correlations between heavy viewing and other variables. Niterói has had television even longer than Americana, but has more correlations. These reflect, I think, not just TV impact but the fact that what Globo produces in Rio actually is much more similar to what goes on in its suburb Niterói than to local culture in any of our other field sites. However, the difference in number of significant correlations is also partially attributable to a smaller sample size in Americana.

4. The only communities in our study with significant traditions of reading were Ibirama—settled initially by Germans, including many Protestants—and Americana–Santa Barbara, whose American settlers were mainly Protestants.

5. Usual daily household TV-set-on hours was the first predictor variable entered, before darker skin color and higher household income, in our standard

multiple regression equation, with number of weekly visitors as the dependent variable. Household viewing hours produced an R^2 change of just 1.6 percent, and a beta (and r) of .13, which, however, is significant at the .001 confidence level.

6. According to an interview with Otavio Costa Eduardo, an American-trained anthropologist who now heads a Brazilian market research firm.

7. Fewer current viewing hours was the third predictor variable entered, after greater religiosity and lighter skin color, in our standard multiple regression equation, with agreement with the statement that marriage is important as the dependent variable. Current viewing hours produced an R^2 change of 2 percent, and a beta of $-.3$.

8. Overall, children had the highest rank, followed by partner, and then (in a virtual tie with partner) parents, with siblings last. In this set of questions, the televiewing variables told us nothing statistically significant about the rank of children and siblings.

　　Another question, "Who's more important, your siblings or your friends?" produced a rare set of correlations in which religiosity and current viewing hours ran in the *same* direction: Religious, younger, heavier viewers with less home exposure tended to value siblings over friends. Final betas were $-.09$ for HOMEEXPO and .09 for current viewing hours, with value of siblings over friends as the dependent variable.

9. Current viewing hours was entered first, followed by less religiosity and more education, with a final multiple R of .19, highest for this set of social distance questions.

10. Pearson's r of .22 is significant at the .001 confidence level.

11. Current average daily televiewing hours was the best predictor (among the usual nine tested) of the perception that "your parents are very different from you."

　　Years of home exposure was the second significant predictor (of three) of closeness to friends. Being dark-skinned and female were the other two variables associated with seeing friends as different from oneself.

12. We constructed our scale of "perceived social distance" by adding together degrees of agreement with the following statements:

Your parents are (were) (very, somewhat, a bit, not at all) different from you.

Your children are different from you.

Your relatives are different from you.

Your friends are different from you.

Your neighbors are different from you.

　　The fact that none of our usual predictor variables had much of an effect on this index suggests that feelings of closeness to the different categories we asked about (parents, children, relatives, neighbors, friends) run in opposite directions.

　　With respect to this set of questions, religiosity, which *was* associated with stated feelings of closeness to parents, relatives, and network members in general, was the best overall predictor variable.

Education, the second best overall predictor of perceived social distance, had opposite effects from religion, being associated with greater distance from neighbors, parents, and overall.

13. In a multiple regression analysis, with the contact index as the dependent variable, 46 percent of the variance (R^2) was explained by number of years the respondent had watched television in the home (beta = .25). Current average daily viewing hours—the fifth variable entered stepwise after (in order) years of home exposure, education, local class, and household income—produced an R change of .005 and a beta of .08.

14. Somewhat paradoxically, such an external orientation may encompass many different sorts of preoccupation with the external world—fears about the world, fascination with the world, desires to participate in the world, or wishes to keep informed about the world while avoiding it.

15. Eagleton (1983:25, fn. 10, quoting J. C. Collins, *The Study of English Literature* [1891]).

16. Early contentions about this are reviewed by Klapper (1960: 110–111).

17. However, the overall positive effects of televiewing were unclear. There was no evidence that TV stimulated children to engage in a greater range of hobbies or active pursuits than did nonviewers (Klapper 1960: 245–246).

18. Those who said they liked to be alone tended to be better educated, less religious, of higher local class, and younger. These were the only variables from our standard multiple regression equation that predicted a positive response to "Do you like to be alone?" (the dependent variable). Education produced an initial R^2 change of 6.0 percent, and a final beta of .15. (The final multiple R was .28.)

19. There was actually a tendency for membership in clubs and associations to rise with televiewing level. This finding is just the opposite of one in the Williams (1986) study of three Canadian towns.

   However, this association in our Brazilian data did not take intercorrelation (multi-collinearity) into account. Televiewing in Brazilian communities is strongly correlated with greater education and higher local class, both of which are much better predictors of club membership than are TV variables per se.

   A statistical analysis (multiple regression) that separates the effects of education and class from that of viewing shows that TV variables make no significant independent contribution to membership. The variables that predicted membership in one or more club or association (SODALIND) were (in order): greater education, male sex, higher local class, older age, and greater religiosity (with a final multiple R of .41).

20. Televiewing was also strongly correlated with literacy (personal literacy, literacy of household head, number of books in home, and allied measures) throughout our sample—among both lower- and higher-income people and in four of our six communities.

21. In the overall sample, current viewing hours was the second of only two predictor variables entered (after education, which had a much greater effect) in our standard multiple regression equation, with the reading index (based on whether the respondent regularly reads books plus magazines plus news-

papers) as the dependent variable. Current viewing hours produced a final beta of .11, with a final multiple R of .64.

The predictive value of current daily televiewing was even more dramatic in Cunha, where there is higher literacy and greater print availability. There, current viewing hours had a final beta of .25 and produced an R^2 change of 4 percent. (The final multiple R was .66.)

CHAPTER TEN

1. Our six field sites were coded to permit various kinds of statistical analyses. They can be treated as categorical and dummy variables (for example, one site versus all the others). They have also been coded from 1 (Gurupá) to 6 (Americana) so that, when useful for analysis, site may be treated as a linear variable reflecting order of television penetration, from earliest to most recent. We used similar procedures for the 15 neighborhoods into which our six sites are divided.

2. Specifically, we asked when the set was turned on and off the first and second times usually, yesterday, and weekends.

3. For individual respondents, the averages were: 2.0 for weekday hours, 2.1 for Saturdays, 2.4 for Sundays, and 1.5 for yesterday.

4. This was an interval variable, which could be correlated with other interval (and ordinal) variables using measures of linear and curvilinear association, such as Pearson's r or eta^2. More simply, we might also have used the informant's answer to the question "How many hours of television do you usually watch?"

5. Average daily household hours were greatest in Arembepe and Americana, lowest in Gurupá.

6. The lifeshare mean was highest in Niterói (5.6 percent), followed by 4.0 percent in Americana, 3.5 percent in Ibirama, 2.8 percent in Arembepe, 1.6 percent in Cunha, and .25 percent in recently exposed Gurupá.

7. Our *household* levels (actually 2.0001 and 6.0001 hours) have the same cutoffs as those used by the Gerbner researchers for American *individuals*.

8. For a "yes" answer to "Is it sometimes necessary to hit a child?" the only significant predictor variables were sex (females answered yes more often) and less home TV exposure. The final betas, however, were only .09 and −.07, respectively, with a final multiple R of .11.

   TV variables told us nothing about a "yes" answer to "Is it sometimes necessary to hit an adult?" The significant predictors were younger age, less religiosity, and higher local class. Again, the final betas were minuscule, with a final multiple R of .15.

   There was more of a TV effect with respect to "Have you ever hit someone?" for which the following predictor variables (in order) made significant independent contributions: male sex, younger age, greater current viewing level, and less religiosity. The final betas were .17 for male sex and .07 for current televiewing hours, with a final multiple R of .24.

9. Pearson product–moment correlations, Pearson's r. Appendix 2 lists only those correlations that are highly significant, that is, significant at the .001 level of confidence.

10. We added responses to the questions: Is the world (very—3, somewhat—2, a bit—1, or not at all—0) dangerous? Is (name of your community) (very, somewhat, a bit, or not at all) dangerous?

11. Of the five questions about door locking, one (Do you always lock your doors?) was eliminated from the scale because it was subsumed by the others: Do you lock the doors of your home during the day? At night? When there's no one at home? When there's someone home? We decided, however, to include each of these four answers as a separate scale component because each action seemed to indicate a somewhat different kind of fear, and all together they indicated increasing levels of fear. That is, a person who locks his or her doors all the time in a small, relatively crime-free community is significantly more fearful than someone who locks them only when no one is home.

12. Weighted to account for the fact that the danger scale components were rated 0 to 3, whereas those on the fear scale were rated 0 to 2.

13. Female gender and older age were the only factors that influenced the fear index.

14. The last variable entered in our multiple regression equation, producing a detectable, but minuscule R^2 change.

15. Home exposure was the third predictor variable entered in our multiple regression equation with community danger dependent (2 percent R^2 change).

16. Sex, religiosity, and lower local class were the only predictor variables entered in our standard multiple regression equation, with a "yes" response to "Are you afraid of the streets at night?" as the dependent variable. The final multiple R was .38.

17. Lighter viewers were more likely to own guns. Five variables (in order) were entered in our standard regression equation with gun ownership the dependent variable: male sex, higher income, older age, higher class, lower current viewing level.

18. Our trust indices, constructed from component variables that use a four-point scale from 3 (very much) to 0 (not at all), are as follows:

    Network trust (TRCLOSE) sums responses to five questions assessing degree to which respondents say they trust family, neighbors, friends, and friends of friends, and value the neighbor relationship.

    Institutional trust (TRINSTS) sums the extent to which the respondent trusts government in general, local leaders, priest, and information on television.

    Total trust (TRUST) sums indices of network and institutional trust.

19. Dark skin color was the only variable that affected the amount of trust (more) that people said they had in TV information (final R of .12).

20. Four variables out of the nine in our standard multiple regression equation predicted the response to "How much confidence do you have in the government?" (the dependent variable, with a scale of 0 to 3). In order the predictors of *less* trust in government were more home exposure (7 percent of the variance), younger age, less religiosity, and higher local class. In other words, long-exposed, younger, less religious people of higher local class had less confidence in the Brazilian government. (The final multiple R was .36.)

21. The characteristics that increased voting were higher local class, being male, greater education, and older age. (Final multiple R of .25.)

22. We also asked our informants if they agreed or not with the following statements:

    It's usual to get along with your neighbors.
    Your siblings are more important in your life than your friends.
    A friend of a friend is also a friend.

23. Because there were radical differences in average income from site to site, we could not simply divide our total sample by income. Had we done so, the more cash-oriented sites (Ibirama, Niterói, and Americana) would have been drastically overrepresented in the richer half. Rather, our first procedure was to divide the sample for each site into higher- and lower-income groups. The six higher segments were then added together, as were the lower ones, to form two income-differentiated samples of 400+ and 500+ individuals respectively.

24. In predicting scores on the liberal sex–gender social issues index, length of respondent's home exposure was entered second in the stepwise multiple regression. Current viewing level was entered fourth. The stepwise order of the predictor variables entered (multiple R = .61) was as follows: years of education, years of home exposure (beta = .18, R^2 change of 5 percent), sex (female), daily viewing hours (beta = .11, R^2 change of 1 percent), religiosity (negatively correlated), and household income.

25. In contrast to Portugal (or France) where second person pronouns and verbs (tu, vos; tu, vous) are used, the "you" forms in Brazil are all grammatically third person: formal—*o senhor,* when addressing a man, and *a senhora,* when addressing a woman, and the informal "you" form—*você.* (Sometimes in southern Brazil, including our Ibirama field site, *tu* rather than *você* is used as the informal "you," but with third person verbs.)

26. Linguistic informality was associated with being well educated and nonreligious and with relatively heavy viewing, long exposure, youth, income, and lighter skin (in that order). These were the seven significant predictor variables entered from our standard multiple regression equation, with an index of linguistic formality (FORMAL, derived from questions about how informants addressed their parents and how their own children addressed them) as the dependent variable. Education produced a huge R^2 change of 21 percent, and a final beta of .21. Current viewing level and years of home exposure had final betas of .13 and .12, respectively. (The final multiple R was .55.)

    A higher correlation (and similar predictors) were found for answers to the individual question of "How (with which pronouns) do your children address you?" Here education produced an initial R^2 change of 20.7 percent, and a final beta of .20. Current viewing level and years of home exposure had final betas of .15 and .14, respectively. (The final multiple R was .56.)

27. These answers were ranked 3 highest, 1 lowest. With respect to the relative value attributed to what one learns in these three arenas, our Brazilian informants ranked family highest (with a mean score of 2.6 on a scale of 0 to 3), with school (2.2) and street (1.2) trailing.

In this set of questions, though not in others, heavy viewers tended to give *less* importance to the family. Viewing level was the third of four predictor variables entered in our standard multiple regression equation, with a higher rank for "importance of what you learn in the family" as the dependent variable. In order, the variables predicting a high value of family learning were light skin color, female sex, fewer current viewing hours, and greater religiosity. Current viewing hours produced a final beta of $-.07$. (The final multiple R was .27.)

28. Length of home exposure was the fourth and final predictor variable entered in our standard multiple regression equation, with a higher rank for "importance of what you learn in the street" as the dependent variable. In order, the variables predicting a high value of street learning were less religiosity, more education, male sex, and longer home exposure (homeexpo). Homeexpo produced a final beta of .08. (The final multiple R was .29.)

    Length of home exposure was the second of three predictors entered (negatively, in this case) in our standard multiple regression equation, with a higher rank for "importance of what you learn in school" as the dependent variable. In order, the variables predicting a high value of school learning were dark skin color, less home exposure, and male sex. Homeexpo produced a final beta of $-.08$. (The final multiple R was .18.)

29. Being poorer, younger, and male were the only factors that raised love over honor. The same three factors were also the only ones that increased the value of education over honor. The multiple R's were .18 for love and .13 for education over honor. Both were barely significant, only at the .05 confidence level.

    Years of education was the only predictor variable that raised the relative value of self-fulfillment. But the R^2 change was only 2.7 percent, with a minuscule R of .16.

    With respect to family, longer home exposure was the third predictor variable entered, after less education and greater religiosity, in our standard multiple regression equation, with agreement with the statement that family is important as the dependent variable. However, years of home exposure produced an R^2 change of less than 1 percent.

    We also asked: "To succeed in life, what is most important: (1) ability, (2) luck, or (3) connections ('pull')?" Our informants ranked personal ability highest (with a mean score of 2.5 on a scale of 0 to 3), with luck (2.0) and connections (1.6) ranking lower. Here again, TV had no effect on answers. We had supposed that connections might be valued more by people who watched a lot of TV, but this wasn't so. Indeed, connections weren't valued much by anyone.

    There was a very weak relationship (.1) between the value placed on connections and greater education, which was the only predictor variable entered from our standard multiple regression equation.

    The importance of personal ability was stressed most by well-educated, light-skinned, higher-class, religious, younger people—producing a multiple R of .35.

    Luck was valued more by less well-educated, darker-skinned people of lower social class and *higher* incomes—producing a multiple R of .38. Thus, we see that in the local class structures of our Brazilian communities, the less successful people stress luck, whereas those who have certain social advantages stress personal ability. This finding, which I previously arrived at through qualitative and case analysis (Kottak 1983) therefore is confirmed statistically.

30. Skin color (lighter) was the only predictor variable entered from our standard set for the work index.

31. Using an identical regression equation (the same potential predictor variables) with LIBJOBST (liberal job stereotyping) as dependent, the multiple R was .24 for LIBJOBST versus .61 for LIBERAL—the liberal sex–gender score for ten *social* issues.

32. Length of home TV exposure was the first predictor variable entered from our standard multiple regression formula, with the next two (and only) being sex and household income, with liberal sex–gender job stereotyping as dependent.

33. Years of home exposure explained 3 percent of the variance in job stereotyping (LIBJOBST), versus 5 percent with respect to social issues (LIBERAL).

34. For our attributed job prestige index, TV's influence runs opposite that of age, female sex, dark skin color, and religiosity. Unlike heavy viewing, years of home exposure did not affect the attributed job index. Scores declined as viewing increased in Arembepe, Ibirama, Niterói, and rose with viewing in none of the communities.

35. The prestige of fishing declines particularly dramatically with increased televiewing in Arembepe, where fishing was once the mainstay of the local economy. This may explain why so many young men in that community refuse to enter their father's profession and are, instead, unemployed or working in local construction activities aimed at tourists.

    Viewing level had little to do with prestige of physicians, nurses, politicians, teachers, and writers.

36. Current viewing hours was the second predictor variable entered, after darker skin color, in our standard multiple regression equation, with a "yes" answer to "If you won the lottery would you stop work?" as dependent variable. Current viewing hours produced an R^2 change of 1.8 percent, and a beta of .13. Religiosity and education also affected responses here. In the overall sample, darker-skinned heavier viewers who are less religious and less well educated were more likely to give "yes" answers to this question.

    "Stop work" responses rose with viewing level in Gurupá, Cunha, Arembepe, Ibirama, and Americana, and declined only in Niterói. Current viewing level rather than length of home exposure is associated with an antiwork bias. HOMEEXPO was positively correlated (final beta of .09) with a "yes" response to our question "Is it important to work if you're rich?" The three predictors of this response were higher local class, lighter skin color, and longer home exposure. (Multiple R of .23.)

37. The respondent's own greater education, income, and class, and younger age were the main factors predicting "yes" responses to the question "Do you think there's a chance your children will attend college?" Respondent's education explained 10 percent of the variance in answers concerning the possibility of

his/her children's college. The final multiple R (after education, younger age, income, and class had been entered as predictors) was .36.

38. Before controlling for the association between income and viewing level. The "start work" age rose obviously with viewing level in Gurupá, Cunha, and Arembepe.

39. More education, darker skin color, years of home TV exposure, less religiosity, higher income, younger age, more current viewing hours (final beta .11), and being female all made significant independent contributions (in that order) toward predicting our respondents' opinion about the proper age for children to begin work. Years of home exposure produced an R^2 change of 1.9 percent, with a final beta of .12, and a final multiple R of .42.

40. Dark skin color and more education were the only factors that increased "yeses" in response to "Do TV *ads* influence you?"

41. Current viewing hours was the second of seven predictor variables entered in our standard multiple regression equation, with a "yes" response to "Do you have a savings account?" as the dependent variable. In order of predictive value of the variables, people with savings accounts tended to be of higher local class, heavier viewers, well educated, male, religious, light skinned, and to have (controlling for associated variables just listed) *lower* household income. Current viewing hours had a final beta of .14. (The final multiple R was .35.)

42. One million automobiles were manufactured and sold in Brazil in 1979. This domestic sales level has not been attained since, and today's still-thriving Brazilian auto industry aims its products toward the export market.

43. Greater education, younger age, and higher social class (in that order) were even stronger predictors of early weaning than was TV. Then came average current TV hours. Education, class, and televiewing are inversely correlated with breastfeeding, and age is positively correlated.

44. Some of the questions we asked were:

How do you imagine life in

Rio?

São Paulo?

The state capital?

Would you like to visit each of them?

Would you like to live in any of those places?

In which of the three would you most/least like to live?

Would you want your children to live in those cities?

45. We found dark-skinned people of lower social class to have the most positive images of Rio and São Paulo. Such people may well be the most likely emigrants to Brazilian cities.

Dark skin color and lower local class were the only predictor variables entered in our standard multiple regression equation, with positive image of São Paulo as the dependent variable. Skin color produced an R^2 change of 4.7 percent, and a final beta of .18. (The final multiple R was .24.)

With respect to image of Rio de Janeiro, dark skin color was again entered first, with lower religiosity second, lower local class third, and greater income fourth. Skin color produced an R^2 change of 5.0 percent, and a final beta of .21. (The final multiple R was .26.)

46. Darker skin color, male sex, and younger age were associated with "yes" responses. The final multiple R was .19, with skin color associated with most (1.9 percent) of the variance.

47. We asked about various links with the external world, including telephone use, frequency of travel outside, destination and purpose of trips, military service, and prior urban residence. Our questionnaires contained several queries concerning information sources other than television, including newspapers, magazines, books, radio, and movies.

CHAPTER ELEVEN

1. Beauty contests are shown on Sílvio Santos.

2. In March 1984, Rio's Manchête channel covered Carnival for 84 continuous hours (Saturday through Wednesday). Coverage resumed the next Saturday night and Sunday morning, when runoffs were held and samba schools competed for the prize. In most time periods, Manchête's Carnival coverage clobbered Globo, which stuck to its normal schedule. In downtown Rio Manchête achieved an average 70 percent share (of televisions in use) versus 6–8 percent for Globo (*Veja* Mar. 14, 1984:114).

   Manchête commissioned the poll by IBOPE, which had not worked during Carnival for six years. (Polling was only done in downtown Rio.) Globo's popular Sunday-night variety–news program *Fantástico* was beaten (during its entire two-hour time slot) for the first time ever. Manchête's success contradicted the received wisdom that *carioca* televiewers find Carnival parades boring and would not watch them. Among some 2 million TV households in the Rio metropolitan area, the overwhelming preference was for Manchête.

   Celebrating its victory, Manchête ran ads in *O Globo* the Sunday and Monday after Carnival, listing audience shares for different time periods. *O Globo's* arch rival *Jornal do Brasil* reported Manchête's victory, but *O Globo's* only mention of it was in ads paid for by Manchête. This Carnival ratings victory coincided with Manchête's plans for national expansion, also helping inaugurate its new outlet in Recife, another Carnival center. One Manchête official proclaimed, "We won by going into the streets, by popularizing."

3. I use the terms *transvestite* and *transsexual* interchangeably here, as Brazilians do.

4. From the viewpoint of this analysis it is irrelevant that these singers were English (Beatles) or Australian (Bee Gees), because it is their popularity within the United States—the value that American culture bestowed on them—that is being discussed.

5. This account of male homosexuality in Brazil draws on an analysis by Peter Fry (1982).

6. Brazil now has the Western Hemisphere's, and perhaps the world's, second largest number of AIDS cases.

7. My colleague Alberto Costa thinks that this apparent tolerance for the homosexuality of Brazilian performers may actually be something quite different—accusations leveled against famous people, particularly against well-known females. Costa has written that during the 1950s certain female singers were called prostitutes *(putas)*. He thinks that successful Brazilian public women, almost always performers, risk being labeled either promiscuous or masculine. Thus, some well-known contemporary Brazilian female singers are called lesbians. Roberta Close, who in truth is masculine (because she is a man and considered promiscuous) would fit Costa's theory.

8. This effect of TV on Christmas gift-giving remains after controlling for intercorrelated variables, such as income.

    Current televiewing hours was the fourth of five predictor variables entered in our standard multiple regression equation, with a positive answer to "Do you give Christmas presents?" as the dependent variable. In order, the variables predicting a "yes" response to this question were higher local class, more education, lighter skin color, more current viewing, and greater religiosity. Current viewing hours produced a final beta of .10. (The final multiple R was .29.)

9. Televiewing (in this case, length of home exposure, rather than current viewing hours) was also statistically associated with birthday giving. Although viewing was associated, therefore, with holiday giving, local social class and education were better predictors of gifts. The impact of religiosity, however, was less than that of televiewing.

    Specifically, length of home exposure was the fifth of six predictor variables entered in our standard multiple regression equation, with a positive answer to "Do you give birthday presents?" as the dependent variable. In order, the variables predicting a "yes" response were more education, higher local class, female sex, younger age, longer home exposure (homeexpo), and greater religiosity. Homeexpo produced a final beta of .10. (The final multiple R was .35.)

10. Manger scenes, for instance, probably came from Italian Catholic churches. The Nativity scene is associated with Francis of Assisi.

11. We determined each individual's religious affiliation (which was generally Roman Catholic, except in Ibirama and Americana, whose populations include a significant number of Protestants). We also asked:

    How important is religion in your life (on a scale of 0–3)?
    Do you go to church? How often?
    Do you participate in *candomblé* (Afro-Brazilian religion)? How often? When was the last time you attended *candomblé*?

12. Years of home exposure was (negatively) the first of three predictor variables entered in our standard multiple regression equation, with relative importance of the main local celebration, in comparison with (inter)national festivals, as the dependent variable. Length of home exposure and education (the third predictor variable entered) were negatively correlated with importance of the local event. Darker skin color, the second predictor, was the only statistically significant variable that was positively correlated with importance of the local ceremony. Years of home exposure produced an R^2 change of 8 percent.

13. Length of home exposure was the third variable entered (positively), after religiosity (associated with a lower ranking of Carnival) and education (positively) in our standard regression formula. Homeexpo had a final beta of .10.

  Televiewing produced no statistically significant difference with respect to the ranking of Christmas. Religiosity and light skin color were the only variables that predicted a statistically significant higher rank for Christmas on the basis of our standard multiple regression equation.

EPILOGUE

1. Another reason why Globo is more successful than American networks may be that it doesn't bore its audience with summer reruns.

References

ADLER, RICHARD P., ed.

1981   Understanding Television: Essays on Television as a Social and Cultural Force. New York: Praeger.

ANDREWS, FRANK M.

1984   Construct Validity and Error Components of Survey Measures: A Structural Modeling Approach. Public Opinion Quarterly. 48:409–442.

ALBERSCHEIM, URSULA

1962   Uma Comunidade Teuto-Brasileiro. Rio de Janeiro: Centro Brasileira de Pesquisas Educacionais, INEP, MEC. (Field site Ibirama.)

ANN ARBOR NEWS

1984   Violence in Summer Movies. October 28, p. C1.

1985a   More Young Adults Are Postponing Marriage, Living with Their Parents (from UPI). November 10.

1985b   Too Much TV Time Linked to Obesity in Children, Teens. May 6.

ANOS 70 SERIES

1981   Televisão: Anos 70, #7. Rio de Janeiro: Europa.

ARENS, W., AND SUSAN P. MONTAGUE, eds.

1981   The American Dimension: Cultural Myths and Social Realities. Sherman Oaks, CA: Alfred.

AXHELM, PETE

1984a   Fans and Athletes Prove Their Mettle in a Week of Surprises—the Spirit. Newsweek. August 11.

1984b   The Glory of Los Angeles. Newsweek. August 20.

BERGER, ARTHUR ASA

1980   Television as an Instrument of Terror. New Brunswick: Transaction Books.

1988   "Star Trek": A Romance of Inner Space. In Media USA: Process and Effect. A. A. Berger, ed. Pp. 235–243. New York: Longman.

BERNIKOW, LOUISE

1986   Is TV a Pal—or a Danger—for Lonely People? TV Guide. October 25:5–6.

BURT, RONALD

1980   Models of Network Structure. Annual Review of Sociology 6: 79–141.

CAREY, JAMES W.

1989   Communication as Culture: Essays on Media and Society. Boston: Unwin Hyman.

CARVALHO, ELISABETH

1981   Telejornalismo: A Década do Jornal da Tranquilidade. In Anos 70, #7: Televisão. Pp. 31–47. Rio de Janeiro: Europa.

COMSTOCK, GEORGE, et al.

1978   Television and Human Behavior. New York: Columbia University Press.

COSTA, ALBERTO C. G.

n.d   A Voice for the Silence: Television, Culture, and Change in Ibirama. Unpublished paper. *To appear in* Television's Social Impact in Brazil. Conrad Phillip Kottak, ed. (Field site Ibirama)

COY, PETER

1984   Once There Was No American Christmas. Cites Christmas in America: the Fabrication of Tradition. Karin Calvert, author. (From Associated Press). Ann Arbor News. December 25: D1, D11.

DAMATTA, ROBERTO

1981   Carnavais, Malandros, e Heróis. Rio de Janeiro: Zahar.

1983   An Interpretation of Carnival. Ray Green, transl. Substance 37/38. Vols. 11(4) and 12(1). Madison: University of Wisconsin.

1987   A Casa e a Rua, 2nd ed. Rio de Janeiro: Guanabara.

DEFLEUR, M.

1964   Occupational Roles as Portrayed on Television. Public Opinion Quarterly 28: 57–74.

DUNDES, ALAN

1975   Seeing Is Believing. *In* The Nacirema: Readings on American Culture. James P. Spradley and Michael A. Rynkiewich, eds. Pp. 14–18. Boston: Little Brown.

EAGLETON, TERRY

1983   Literary Theory: An Introduction. Minneapolis: University of Minnesota Press.

FOLHA DE SÃO PAULO

1983   December 12.

THE FORD FOUNDATION

1976   Television and Children: Priorities for Research. Report of a Conference in Reston, Virginia, November 5–7, 1975. New York: The Ford Foundation.

FREEDMAN, JONATHAN L.

1984   Effect of Television Violence on Aggressiveness. Psychological Bulletin 96(2): 227–246.

FRY, PETER

1982   Para Inglês Ver. Rio de Janeiro: Zahar.

GEERTZ, CLIFFORD

1973   The Interpretation of Cultures. New York: Basic Books.

1983   Local Knowledge. New York: Basic Books.

GERARD, JEREMY

1989   3 Networks Forming Trade Alliance. New York Times, February 13, p. 27.

GERBNER, GEORGE

1967   An Institutional Approach to Mass Communication Research. *In* Communication: Theory and Research. L. Thayer, ed. Springfield, IL: Charles C Thomas.

GERBNER, GEORGE, AND LARRY GROSS

1976a Living with Television: The Violence Profile. Journal of Communication 26: 173–199.

1976b The Scary World of TV's Heavy Viewer. Psychology Today April: 41–45, 89.

GERBNER, GEORGE, et al.

1978 Cultural Indicators: Violence Profile No. 9. Journal of Communication 28: 176–207.
1979 Violence Profile Number 10: Trends in Network Television Drama and Viewer Conceptions of Social Reality. Philadelphia: Annenberg School of Communications, University of Pennsylvania.
1980 The "Mainstreaming" of America: Violence Profile Number 11. Journal of Communication 30: 10–29.

GLENNON, L. M., AND R. J. BUTSCH

1979 The Devaluation of Working Class Lifestyle in Television's Family Series, 1947–1977. Paper presented at the Meeting of the Popular Culture Association.

GOODMAN, ELLEN

1986 TV's Forbidden Word: Contraception. Ann Arbor News, December 5.

GRANZBERG, G., AND J. STEINBRING, eds.

1980 Television and the Canadian Indian. Winnipeg: University of Winnipeg.

GRAY, JERRY

1986 With a Few Exceptions, Television in Africa Fails to Educate and Enlighten. Ann Arbor News. December 8.

GREENBERG, B. S.

1982 Television and Role Socialization: An Overview. *In* Television and Behavior: Ten Years of Scientific Progress and Implications for the Eighties, Vol. 2, Technical Reports. D. Pearl, L. Bouthilet, and J. Lazar, eds. Pp. 179–199. Rockville, MD: National Institutes of Mental Health.

GREENBERG, B. S., ed.

1980 Life on Television. Norwood, NJ: Ablex.

GUNTER, BARRIE

1986 Television and Sex Role Stereotyping. London: John Libbey.

GUNTER, BARRIE, AND MICHAEL SVENNEVIG

1987 Behind and in Front of the Screen: Television's Involvement with Family Life. London: John Libbey.

GUTIS, PHILIP S.

1987 American TV Isn't Traveling So Well. The New York Times.

HALFOUN, ELI

1984 Weekly column, January 20. Amiga. Rio de Janeiro: Bloch.

HARRIS, MARVIN

1964 Patterns of Race in the Americas. New York: Walker.
1970 Referential Ambiguity in the Calculus of Brazilian Racial Identity. Southwestern Journal of Anthropology 26(1): 1–14.

HARRIS, MARVIN, AND CONRAD P. KOTTAK.

1963 The Structural Significance of Brazilian Racial Categories. Sociologia 25: 203–209.

HAWKINS, ROBERT P., AND SUZANNE PINGREE

1980   Some Processes in the Cultivation Effect. Communications Research 7: 193–226.

1982   Television's Influence on Social Reality. *In* Television and Behavior: Ten Years of Scientific Progress and Implications for the Eighties, Vol. 2, Technical Reports. D. Pearl, L. Bouthilet, and J. Lazar, eds. Pp. 224–247. Rockville, MD: National Institutes of Mental Health.

HERZ, DANIEL

1987   A História Secreta da Rede Globo. Porto Alegre: Tchê.

HILL, CHRISTINA D.

1982   Blacks on Daytime Television. *In* Researching American Culture: A Guide for Student Anthropologists. Conrad P. Kottak, ed. Pp. 245–258. Ann Arbor: University of Michigan Press.

HIMMELWEIT, HILDE T., A. N. OPPENHEIM, AND PAMELA VINCE

1958   Television and the Child. New York: Oxford University Press.

HIRSCH, PAUL M.

1979   The Role of Television and Popular Culture in Contemporary Society. *In* Television: The Critical View. Horace Newcomb, ed. Pp. 249–279. New York: Oxford University Press.

HOLSTI, O. R.

1968   Content Analysis. *In* Handbook of Social Psychology. Vol. 2. G. Lindzey and E. Aranson, eds. Reading, MA: Addison-Wesley.

HOOD, STUART

1987   On Television, 3rd ed. London: Pluto.

HSU, FRANCIS L. K.

1975   American Core Values and National Character. *In* The Nacirema: Readings on American Culture. James P. Spradley and Michael A. Rynkiewich, eds. Pp. 378–394. Boston: Little Brown.

HUJANEN, T.

1976   Immigrant Broadcasting and Migration Control in Western Europe. Tampere, Finland: Institute of Journalism and Mass Communication, University of Tampere.

ISTO E

1984   Olimpíadas. August 8.

JORGENSEN, JOSEPH

1982   Methods, Standards, and Assumptions: Ethnographic Field Data Collection and Analysis. Technical Memorandum No. 1, The Harvest Disruption Sociocultural Impacts. Anchorage: U.S. Department of the Interior, OCS Office.

KEHL, MARIA RITA

1981a   Mil e Uma Noites para as Multidões. *In* Anos 70, #7: Televisão. Pp. 49–73. Rio de Janeiro: Europa.

1981b   Um só Povo, uma só Cabeça, uma só Nação. *In* Anos 70, #7: Televisão. Pp. 5–29. Rio de Janeiro: Europa.

KLAPPER, JOSEPH T.

1960   The Effects of Mass Communication. Glencoe, IL: The Free Press.

KOTTAK, CONRAD PHILLIP

1978   Rituals at McDonald's. Natural History, January: 74–83.

1980   The Past in the Present: History, Ecology and Cultural Variation in Highland Madagascar. Ann Arbor: University of Michigan Press.

1983   Assault on Paradise: Social Change in a Brazilian Village. New York: Random House. (Field site Arembepe.)

KOTTAK, CONRAD P., ed.

1982   Researching American Culture: A Guide for Student Anthropologists. Ann Arbor: University of Michigan Press.

KRIPPENDORFF, K.

1980   Content Analysis: An Introduction to Its Methodology. Beverly Hills: Sage.

LAMBERT, JACQUES

1967   Latin America: Structures and Political Institutions. Helen Katel, transl. Berkeley: University of California Press.

LANG, K., AND G. E. LANG

1953   The Unique Perspective of Television and Its Effects: A Pilot Study. American Sociological Review 18: 3–12.

LAZARSFELD, P. F., AND R. K. MERTON

1971   Mass Communication, Popular Taste, and Organized Social Action. *In* The Process and Effects of Mass Communications, rev. ed. W. Schramm and D. F. Roberts, eds. Pp. 554–578. Urbana: University of Illinois Press.

MAINE, HENRY SUMNER

1861   Ancient Law. London: John Murray.

MARCUS, GEORGE E., AND MICHAEL M. J. FISCHER

1986   Anthropology as Cultural Critique. An Experimental Moment in the Human Sciences. Chicago: The University of Chicago Press.

MARCUS, RUTH, AND KENNETH E. JOHN

1986   In the Voice of Public Opinion, Lawyers Rank Low. The Washington Post, National Weekly Edition. September 1.

MCDONALD, GREGORY

1984   Carioca Fletch. New York: Warner Books.

MCDOWELL, EDWIN

1986   Books Linked to Series a New Sideline for Public Television. The New York Times. November 29.

MEAD, MARGARET

1961   Coming of Age in Samoa. New York: Morrow Quill. (Orig. 1928)

MEYEROWITZ, JOSHUA

1985   No Sense of Place: The Impact of Electronic Media on Social Behavior. New York: Oxford University Press.

MIDDLETON, JOHN

1967   Introduction. *In* Myth and Cosmos: Readings in Mythology and Symbolism. John Middleton, ed. Pp. ix–xi. Garden City, NY: The Natural History Press.

MIRANDA, RICARDO, AND CARLOS ALBERTO M. PEREIRA

1983   Televisão: o Nacional e o Popular na Cultura Brasileira. São Paulo: Brasiliense.

MORGAN, THOMAS

1986   Black TV Viewers Seen as Major Force by Networks. Ann Arbor News. December 7: F11.

MORRISON, PATT

1986   MTV with a Twist. *Ann Arbor News*. December 14.

MURRAY, J. P., AND S. KIPPAX

1978   Children's Social Behavior in Three Towns with Differing Television Experience. Journal of Communication 29: 31–43.

1979   From the Early Window to the Late Night Show: International Trends in the Study of Television's Impact on Children and Adults. *In* Advances in Experimental Social Psychology. L. Berkowitz, ed. New York: Academic Press.

MYERS, JANE

1985   Sorry Walter, but Your Name Let You Down. Ann Arbor News. February 10: E1–2.

NATIONAL COMMISSION ON WORKING WOMEN

1984   Women in Focus: An Analysis of TV's Female Characters and Their Jobs. November 26.

NEWCOMB, HORACE

1974   TV: The Most Popular Art. Garden City, NY: Doubleday, Anchor.

NEWSWEEK

1984a   August 13.
1984b   Autust 20.

PACE, RICHARD B.

1987   Economic and Political Change in the Amazonian Community of Itá, Brazil. Ph. D. dissertation, Department of Anthropology, University of Florida. Ann Arbor: UMI. (Field site Itá)

n.d.   Unpublished paper. To appear *in* Television's Social Impact in Brazil. Conrad Phillip Kottak, ed. (Field site Itá).

PARENTI, MICHAEL

1986   Inventing Reality: The Politics of the Mass Media. New York: Saint Martins.

PEARL, D., L. BOUTHILET, AND J. LAZAR, eds.

1982   Television and Behavior: Ten Years of Scientific Progress and Implications for the Eighties. Vols. 1 and 2. Rockville, MD: National Institutes of Mental Health.

PRADO, ROSANE M.

1986   Mulher de Novela e Mulher de Verdade: Estudo sobre Cidade Pequena, Mulher, e Telenovela. Rio de Janeiro: Master's dissertation. Programa de Pos-Graduacão em Antropólogia Social, Museu Nacional, Universidade Federal do Rio de Janeiro. (Field site Cunha)

RAMOS, ROBERTO

1986   Grãfinos na Globo. Petrópolis: Vozes.

ROBERTS, E. J.

1982   Television and Sexual Learning in Childhood. *In* Television and Behavior: Ten Years of Scientific Progress and Implications for the Eighties, Vol. 2,

Technical Reports. D. Pearl, L. Bouthilet, and J. Lazar, eds. Pp. 209–223. Rockville, MD: National Institutes of Mental Health.

ROTHENBERG, RANDALL

1989   3 Networks See Declines Continuing. New York Times, February 8, pp. 25–45.

SALDICH, ANNE RAWLEY

1979   Electronic Democracy: Television's Impact on the American Political Process. New York: Praeger.

SCHONAUER, DAVID

1988   "Star Trek" Sails Boldly On. The New York Times. March 27: Section 2, p. 43.

SHIRLEY, ROBERT W.

1971   The End of Tradition: Culture Change and Development in the Municipio of Cunha, São Paulo, Brazil. New York: Columbia University Press. (Field site Cunha)

SIGNORIELLI, N., L. GROSS, AND M. MORGAN

1982   Violence in Television Programs: Ten Years Later. *In* Television and Behavior: Ten Years of Scientific Progress and Implications for the Eighties, Vol. 2, Technical Reports. D. Pearl, L. Bouthilet, and J. Lazar, eds. Pp. 158–173. Rockville, MD: National Institutes of Mental Health.

SMITH, SALLY BEDELL

1985   Why TV Won't Let Up on Violence. The New York Times. Sunday, January 13: Section 2, pp. 1, 25.

SMYTHE, D.

1954   Reality as Presented on Television. Public Opinion Quarterly 18: 143–156.

SURGEON GENERAL'S SCIENTIFIC ADVISORY COMMITTEE ON TELEVISION AND SOCIAL BEHAVIOR

1974   Television and Growing Up: The Impact of Televised Violence. Report to the Surgeon General, United States Public Health Service. Washington: Government Printing Office.

STRAUBHAAR, JOSEPH D.

1982   The Development of the Telenovela as the Pre-eminent Form of Popular Culture in Brazil. Studies in Latin American Popular Culture 1: 138–150.

1983   Estimating the Impact of Imported Versus National Television Programming in Brazil. *In* Studies in Communication. Vol. 1. Sari Thomas, ed. Norwood, NJ: Ablex, Pp. 34–45.

TANNENBAUM, PERCY H., ed.

1980   The Entertainment Functions of Television. Hillsdale, NJ: Lawrence Erlbaum Associates.

TÁVOLA, ARTUR DA

1983a   Globo and Its Pattern of Production, I. O Globo. October 3, p. 28.

1983b   Globo and Its Pattern of Production, II. O Globo. October 4, p. 30.

1983c   Obituary of Janete Clair. Weekly column, December 3. Rio de Janeiro: Manchête.

1983d   Speaking of the Novela on the Night of a Debut (Eu Prometo). O Globo. September 19, p. 26.

1983e   Weekly column. Têve. September 25. Rio de Janeiro: O Globo.

1984   A Liberdade do Ver. Rio de Janeiro: Novo Fronteira.

THORBURN, DAVID

1988   Television as an Aesthetic Medium. *In* Media, Myths and Narratives: Television and the Press. James W. Carey, ed. Pp. 48–66. Newbury Park, CA: Sage.

TIME

1986   Networks Face Challenge. September 22: 69–72.

TURNER, VICTOR W.

1974   The Ritual Process. Harmondsworth, England: Penguin.

TV GUIDE (DETROIT EDITION)

1986a   The Best and the Worst by the Numbers. July 12–18:14.

1986b   More Enjoy TV Than Sex, Says Ad Agency Study. News Update Section. July 12–18:A1.

USA TODAY

1985   February 14. P. B1.

VEJA

1984a   March 14. P. 12.

1984b   Olimpíadas. August 8. Pp. 36–50.

1984c   Victórias no Tatame. August 15. P. 61.

1984d   Brazil de Ouroe de Prata. August 15. P. 48.

WAGLEY, CHARLES

1953   Amazon Town: A Study of Man in the Tropics. New York: Macmillan. (Field site Itá)

1963   An Introduction to Brazil. New York: Columbia University Press.

1976   Amazon Town: A Study of Man in the Tropics. With a new chapter by Darrel L. Miller. New York: Oxford University Press. (Field site Itá)

WAGLEY, CHARLES, ed.

1952   Race and Class in Rural Brazil. Paris: UNESCO.

WATERS, HARRY F.

1988   The Future of Television. Newsweek. October 17:84–86.

WILLEMS, EMILIO

1947   Cunha: Tradicão e Transicão em uma Cultura Rural do Brasil. São Paulo: Secretaria da Agricultura. (Field site Cunha)

WILLIAMS, RAYMOND

1975   Television: Technology and Cultural Form. New York: Schocken.

WILLIAMS, TANNIS MACBETH, ed.

1986   The Impact of Television: A Natural Experiment in Three Communities. Orlando, FL: Academic Press.

WITHEY, STEPHEN B., and RONALD P. ABELES, eds.

1980   Television and Social Behavior: Beyond Violence and Children. Hillsdale, NJ: Lawrence Erlbaum Associates.

WOLF, ERIC

1982   Europe and the People Without History. Berkeley: University of California Press.

Index

PN 1992.6 .K67 1990
Kottak, Conrad Phillip.
Prime-time society

OCT 8	DATE DUE	
JAN 03 2001		
JAN 08 2001		
JAN 0 7 2002		